BUILDING BLOCKS

OTHER BOOKS BY GENE I. MAEROFF

A Classroom of One (2003)

The Learning Connection (2001),
editor, with Patrick M. Callan and
Michael D. Usdan

Imaging Education (1998), editor

Altered Destinies (1998)

Scholarship Assessed (1997),
with Charles E. Glassick and Mary Taylor Huber

Team Building for School Change (1993)

Sources of Inspiration (1992), editor

The School Smart Parent (1989)

The Empowerment of Teachers (1988)

School and College (1983)

Don't Blame the Kids (1981)

The Guide to Suburban Public Schools (1975),
with Leonard Buder

BUILDING BLOCKS

Making Children Successful in the Early Years of School

GENE I. MAEROFF

First published in 2006 by
PALGRAVE MACMILLAN™
175 Fifth Avenue, New York, N.Y. 10010 and
Houndmills, Basingstoke, Hampshire, England RG21 6XS.
Companies and representatives throughout the world.

PALGRAVE MACMILLAN is the global academic imprint of the
Palgrave Macmillan division of St. Martin's Press, LLC and of Palgrave
Macmillan Ltd. Macmillan® is a registered trademark in the United
States, United Kingdom and other countries. Palgrave is a registered
trademark in the European Union and other countries.

ISBN-13: 978-1-4039-6994-1
ISBN-10: 1-4039-6994-9

Library of Congress Cataloging-in-Publication Data
Maeroff, Gene I.
    Building blocks : making children successful in the early years of school
/ Gene I. Maeroff.
        p.   cm.
    Includes bibliographical references and index.
    ISBN 1-4039-6994-9 (alk. paper)
    1. Early childhood education.   I. Title.
LB1139.23.M34   2006
372.21—dc22
                                                                        2006043206

A catalogue record of the book is available from the British Library.

Design by Letra Libre Inc.

First edition: September, 2006
10   9   8   7   6   5   4   3   2   1
Printed in the United States of America.

For Joyce and Rachel

Contents

Preface

My granddaughter Chloe was in the first of her two years of preschool when I began work on this book. She will be in first grade as the book is published. Naturally, Chloe's entry into the world of formal learning helped pique my interest in writing about the primary grades. Equally as motivating for me has been my impression, formed over decades of observations in classrooms, that students may have a lifetime of troubles awaiting them if schools don't get it right at the beginning.

Most Americans find it perfectly reasonable to assemble students at various points in their education in places that focus on a particular phase of learning—graduate and professional schools, undergraduate colleges, high schools, and middle schools and junior highs. The elementary school, though, lumps together children as young as 3 or 4 with those who might be as old as 10, 11, 12, 13, or 14, depending on the span that the school serves. Such an arrangement does little to assure that the youngest children will receive concentrated attention during the most crucial part of their education.

If one believes that early education has a particular role to play in setting the table for all the intellectual meals that follow, then surely the youngest learners deserve an arrangement that does more to recognize their special needs. Similarly, teachers who work in such a milieu can devote themselves in a single-minded way to laying the foundation for literacy and numeracy.

Ideally, a school that serves only the years from prekindergarten through third grade (PK–3) could do this well for reasons that I explain during the remainder of this book. In the absence of separate buildings for young children, school districts could at least give the primary grades their own standing in a building housing other grades. Education officials could accomplish this by turning over part of the building to

PK–3 classrooms, assigning an assistant principal or head teacher to supervise these grades, and enabling those involved in the education of young children to pursue their work in the collaborative ways that I describe on these pages.

I made field visits to schools in more than a dozen states during 2004 and 2005 to observe situations that illustrate the powerful potential of the PK–3 approach. I spent time in classrooms from California to Delaware, from Massachusetts to Texas for this project. An emphasis on the primary years has extra appeal for those children who get the least out of the current arrangement. Their progress in the future depends on their receiving enhanced attention during the formative years of learning. That said, I want to stress that PK–3 would be a boon to all children, regardless of socioeconomic circumstances.

I learned that the Foundation for Child Development in New York City shared my interest in focusing on the primary grades. The foundation, led by Ruby Takanishi, its president, has sponsored meetings devoted to the PK–3 concept, published papers on the idea, and made grants to organizations and scholars to address the topic. A grant by the foundation to the Institute for Educational Leadership in Washington permitted me to devote these many months to my work and to travel widely in search of people, programs, and schools that would inform this book.

My travels enabled me to interview people, to observe them at work, to sit in on their meetings, and to hear them make presentations in various settings. Throughout the book much of what they said appears without citation as the statements were made to me or in my presence.

I will not try to thank by name the many individuals around the United States who facilitated these visits. Their help made my work immeasurably easier and saved me a great deal of time. Every time I carry out a project of this magnitude, I am impressed anew with the openness and candor that I encounter along the way. On the other hand, it required persistence to set up some of the visits. There were even a few that I never made as I simply ran out of time for circumventing some of the obstacles set in my path by those not inclined to open their schools and school systems to scrutiny. By and large, though, assembling this picture of the possibilities for PK–3 education was an exciting and rewarding venture that brought me in contact with many admirable men and women who are making wonderful contributions to learning and to the children in American classrooms.

Being situated at Teachers College, Columbia University, also aided me greatly. Certain colleagues and the fine library helped at various points. My work with the Hechinger Institute on Education and the Media at Teachers College involved activities that included topics pertinent to the scope of this book. I am also grateful to Palgrave Macmillan for once again publishing my work. This is my third book for this publisher and I appreciate the confidence and support I have received.

Gene I. Maeroff
Teachers College, Columbia University
New York City

A WORLD OF NEW BEGINNINGS

When Lillian Emery Elementary School in Indiana died in 2005, it was almost immediately reborn as the Children's Academy of New Albany. Shorn of its fourth and fifth grades, it became a PK-3 school, serving only prekindergarten through third grade. This new configuration meant that the Children's Academy could tighten its focus on primary education, a vital goal for a school that had ended the year with the lowest-ranking fourth graders of all of southern Indiana's elementary schools.[1]

In light of abundant evidence that students who complete third grade as poor readers face an almost certain struggle for the remainder of their schooling, the entire faculty was dismissed and members had to reapply for their jobs, along with others who wanted to work at the reconstituted school. The New Albany–Floyd County Consolidated School Corporation had concluded that the Children's Academy would need the best teachers it could find, new leadership, a curriculum stressing language and literacy, and the expectation that every student could learn to read proficiently.

Without fourth and fifth graders in the building, the entire atmosphere and orientation of the Children's Academy shifted and the staff could concentrate exclusively on the needs of students in the early elementary grades. This change was important to a school in which in the previous year teachers had made 1,200 referrals to the principal's office for discipline. Placing unprecedented emphasis on literacy instruction, the new Children's Academy fashioned a school day that gave teachers time for professional development and collaborative planning. Everything pointed toward third grade: by the end of that year pupils everywhere, not only in New Albany, must shift from learning to read to reading to learn.

Critics of American education cite lagging test scores, high dropout rates, and the need for remedial courses in college as signs of the deficiencies of public schools. If nothing changes in schools, the income of workers in the United States will decline as the least educated portion of the population continues to grow fastest.[2] Meanwhile, India, China, and other countries that compete with the United States on a host of fronts are gaining rapidly in education, graduating increasing numbers from colleges and universities.

Seldom do those alarmed by such trends pay enough attention to what happens at the beginning, when the foundation is put in place for all that follows. Actually, Thomas Jefferson recognized this imperative as long ago as the eighteenth century, observing that democracy depends on an educated electorate. He called for establishing elementary schools to teach reading, writing, and arithmetic and proposed that "every child was to be taught gratis for three years."[3] Surely, a solid foundation and a commitment to learning put in place during the early years will contribute much to stem the rate of high school dropouts and to boost the numbers entering and completing college.

Above all, education in the earliest years should concern itself with preparing youngsters to become confident readers and adept at mathematics in the ensuing years. Schools must organize themselves around this mission. "[A] consensus has emerged over the last 20 years about the critical nature of the primary grades—preK-3—in terms of literacy development," Joseph Murphy, an authority on educational leadership, writes in a book that examines the role of principals in leading reading instruction.[4]

A PK-3 school encompasses preschool, kindergarten, and the first three grades, positing its rationale on the commonalities of these grades and the opportunity that such an approach gives administrators and teachers to enhance child development at its most fragile and potentially most productive time. The fragility is especially pronounced at the new Children's Academy, which draws 40 percent of its students from three publicly subsidized housing projects and where poverty is so pervasive that more than nine out of ten students qualify for federally subsidized meals.

But a configuration emphasizing the early years is by no means an act of desperation, whether it happens at a troubled school like the Children's Academy or at high-achieving PK-2 schools like those in affluent Glen Ridge, New Jersey, where nine out of ten students score at or above the proficient level and two-thirds of the adults have bachelor's degrees. A PK-3 approach fortifies early education in the following ways:

1. EMPHASIS—Designation of pre-K through grade 3 as a unit unto itself with specific goals is a first step toward assuring that the youngest children do not get shunted aside as older students receive precedence.
2. TEAMWORK—In a PK-3 school or unit of their own, staff can more readily plan across grade levels and classrooms, viewing the youngsters as one unified learning community. They can form both horizontal teams for teachers of a particular grade level and vertical teams with one teacher from each grade level, preschool through third grade.
3. GROUPING—Flexible small-group instruction of pupils that reaches beyond a single classroom and crosses grade levels acknowledges the uneven progress of students at these ages.
4. STAFF DEVELOPMENT—Educators at this level share common professional interests best addressed through joint continuing education that recognizes the interlocking nature of their work.
5. CULMINATION—Third grade, as a concluding point, takes on significance as the juncture at which to gather the fruits of early learning to make success more likely in the grades that follow.

Unprecedented attention to schooling from preschool through third grade offers greater promise for improving outcomes than almost any other step that educators might take. Doing it right in the first place is the most obvious way to give students what they will need to prosper in the classroom. Otherwise, every intervention afterward becomes remedial—expensive, difficult, bruising to children. As prekindergarten grows universal and kindergarten expands to fill the entire school day, schools will best sustain early gains by reinforcing the entirety of primary education. *Coordination* should be the watchword of this effort, with standards, curriculum, instruction, and assessment aligned across the PK-3 continuum like the moving parts of a finely designed mechanical clock.

Students who come out of third grade as fluent readers can approach much of the rest of the curriculum with confidence. Learning to reason with numbers during the primary years will not make an Einstein of every child, but it will lift the mystery from mathematics and enhance their prospects. A PK-3 structure, by reducing the need for remediation, can lead to more productive learning in the upper elementary grades and in secondary school. An approach that emphasizes reading and math by no means implies that schools ought to ignore other subjects. Teachers can offer social studies and science in tandem with reading and math. The arts, as well, have a place in the education of young children.

Strengthening early childhood education is possible by looking at schooling from preschool through third grade as a distinct period of schooling. Educators could devote separate schools to children from about the age of three or four to the age of eight or nine. Or, the primary grades could have their own discrete identity in the elementary school with, perhaps, their own assistant principal. In such a setting everything would revolve around this age group.

Such an idea is neither new nor untried. The National Association of State Boards of Education in 1988 called on the nation's elementary schools to create early childhood units to serve children from the ages of four through eight.[5] Even ten years earlier, Edward Zigler of Yale University, an originator of Head Start, proposed aligning preschool with the early elementary grades.[6] He thought that efforts to raise achievement, especially among the poorest children, depended on programs from birth to age three similar to Early Head Start, followed by preschool, and then by a focus on the primary grades. He wanted schools to "provide quality education through grade three so that children read on grade level by the end of third grade."[7]

The prestigious National Academy of Sciences said that advances in knowledge and changing circumstances call for a fundamental reexamination of the nation's ways of dealing with young children and their families. This group of experts pointed out that society continues to use outdated policies and strategies that do not recognize what has been learned about young children through research.[8] A PK-3 approach represents an appropriate fresh response.

Prekindergarten amounts to a new grade added to formal schooling—at the beginning rather than the end. What has been a journey of 13 years will extend to 14 years—or 15 years if pre-K includes three-year-olds. This is monumental. Kindergarten is the most recent addition to the continuum, which until a half-century ago started in most places with first grade. The period of years that begins with preschool and runs through the end of third grade accounts for more than a third of elementary and secondary education. No other phase of a student's schooling figures more prominently in shaping the child's future.

Ideally, a PK-3 school could underscore its connection to what occurs in the lives of children from birth to age three by reaching out to help young parents enrich settings for infants and toddlers. Many of these mothers and fathers have never before prepared a child for school. Then, it would make preschool available to children starting at the age of three, provide full-day kindergarten, and align the academic work through the third grade, letting pupils move through the continuum at rates appropriate to their social, emotional, and educational development. High-quality child care, infused with learning opportunities, would be available before and after classes, recognizing the needs of today's families.

Schools in the United States have sometimes organized themselves to emphasize the early grades, and other countries, notably the United Kingdom, have also used this configuration. The British infant school—designed specifically to accommodate children between the ages of five and seven—dates back to the 1820s and became official in the 1870s. As recently as 1988, in the Education Reform Act, the British government identified schools and departments for children from five to seven years old as the first key stage of the educational process.[9]

Separate infant departments in elementary schools or freestanding infant schools continue to serve some children until they move to the second key stage, from the age of 7 through 11, but fiscal pressures in the United Kingdom have forced the consolidation of smaller infant programs into elementary schools that include a longer age span. Still, thousands of youngsters in the age group attend schools that focus on young children who then transfer into an upper elementary school at the age of seven, eight, or nine.[10]

A self-contained PK-3 continuum could also be a vehicle for a nongraded, interage program, letting youngsters progress at rates appropriate to their individual development, with less concern about grade-to-grade promotion. This would allow for more emphasis on assuring that students reach a specified threshold of learning by the end of third grade. Currently, some parents delay the entrance of five-year-olds into kindergarten for a year to give them more time to gain maturity, and some schools hold over pupils deemed unprepared for first grade for a second year of kindergarten. Measures of this sort would be largely unnecessary in a PK-3 setup, where multiage grouping could provide a more flexible learning ladder for children to climb. Such schools could also give closer attention to the uneven progression of special education students and English-language learners.

For decades, education in the United States operated in lock-step fashion, with students taking a precise length of time to pass through each stage. The lock-step has been flying apart for years at its upper levels—high school and college—in a seemingly contradictory way. Some students take longer to complete their studies and some do it more rapidly. The practice of repeating a grade to get a better grounding and improve marks, for instance, has become ever more widespread at elite boarding schools, which have long offered a post–senior year to public high school graduates who want to burnish their records. Many students, particularly in big cities, fail to get their diplomas in four years, requiring five or six years to do so. Clifford B. Janey, school superintendent in Washington, D.C., proposed flexible programs for high school students so that they might take five years or more to complete the four years of high school. He had earlier used the approach as superintendent in Rochester, N.Y., to increase graduation rates.

One-third of the students who enter college take remedial courses that, in effect, are high-school-level studies, further extending the time to degree completion. People no longer look askance if a student does not earn a baccalaureate in four years, which only 43 percent of students now do. The average time from start to finish has expanded to five years, according to Clifford Adelman, an analyst with the U.S. Department of Education. These various developments represent a slowing down of the academic progression.

Meanwhile, other students speed up the process by blending high school and college. Between 10 and 30 percent of high school juniors and seniors take college-level work while still enrolled in high school,[11] through such programs as Advanced Placement, dual enrollment, early-college high schools, and examination-based college credits. Florida even lets some students skip the senior year of high school and move on to college.

Yet, the early elementary years remain largely untouched by such trends. Despite huge developmental differences among young children, schools make few accommodations for differences in their social, emotional, and academic growth. The flexibility of the PK-3 continuum could change this. Not only might some children spend extra time in preschool or the first grade, for example, but in appropriate instances they could attend classes on more than one grade level during a single day. In any event, PK-3 offers a chance to have fewer controversies over social promotion or nonpromotion. Teachers can freely guide students through the work they need at rates suited to each child.

EMPHASIZING THE EARLY GRADES

Not all schools that opt to focus on the early grades adopt a PK-3 or PK-2 configuration. More often, in fact, this emphasis arises from giving closer attention to the younger children in schools that run through fifth, sixth, or eighth grade. It occurs when school districts recognize that outcomes at the upper grades will not improve without bolstering the education of children before they reach the middle years of elementary school.

Montgomery County, Maryland:
To Close the Achievement Gap

Jerry D. Weast, superintendent of Montgomery County Public Schools in the suburbs just north of Washington, D.C., saw the need to reach children in the earliest grades if he were to improve the system, which hid its problems under a veneer of affluence. The mansions of Potomac and the glittery shops and upscale restaurants of Bethesda made it easy to overlook the poverty of Silver Spring and Takoma Park and the growing influx of blue-collar, Spanish-speaking immigrants from Latin America. Residents did little more than grumble as an achievement gap of monumental proportions carved a schism through the spine of the sprawling school district of 140,000 students.

It took the arrival of Weast as an impertinent new superintendent in 1999 to force residents to confront—and do something about—the mounting difficulties in their schools. Fresh from having merged three school systems in North Carolina to create the Guilford County Schools and armed with insights gained during 27 years as a superintendent, Weast set out to seek improvement in Montgomery County by rubbing the noses of residents in the egregious situation they had chosen to overlook. He recognized that the Montgomery County Public Schools

(MCPS) had, in effect, turned into what amounted to two separate school systems. He decided that the only way to fix the situation was by emphasizing the earliest years of schooling.

Weast gathered all the data he could find, going beyond household income to ferret out statistics on such details as mobility, rental housing, ambulance runs, mental health services, homeless shelters, bus routes, and other factors to highlight differences between the haves and the have-nots. He cast the findings in map form—green for affluence and all that went with it, red for poverty and its dire accompaniments.

The red area coincided with the center of the school district, extending north in a swath from the District of Columbia border to Gaithersburg and containing the oldest housing, much of it comprised of multiple dwellings. He superimposed green and all it represented over the rest of the district, westerly and northerly, with multimillion-dollar houses and families whose children lust for Ivy League acceptances. Weast set the map on an easel and displayed it at a series of almost a dozen public meetings. He had found his mantra: his mission was to "green the red zone."

"These are pretty smart people," Weast said of residents of the green zone. He told them that district-wide achievement was "flattening and deteriorating." He was about to ask them to increase their taxes so that the school system could launch an initiative to boost student performance, particularly in the schools with the most impoverished children and the greatest concentration of minority students. "One thing that appealed to everybody was that if we built a strong educational system it had a positive correlation to their housing values," he said, reflecting on his efforts.

And so it was that MCPS launched a "kindergarten initiative," capping class size at 15 pupils in the 56 of the system's 125 elementary schools containing the neediest children. The initiative provided for full-day kindergarten in these schools. Almost everything that happened in kindergarten was going to be about literacy. Four essential questions drove school reform in Montgomery County:

1. What do students need to know and be able to do?
2. How will we know they have learned it?
3. What will we do when they haven't?
4. What will we do when they already know it?

Weast used kindergarten as the fulcrum, balancing an expansion of preschool on one side and an early success performance plan for first and second grades on the other side. His approach encapsulated the crucial four-year period at the outset of schooling, with fluency in reading by third grade as his goal. Weast aimed to help the children—like an army entering combat—make breakthroughs before they "hit the Draconian test stuff," as he referred to the federal government's No Child Left Behind testing requirements that start at third grade.

He revised the curriculum to increase rigor, aligning the work from grade to grade to make it more likely that success in one grade would lead to success in the next one. Assessment became a tool for monitoring pupil progress, and staffs learned more about what they were to teach and how to teach it. The district reduced class size in first and second grades to 17-to-1 in the 56 target elementary schools.

"Early childhood is the way to stop the hemorrhaging," the plain-spoken superintendent said of the plan. Weast, who grew up on a farm in Kansas and whose mother taught in a one-room schoolhouse on the prairie, relishes explaining his actions from the vantage of his origins. He used a rural analogy to justify investing more heavily in certain areas of the school district: If you take a look at your farm, it has all sorts of pieces of land. Some need more fertilizer and some need less. Some of them grow this kind of crop, some grow that kind. The overall yield is what you're looking for. You don't ask one piece of land to grow less wheat, but if 50 bushels of wheat is what you want all over your farm, you have to do different things in different areas to get the same 50 bushels. If you do those things and do them right, where you were growing 50 bushels, you'll grow 70, and where you were growing 30 bushels of wheat, you'll grow 55. So, you're moving everything beyond the standard of 50. You're closing the gap and raising the bar."

And he used a PK-3 focus to do it.

New Albany, Indiana: To Build a Learning Foundation

Teresa Perkins, who oversaw curriculum and instruction for New Albany's schools, viewed the creation of the Children's Academy as a PK-3 school as an attempt "to get innocence back in the building." Most everything could then be about helping little children learn to read. Older elementary students who had failed to learn to read were no longer there to act out, monopolizing the time and attention of the staff. "It's scary if you're in fourth grade and a nonreader," said Merla Braune, a reading teacher at the school, which she attended when she was a youngster living in the projects.

The focus on the primary grades and, by extension, on reading meant that the Children's Academy could devote professional development largely to discussions of early literacy. The reformulated school built a schedule that allowed for daily meetings of the three teachers who taught on each grade level, as well as after-school meetings twice a week of the entire faculty. The school became the only one of New Albany's 13 elementary schools with full-time teachers of art, music, and physical education whose courses freed the classroom teachers for meetings during the school day. Two teachers from the intensive program known as Reading Recovery spent half the day tutoring individual first graders and the other half working with children from other grades.

The Children's Academy sought to build a strong learning foundation from the moment that pupils entered the school. What had been a half-day pre-K program with one class in the morning and one in the afternoon became three full-day prekindergartens. The school also began to offer full-day kindergarten, still a luxury in the many parts of the United States that have only half-day programs. For the first time, transportation became available for the many children whose fourth- and fifth-grade siblings, now located at another school, were unavailable to walk with them between school and home. The Children's Academy also added a counselor to work with students and a social worker to help families.

Lives could be changed more readily inside the two-story, red-brick school than outside, where the homes to which children returned each day often did not provide the kind of preparation and reinforcement that contribute so greatly to academic success. The school had no functioning parents' organization. With an enrollment of 243, roughly half white and half black, the school served as testimony to the proposition that poverty can be an equal opportunity affliction. The nearby projects, home to so many of the students, were dreary places with barrackslike structures instead of the high rises that city people associate with subsidized housing. Other pupils lived in the modest houses on the surrounding streets. Sheila Rohr, the new principal, encountered one of the worst features of Midwest rural poverty when she drove up to school one morning to see the flashing dome lights of police cruisers. Officers were raiding a meth lab in the garage behind a home across from the school.

It seemed no accident that the Children's Academy, like its predecessor, Lillian Emery Elementary, had an enrollment that was the poorest and the blackest in New Albany. The school's zoning lines, similar to those for a gerrymandered election district, looped around what appeared to be more prosperous homes, consigning their occupants to other elementary schools, but making sure to encircle the projects. As the ultimate indignity, one of the projects faced the fenced-in New Albany Country Club and its lush green fairways, where golf carts sped about in full view of the subsidized residents.

AMERICA'S SCHOOLS: FROM ONE ROOM TO AGE-SPECIFIC SCHOOLS

There was a time, of course, when youngsters of all ages studied their subjects together, attending class in a one-room schoolhouse. This arrangement especially suited rural areas with scattered populations and not all that many children of any particular age group. Given the growing concentration of pupils in cities, though, educators sought new ways to group them, and age-graded schools appeared in urban areas by the mid-nineteenth century. People of the era looked on this situation as more modern than the one-room schoolhouse: it conformed to the factory model of production that had emerged after the Industrial Revolution. The ability to tailor books, materials, and lessons to a single age group represented a sort of efficiency.

Frequently, an age-graded school housed students until they reached the early teens, marking an end to formal education for the many who gravitated into the workforce at that point. By 1920, schools enrolled more than 90 percent of American children from the age of 7 to 13, a situation prompted by the fact that every state by then had a compulsory schooling law[12] to accompany statutes banning child labor. As late as 1940, young adults between the ages of 25 and 29 had completed an average of only 10.3 years of schooling.[13] This was all that most Americans needed until the mid-twentieth century to advance to jobs leading to working-class respectability.

The junior high school, accommodating youngsters from the seventh through the ninth grades, emerged early in the twentieth century. Specifically modeled after the high school, with teachers specializing in subjects and students changing classes, junior high spanned a transition period for pupils regarded as too old to be with younger children and too young to be with older students. The 6–3–3 configuration of the grades became the paradigm in many locales from World War I until long after World War II. Historians point out that "[h]ere and there educators experimented with more sweeping alternatives," including K-3 as a pedagogical continuum. Mostly, though, "school districts made incremental rather than fundamental changes in the graded school."[14]

Perhaps elementary schools should have taken steps long ago to accommodate prekindergarteners and to pay closer attention to the primary continuum, but this was not the case. The very word *preschool* attests to the longstanding belief that four-year-olds should not figure in the "regular" school program. Only now—with growing awareness of the value of pre-K and its spread—is a shift occurring. A sign of an attitudinal shift was the report in 2005 by the National Association of Elementary School Principals calling on their colleagues to provide a coherent program during the primary years as "part of a continuum of learning that extends from pre-kindergarten through third grade."[15]

The current push to include four-year-olds and even three-year-olds in school actually signifies a return to what existed in America through the first third of the nineteenth century. In colonial times, three- and four-year-olds sat in one-room schoolhouses with older children. These youngsters figured in America's infant school movement of the 1820s, helping lift enrollments to the point that 40 percent of three-year-olds in Massachusetts were in school. But there was already a backlash against early childhood education, with opponents arguing that young children belonged at home with their parents and that subjecting them to school "weakened their growing minds and eventually led to insanity."[16] Public schools acted to set minimum ages for entering school and to delay the start of formal education, policies that advocates of kindergarten took more than a century to overcome in districts across the country.

INTERLOCKING SCHOOLS BY PAIRS

Children benefit most from an early emphasis when they continue into the upper elementary grades at a school that builds on and collaborates with the efforts of the lower school. School systems usually cannot mandate this sort of closeness; it flows best from the colleagueship of educators at the two separate levels. A structure of paired schools facilitates collaborative efforts. This paired approach is seen in the Greece Central School District in upstate New York, seven miles west of Rochester, and in Chicago. The district of 13,500 students is the kind of stable community where 93 percent of the youngsters remain enrolled from year to year, and more than two-thirds of the population is of Italian, German, and Irish stock.

Greece had four pairs of schools during the 2005–06 school year; each pair had one school that served children through second grade and one for grades 3 through 5. In one of those pairs, Paddy Hill Elementary School had 359 pupils from prekindergarten through second grade, and Kirk Road Elementary School housed youngsters in third, fourth, and fifth grades.

The paired schools had a combined school improvement plan, shared staff, joint professional development, aligned committees and teams, and a common educational theme. Under a unified school improvement plan, for example, the two schools targeted, year by year, the percentage of students expected to meet or exceed learning standards— goals that Kirk Road could most readily meet if Paddy Hill did its part by getting pupils ready in the primary grades. The two schools shared an assistant principal, a psychologist, and a counselor, all of whom spent half their time in each building. While teachers worked at only one school or the other, the two principals held joint professional development sessions at various points throughout the year and met regularly for planning sessions.

The common educational theme—which included physical and social-emotional growth along with the cognitive—was informed by the writings of Howard Gardner and Mel Levine. In this connection, teachers at Paddy Hill prepared learning profiles on second graders who fell below expectations and passed them along to third grade teachers at Kirk Road so that the upper elementary school could give extra attention to those children.

"The principal of Paddy Hill and I have forged a close working relationship," Caroline A. Critchlow, principal of Kirk Road, said of Jean Biondolillo. "We are committed to a strong connection between the schools. We have committed to common instructional strategies. We work hard to ensure a smooth second grade to third grade transition. Second graders visit the third grade classrooms and last year we facilitated teacher visits between classrooms. Second grade teachers [from the lower school] worked with me and the third grade teachers to score a third grade district assessment." During the previous two years, teachers from Paddy Hill observed the science assessment process at Kirk Road to gain firsthand knowledge of the expectations that awaited their pupils.

Such experience, becoming familiar with assessments that their students will encounter in the next grade at the next school, helps teachers in the earlier grades better prepare children for the future. Student success at Kirk Road depended a great deal on the earlier work of teachers at Paddy Hill, especially when it came time for students to take tests required for No Child Left Behind. Children first faced the tests in third grade but results were listed as outcomes for Paddy Hill/Kirk Road, thereby acknowledging the contribution of the primary grades in shaping outcomes that appear down the line. "Collaboration between the principals has strengthened connections between the two schools and provided a smoother transition for students and parents," Biondolillo said.

In Chicago, two neighboring K-8 schools near the lakefront, south of downtown, that the superintendent had closed, reopened in 2005 as paired schools, putting each in a better position to improve by concentrating on a narrower slice of students. Thus, the former Pershing Magnet School became Pershing East, a PK-3 school, and the former Douglas Academy became Pershing West, a 4–8 school into which Pershing East fed its children. "They love being the oldest ones in the school," Ashanti Howard said of her third graders. "They feel like seniors."

The building housing Pershing East offers a perfect setting for a PK-3 school of 226 pupils and probably should never have had a full array of elementary grades. A one-story, buff-brick structure of plentiful glass, designed in the 1950s by Skidmore, Owings, and Merrill, the school has just 10 classrooms, allowing for two classes at each grade level—in each case side by side—from preschool through third grade. It occupies a corner of Lake Meadows Park and draws most of its students from the towering apartment buildings on adjacent blocks. Having served older children, the building has a spacious library. The school converted what had been a science laboratory to a fine arts room, staffed by a full-time teacher. A separate computer room supplements the single computer situated in each classroom.

Pershing East was still finding its niche as a PK-3 school during the 2005–06 school year, but teachers already recognized the potential advantage of the more targeted and more finely focused professional development that the University of Chicago helped carry out for them. A block of time devoted to literacy instruction every morning from 9 to 11 signified the mission of the school, where Principal Katherine Volk said: "If they're not reading by the end of second grade, we have a problem on our hands. And I'm not talking about the test they have to take in third grade."

INTERLOCKING THE P-16 PROGRESSION

In the 1990s, some educators and policymakers began stressing the need for connections along the educational continuum by referring to the interlocking nature of the years from prekindergarten through college, the time when parents watch their offspring grow from learning to tie their shoelaces to assuming adult responsibilities. In such states as Georgia and Maryland, government officials formed P-16 Councils to explore and sponsor policy initiatives that addressed the entire continuum. Joel Klein, New York City Schools chancellor, pointing out how one level of education builds on another, put it this way: "The better job we do of educating our children in the lower grades, the more prepared they'll be in the higher grades."[17]

The Education Commission of the States propounded a P-16 vision with an emphasis on aligning the years that make up the PK-3 portion of the continuum, initially to assure readiness for the first grade, and then to result in children who can read by the end of the third grade.[18] In keeping with this philosophy, a California master plan[19] that included 19 pages of proposals for school readiness started from birth and continued through the primary grades, so that by third grade youngsters will have gained the reading skills to carry them into the rest of their education. Some parents in California regard the goal of universal preschool as a way to "build down" and thus provide the educational system, like a skyscraper, with deeper footings.

The various pieces of the P-16 continuum have long existed in splendid isolation from each other. Informed observers recognized by the 1970s that a full education required a student to pass through elementary school, junior high or middle school, high school, and the undergraduate years of college. Yet, historically, Americans have largely viewed these elements as separate places to sojourn along the educational journey, each level having little more to do with the others than the countries through which a vacationer might pass during a grand tour of European capitals. And for all too many American children, the first leg of this trip has been a journey to nowhere, leaving them to carry empty baggage for the remainder of their travels through the educational labyrinth.

THE VERY EARLY YEARS

It's drizzling and Kathleen Smith wears her usual attire for such a day, a hooded jacket—the hood her only defense against the raindrops. Smith is a parent educator for Parents as Teachers (PAT), a home visitation program, and when she works she fills her arms with materials and toys that make it impossible to carry an umbrella. She pulls her van to the curb, in front of a small house on a street of small houses. It has no garage, only a covered carport. This is Pattonville, a school district that encompasses several municipalities northwest of St. Louis, near the airport.

Smith is about to make a home visit, underwritten by the state, to Beth and her two children, daughters ages two and three. Beth is a very young-looking 18 and has been homeless several times. A court ordered the father of one of her children to pay a modest amount of child support; the father of the other child pays nothing. Now, she lives with her grandparents, who provide not only shelter, but a modicum of dependability for this young mother and her children whose lives have been filled with disruption and dislocation. Beth completed her high school diploma in an alternative program. Like Beth, one of every ten mothers PAT serves across the country is a teenager.

Part of Smith's work for Parents as Teachers involves teaching a parenting course at the local high school for pregnant students and those who have borne children. She met Beth in such a class. Smith also became a certified doula, allowing her to assist in delivering babies, so that she could attend the births of the infants of the pregnant students she meets. "I am sometimes the only stable person in their lives," says Smith, who assisted in Beth's deliveries. Beth has five brothers and sisters. Just this morning, while at the high school, Smith learned that Beth's 14-year-old sister was pregnant. Smith, whose nurturing seems to know no bounds, remains relentlessly optimistic. She has to be that way: her son is serving in Iraq.

It is just past noon. Beth and the children pad about barefoot in the tiny living room. They all wear loose tee-shirts and baggy clothes, very likely their sleepwear. They all sniffle and Beth announces that they have been ill, one after the other. Her grandfather, a gaunt man who works a night shift, sips coffee in the adjoining kitchen, which opens to the living room.

Beth and Mattie, the two-year-old, get down on the floor, which has crumbs on it, and sit cross-legged. Smith lowers herself to the floor, facing them. The three-year-old, Stacy, drapes herself over one of the two sofas. Smith pours materials onto the floor out of a canvas bag as she begins to show Beth how to teach Mattie about colors and shapes and how to count. Smith talks about getting the children to categorize blocks and other objects and to recognize differences among objects, linking these skills to the importance of recognizing the shapes of various letters as a step toward reading.

More or less following a script, as PAT parent educators are directed to do, Smith reviews what Beth can expect of Mattie at her age, pointing out that the child will be pronouncing words more and more distinctly. They briefly discuss Mattie's progress in toilet training. Then, Smith produces what appears to be a large cookie sheet with magnetic animals stuck to it. She tells Mattie a story as she moves the animals around, demonstrating what Beth could do with a cookie sheet as an aid. "What does a bird say?" Smith asks Mattie as she moves one of the animal figures. Smith goes through the same questions for an assortment of animals—a white dog, a gold fish, a blue horse, and others—reminding Beth that she can ask about the animals' sounds and their colors when she repeats this exercise with her daughter.

Then, Smith takes out a picture book, *Fish Eyes*, and asks Beth to read aloud to Stacy. As Beth reads, Smith helps Stacy count the number of fish on each page. After reaching a page with nine fish (which she counts correctly), Stacy wriggles away, her attention at an end, coughing and looking for a tissue to wipe her nose. "Did you make an appointment to have her screened?" Smith asks Beth, referring to one of the other services provided by Parents as Teachers. Stacy is back; she counts, flawlessly, to 10.

The one hour for the home visit has almost elapsed. "One more thing," Smith says, taking out a manila folder onto which she has drawn the outlines of the shapes of common objects. Smith asks Mattie to put the object on top of the matching shape—an eraser, a comb, a paper clip, a crayon, a clothespin. "It's low tech and homemade," Smith explains. Stacy comes over and makes all the matches even though the activity is meant for her younger sister. Then, as always happens near the end of a PAT visit, Smith dispenses handouts, one explaining to Beth how she can help Mattie learn colors, another identifying how she can cultivate Stacy's thinking skills.

As she rises from the floor to leave, Smith talks to Beth about the federal government's Women, Infants, and Children program, for which Beth thinks she is no longer eligible. She also asks Beth whether she is searching for work and learns that she has looked into a $9-an-hour job at the Dollar Store. Beth tells Smith she made a phone call about getting Stacy into Head Start. "Have you thought about vocational school?" Smith asks, raising the question of Beth's own education. Smith gently dispenses a final bit of advice to the young mother: "You need to wake them early in the morning and get them dressed. If you're not on a schedule, they won't be. This is especially important when you get a job." A round of hugs and Smith, bags and materials in hand, is on the way back to her van and her next home visit.

IT TAKES MORE THAN A SCHOOL

As the description of a home visit shows, school alone does not shape outcomes for children. Their educational success ultimately is the product of family, neighborhood, and economic and social circumstances. Youngsters do not suddenly descend from the planets and appear in classrooms. They have been living in homes, usually in the company of at least one biological parent. Parenting contributes three or four times as much as early child care to the development of young children, and mothers especially have a profound effect on the extent to which youngsters are prepared for school.[1]

While observers pay attention these days to achievement gaps among students, the differences among children before they ever reach school can be enormous. The first three years or so of life place an indelible stamp on youngsters that no amount of later schooling entirely rubs away. James J. Heckman, a professor at the University of Chicago and a Nobel laureate in economics, says that the most important influences on young children's development are family, home, and immediate social circle. He urges parents to take a hard look at how they raise their children, especially in the early years, and to ask how they can improve their parenting practices.[2]

Research on the acquisition of vocabulary illustrates the stakes in child-rearing. Observations of interactions, especially conversations between parents and toddlers, found tremendous variations by the age of three. The number of words a toddler was exposed to during a typical year was 11.2 million in a professional family, 6.5 million in a working-class family, and 3.2 million in a welfare family. By age three, one could predict the language skills that children would possess in the fourth or fifth grade. "Estimating the hours of intervention needed to equalize children's early experience makes clear the enormity of the effort that would be required," the researchers said. "And the longer the effort is put off, the less possible the change becomes."[3]

Such a link to socioeconomic levels is daunting in light of figures showing the growing pervasiveness of poverty. In 2003, for instance, the poverty rate for families with children under the age of 18 rose for the first time since 1998 and median family income for families with children was dropping from its 2000 peak.[4] Bobbie D'Allessandro, former school superintendent in Cambridge, Massachusetts, observes: "We have to realize that the achievement gap happens well before our children even enter school. I worry as a K–12 educator about what we are doing 0–3. How are we going to work to close that gap that occurs much before those children even enter our school systems?"

Thus, a school that concentrates on the primary grades must ultimately contend with forces that affect children long before they reach classrooms. Ideally, PK–3 education would give attention to youngsters almost as soon as they are born. Few schools, however, have contact with children during the years prior to preschool and kindergarten. Schools that choose to act during these years could promote literacy among families with infants and toddlers. They could also become involved in home visits to help parents and even pregnant mothers. Additionally, the extent to which schools influence the quality of child care for infants and toddlers can help determine outcomes in the primary grades.

How PAT Operates

Parents as Teachers grew out of a project founded in 1981 to help families learn how to stimulate the development of newborns. It expanded to cover toddlers up to the age of three and, after that, children up to five. A law enacted in Missouri in 1984 requires the state's school districts to provide parental education and developmental screening for children from birth to kindergarten entry. The legislature appropriated funds to implement Parents as Teachers across the state for 10 percent of families with children up to the age of three. PAT established a national center as a nonprofit organization in 1987.

School systems in Missouri, assisted by the State Education Department, comfortably incorporate Parents as Teachers into their array of early childhood initiatives. In the Ferguson-Florissant district, for example, Joy M. Rouse, the director of early education, includes PAT under her aegis. The program is housed in a large building with child care facilities and classrooms for the system's prekindergarten pupils. The district offers free pre-K but charges families for child care. PAT trained both preschool and child care teachers to perform as parent educators and do home visits. "PAT is the foundation for everything we do in the district," says Rouse.

Parents as Teachers has less-certain funding sources outside Missouri. The organization suggests to local affiliates that they link up with county health departments, churches, the United Way, and other nonprofits, as well as explore state-based funding through early childhood programs. Other possible funding streams flow from such federal programs as Title I, Even Start, Head Start, and Temporary Assistance to Needy Families (TANF). Normally, parent educators like Kathleen Smith make visits geared to the month-by-month development of children from birth to three. In most locales, PAT also offers group meetings. More than two-thirds of the children receive annual health and developmental screenings leading to the identification of problems requiring referrals for 11 percent of them.

Statistics on Parents as Teachers show that 65 percent of the families it reaches are white (like Beth's), 13 percent African American, 12 percent Latino, and the rest from other groups or unidentified. Forty-one percent of the families are low income and almost one in four is a single-parent household. Thus, PAT serves advantaged families as well as needy ones. "Just because you're affluent doesn't mean you know anything about child development," says Debra Smith McCutchen, who coordinates PAT activities in the Ferguson-Florissant School district.

Each parent educator undergoes one week of training. It is a part-time job and the program does not require home visitors to have college degrees. Increasingly since the late 1990s, Parents as Teachers has emphasized findings from brain research. The curriculum has benefited from the input of neuroscientists at Washington University in St. Louis. For example, PAT tells parents of "windows of opportunity" during the early years of life, when a child is most receptive to emotional, social, and intellectual stimulation.

HOME VISITS IN OTHER PROGRAMS

Missouri's experience demonstrates how public schools can incorporate visits to the families of infants and toddlers into their mission as they try to influence school readiness. In Independence, besides using Parents as Teachers, a product of its own state, to send visitors to the homes of 2,972 children under the age of five during 2005, the district had 110 children under three in its Early Head Start program and 286 children under five involved in its family literacy program. Surely, it would be desirable if such programs as those in Independence preceded the PK–3 progression everywhere to provide enhanced developmental experiences for youngsters during the years from birth to preschool.

The Parent-Child Home Program

The Parent-Child Home Program (PCHP) begins with toddlers as young as 16 months. It consists of half-hour home visits twice a week for two years. Usually a school district sponsors the visits, but in some locales—as with PAT—the sponsor might be a social service agency, a community-based organization, or some other entity that deals with children and families. Unlike Parents as Teachers, the program focuses exclusively on families challenged by such obstacles as poverty, limited education, and literacy and language barriers. This has been its focus since its origin in 1965 as a doctoral project carried out in a Long Island community in New York. By 1979, the Carnegie Corporation had praised PCHP for its long-term impact in raising the IQs of participating children and for increasing conversation between mothers and their children.[5]

The parent watches while the home visitor interacts with the child, modeling behaviors that the parent can imitate and continue with the child afterward. On the first of the two visits each week, the home visitor takes along books and toys to use with the child and leaves them with the family as gifts. "Many of the families we serve have no reading materials in the home when they begin the program and the books become the basis of not just the child's library but the family library," says Sarah E. Walzer, executive director of PCHP, based in Port Washington, New York.

The program seeks to improve the quality and quantity of conversation between parents and children. Watching and listening to home visitors as they interact with the children gives parents topics to discuss and language for holding that conversation. Research has found that youngsters who participate in the Parent-Child Home Program do, in fact, show greater readiness for kindergarten as compared with counterparts who were not in the program.[6] Eighty-five percent of the families that enroll remain for the entire two years.

The Nurse-Family Partnership

The Nurse-Family Partnership (NFP) seems almost too good to be true. It calls itself an "evidence-based" home visit program and the evidence shows great success. NFP works exclusively with low-income, first-time mothers, at least half of whom are still in their teens and almost nine out of ten unmarried. Nurses begin meeting with the mothers while they are still pregnant and continue the visits until the child's second birthday.

The program attributes its success largely to three factors: using formally educated nurses, adhering to an intervention model tested in randomized trials, and operating at a sufficient scale by serving about 100 families at each site. The Nurse-Family Partnership seeks to improve pregnancy outcomes, child health and development, and parents' economic self-sufficiency. Sites operate in conjunction with a range of public and nonprofit agencies including health departments, community-based health centers, nursing associations, and hospitals.

The schedule calls for a nurse to visit the mother-to-be once a week for a month at the outset and, then, every other week until the baby is born, concentrating all the while on behaviors that can affect fetal development. Nurses take diet histories during the mother's pregnancy and assess smoking, alcohol, and drug use, seeking reductions in any patterns of substance abuse. Visits continue once a week for six weeks after birth to help the mother through the immediate postpartum period. The nurse then visits every other week until the baby is 21 months old, and monthly afterward. Visits end up, though, occurring only about half the scheduled times, mostly because mothers miss appointments.

The nurses, like the home visitors of PAT, follow visit-by-visit guidelines that reflect changing stages of development. They tell mothers how to improve the physical and emotional care of their babies. As the children grow older, nurses use curriculums that help mothers understand their infants' and toddlers' communicative signals, enhancing parents' ability to interact with the children.

They work with the women to clarify goals and solve problems that may interfere with their education and pursuit of employment. The nurses help the young mothers build supportive relationships with family members and friends and link them to health and human services. While the program does not concern itself with the cognitive development of children as directly as PAT does, it nonetheless encourages mothers to read to their babies, talk with them, and make interactions enjoyable.

Research found the professional nurses more effective as visitors than comparable paraprofessionals with no formal education in the caregiving professions. It also showed that the program reduced child neglect and abuse and increased labor force participation by the mothers. The Nurse-Family Partnership had the highest payoff to society of any of 42 pre-K, child welfare, youth development, mentoring, substance abuse, and teen pregnancy prevention programs studied in 2004.[7]

Nurses enter data on each visit into a computer system that permits supervisors to monitor their work. David Olds, who was then a recent college graduate and has since earned his Ph.D., founded the Nurse-Family Partnership in the 1970s, but the program did not expand nationally until 1996 and is now in more than 20 states. Each site finds its own financial support. Colorado's state legislature, for instance, earmarked $350 million of tobacco-settlement funds to pay for the Nurse-Family Partnership for 25 years.

THE CHILD CARE DILEMMA

While the impact of mothers on child development—positively or negatively—is indisputable, many children younger than four or five spend a large portion of each day away from home even though they do not yet attend school. They are in child care. Once, it was a given that mothers would mind their children during the years before they entered school. When mothers could not discharge this duty, another family member stepped into the breach. That world now seems as distant as the era of cloth diapers.

The increase of single-mother households and working couples has exacerbated the need for child care at all economic levels. More than 60 percent of mothers with children under three work[8] and 73 percent of infants and toddlers of employed mothers are in nonparental care.[9] Furthermore, for mothers with and without jobs outside the home, the growth rate of preschool participation is the same.[10] Most families must pay on their own for child care, but the federal government provides $16 billion—and the states another $4 billion—to help cover costs for low-income families.

The quality of child care and, correspondingly, its effect on development varies greatly. A succession of studies in recent years even raised questions about whether youngsters who were in child care behave more aggressively once they reach school. Findings related to the impact of child care almost certainly depend on such variables as the number of hours a child spends in care, the kind of setting, the qualifications of care givers, and the quality of parenting at home. Differences in the quality of care for the youngest children should be a matter of everyone's concern. Philosopher John Dewey noted a century ago that "what the best and wisest parent wants for his own child that must the community want for all of its children."[11]

The National Research Council's landmark report *Eager to Learn* emphasized that both preschool and child care should combine care with learning.[12] Government-provided child care in combination with education in western Europe illustrates the possibilities for the United States. "To the French," said a report on the system known as the *École Maternelle*, "this preschool attended by 2.5 million children is the crown jewel of the country's educational system. It is a widely shared rite of passage of French childhood."[13]

American authorities, by comparison, give attention to safety provisions but tend to ignore such factors as adult-child ratios, credentials of care givers, and curriculum requirements. It is, in fact, a stretch to apply the word *curriculum* to the many settings in which images on a television screen constitute the educational component. Enforcement of licensing usually pertains only to centers and larger settings and ignores the tens of thousands of private homes in which parents leave children in someone's care every day. Money is the big issue when it comes to the quality of child care. It affects the facilities, but more significantly, it determines the qualifications of the staff.

Thus, infants and toddlers, at a time of greatest risk to their brain development, may end up in compromised settings and in the hands of deficient care givers, not to mention the possibility of having inept parents. One cannot overemphasize the critical importance of experiences and relationships that leave deep impressions during these years. Some windows of opportunity may forever slam shut.

Making Child Care More Educational

An ambitious effort in Pittsburgh to mount a program of early care and education failed, in part, because state officials—whose funding was crucial—viewed the program essentially as expensive baby sitting and not the responsibility of taxpayers.[14] The Heinz Endowments was the moving force behind the $60 million Early Childhood Initiative. Teresa Heinz Kerry, chairman of the endowments, commented in the wake of the inability to secure the state's fiscal backing: "Does investing in children to give them a good start in life make more sense than trying to 'fix' them or the problems they cause later?"[15] Two years later, demonstrating that he was on the same page as his wife, presidential candidate John F. Kerry said in a campaign speech: "We've got to stop being content to spend $50,000 a year of your tax money to house a young person in prison for the rest of their life rather than invest $10,000 a year in Head Start, Early Start, early childhood education, after-school programs."[16]

The real or imagined schism between child care and early education does little to resolve the problem of what to do with children when they are not in school—either because they are not yet old enough or because they need to spend the hours before and after class somewhere. Mark Ginsberg, executive director of the National Association for the Education of Young Children, argues against distinguishing between early care and early education: "We may not understand what we're providing if we think it's possible to somehow separate the two."[17]

Child care providers have been renaming their enterprise "child care and early education," which sometimes is a fair description and other times no more than a deceptive euphemism. Whatever the name on the door, children's minds do not shut off in any setting. Child care always holds potential for learning, however much it may remain unfulfilled. Therefore, efforts to strengthen educational aspects of child care cannot help but benefit children. Parents wonder where to put children during out-of-school time, especially in the case of half-day pre-K and kindergarten programs. Even with the pioneering effort to create universal prekindergarten in Georgia, for instance, the state-sponsored program operates for only 6.5 hours a day and for 180 days a year, paralleling the school day and the school year.

Part of the undoing of the initiative in Pittsburgh was that what founders envisioned as a half-day program grew to a full-day program. Planners underestimated the number of eligible children whose working mothers needed child care. Total cost per child for the fully subsidized program ballooned from a projected $4,407 to $13,612, an increase exacerbated by other mistakes in the business plan as well.

Maryland's Approach: The Judy Centers

In 2000, Maryland established a network of centers devoted to early care and education. Named in memory of Judith P. Hoyer, an advocate for young children and the wife of Congressman Steny Hoyer, the Judy Centers serve youngsters from birth until they enter preschool or kindergarten and strive to ensure that kids get stimulation to strengthen the foundation of their education. The centers collaborate with school systems, child care providers, social service agencies, and counties to upgrade care, coordinate family services, identify situations requiring intervention, and help support Head Start, pre-K, and kindergarten programs. Two of the state's twenty-four Judy Centers are situated within the Montgomery County Public School district and operate in conjunction with nearby elementary schools.

The centers render technical assistance to help child care providers improve to the point that they can seek national or state accreditation. Providers seeking to raise the quality of their services to children and families may get grants to pay for the college tuitions and professional development of staff members, salary enhancements, equipment and materials, and applications fees for accreditation. In turn, Judy Centers provide grants to school systems to purchase child care and family support services from those providers that attain accreditation.

Judy Centers also try to improve the quality of informal child care providers too small to seek accreditation but nonetheless responsible for minding a few children each day. Such private home settings are especially important in Montgomery County, where many families without immigration documents feel more comfortable and also can more easily afford this kind of child care. Latino children comprise the single largest segment of the enrollment in the two Montgomery elementary schools with Judy Centers, Summit Hall and Rosemont. The schools depend on child care providers as wraparound settings. Judy Centers run some child care programs at their own sites on a year-round basis.

Programs serve parents as well as children, sometimes by collaborating with branch libraries. "Parents learn why it's important for their children to come to school, what school provides, and who to talk to about school," says Keith Jones, the principal of Summit Hall Elementary, who is grateful to have a Judy Center next door to his school. He continues: "You're struggling to bring a community in and help them understand their role in the American system of education. We hope to get those families into the Judy Center early and work on language, health, and safety, and then the transition to prekindergarten and kindergarten."

Educare: A Model in the Making

The Buffett Early Childhood Fund and the Ounce of Prevention Fund have mounted an ambitious attempt to demonstrate the potential for intervening early in the lives of children. Calling their venture Educare, they operate centers providing care and education to 150 to 200 children at each location—Chicago's south side, Omaha's north side, and Milwaukee's Metcalfe Park. The program aims to establish such centers in 10 states. Yes, the Warren Buffett family fortune underpins this enterprise.

Private money builds each Educare Center at a cost of 2.3 to 2.5 million dollars. Then, the organization skillfully blends such federal programs as Early Head Start and Early Reading First with state and child care dollars and funds from school districts to operate the centers. Services begin when mothers-to-be are pregnant and continue with programs for infants and toddlers, all the while trying to build trusting and supportive relationships with parents. To emphasize continuity of care and minimize wrenching transitions, the centers use two different models to organize settings for infants and toddlers. One arrangement mixes infants and toddlers of various ages who remain with the same classroom team for three years. The other organizes them into same-age groups that remain with the same teacher for three years.

HOW TO HELP PARENTS
PROMOTE EARLY LITERACY

Learning should be reinforced in the homes of very young children, whatever the quality of child care and early education. Eighteen pre-K classrooms in five Montgomery County elementary schools, part of the Wheaton Cluster, partnered with two outside child care centers and a child development course at a high school to promote school readiness under a federal Early Reading First grant. The effort provided professional development and coaching for the teachers and child care workers and gave parents free books and literacy materials. The Aspen Hill Library collaborated by hosting literacy classes for parents and story times for children. The library also held conversation clubs in Spanish to help build parenting skills.

School officials realized that when they put fresh emphasis on the early years, they should engage the home and therefore decided to put the system's family and community partnerships unit under the curriculum office. Schools could then better coordinate family outreach with English as a Second Language, Title I, preschool, and other educational pursuits. At the request of the County Council, the school system also bolstered its ability to help children from birth to school entry by collaborating with the county's Department of Health and Human Services. The department sponsored literacy learning parties, equipping parents of young children with practical strategies for preparing youngsters for school.

It is imperative to reach families least likely to make reading a part of the household experience. The federal government's Even Start program, which began in 1989, invests in literacy programs for very low-income families, particularly during the years leading up to a child's third birthday. The $220 million that Even Start allotted in fiscal year 2005 supported programs for family literacy, to help parents improve their own literacy, and for early education of children. States receive the funds and then award grants to local projects on a competitive basis. Such programs face enormous challenges, though, as revealed by evaluations showing that the gains of children and parents in Even Start were no greater than those of similar children and parents not in Even Start.[18] So, efforts to boost family literacy during the years leading up to school may not compensate for the differences in the early experiences of children. The Bush administration has proposed to eliminate Even Start.

Officials at California's Peninsula Community Foundation, concerned about the paucity of books in the homes of very young children from low-income families, funded a program in 1999 in San Mateo not only to get books into homes but to get children and adults to enjoy books together. From those origins, Raising a Reader spread through the Silicon Valley and to more than 70 communities in 32 states.

Program sites send red canvas bags of books bearing the inscription "Read to Me" to homes each week with instructions about how to share the books with children of preschool age. The adults don't have to know English. They don't even have to know how to read. The program wants children to become familiar with the existence of books, learning what a book is—feeling it, turning the pages, seeing the pictures, talking about it with an adult. Children and adults discover together that books can be a normative part of homes, and, all the while, parent and child bond through the shared experience.

Raising a Reader calls this "book cuddling," typically a tot sitting in a parent's lap as they look through a book and talk about it. The bags include some of the classics of children's literature. Moreover, for the very youngest children, through the age of two, book bags are filled with hard-board picture books with few words. The program set out to spread an appreciation of books in this manner through child care centers, Head Start, visiting nurse programs, and libraries.

More recently, preschools and kindergartens in public schools have joined the mix. The program includes information that discusses brain development, suggestions of questions to ask children, and activities to carry out related to stories. There is also a video—available in nine languages—that encourages parents to create a language-rich home, not worry about making mistakes in reading to children, get children to participate in the story, and recognize there is no right or wrong way to share a book. Raising a Reader rotates the book bags from home to home, a sort of circulating library that belongs to the sponsoring organization. Each of the 26 bags contains four books, an entirely different set from those in any other bag, making a total of 104 separate books that may eventually reach each home.

Another family literacy program, Avance, began at the Mirasol housing project in San Antonio in 1973, where Gloria G. Rodriguez founded it to help poor Latina mothers promote the literacy of their children from birth through the age of three. The program grew and prospered to the extent that one of its funders, W. K. Kellogg Foundation, singled out Avance as a model grantee when the foundation celebrated its seventy-fifth anniversary in 2005. What began as a program to teach uneducated mothers about the developmental stages of their infants and toddlers took on a dual mission over the decades, encouraging and aiding mothers in advancing their own life prospects. Where 30 years ago most of the mothers remained high school dropouts, now most complete high school or earn an equivalency diploma.

Avance (Spanish for "to advance"), like other family literacy efforts, predicates its existence on a belief that the years before children enter school are too vital to leave to chance, especially when youngsters live in circumstances that might not ordinarily adequately prepare them for the classroom. Using both Spanish and English, instructors carry out the nine-month core program in housing projects, community centers, public schools, and anywhere else that they can get mothers to gather regularly to learn about the emotional, physical, social, and cognitive growth of their children.

After a year in the program, 53 percent of children between the ages of two and four were in the normal range of language development as compared with just 13 percent of them at the outset. Moreover, teachers receiving these children in preschool and kindergarten rated 90 percent of them as at least average on measures of school readiness. None of the pupils in a study sample were held back in first or second grade.[19]

PUTTING THE VERY EARLY YEARS IN PERSPECTIVE

Differences in parenting account for an estimated one-third to one-half of the variation in school outcomes between poor and not-poor children.[20] In other words, it matters a great deal whether adults during the first three years of children's lives foster an environment that promotes healthy social, emotional, physical, and mental development. So, the question is not whether parents ought to improve their child-rearing skills, but how to intervene in the most effective manner to help them do so. This is a question that educators involved in PK–3 education ought to ask as they think about outreach to homes before youngsters reach school.

Home visits—a labor-intensive, one-on-one approach—are a decidedly expensive way to reach children. Apparently, the value of home visits increases with their frequency, which adds to the expense, as does the hiring of more expert visitors. Family literacy programs, which cost less, certainly can benefit children, but in the long run are a pale substitute for sustained, natural conversation between parents and children in a milieu filled with aspiration and rich in all manner of language.

Ultimately, the results of dispatching visitors to meet with parents in their homes—or of sending books home for parents to read to their children—depend on the ability to change adult behavior, which is not an easy task. Anyone who looks back on shattered New Year's resolutions knows how difficult this can be. Home visits may do more to enhance parents' sensitivity to children's needs than to improve cognitive performance and school readiness.[21] Interventions that affect maternal sensitivity, however, may be more fruitful than some realize and can, along with enriching the home environment, mediate poverty's effects on children's cognitive and language performance.[22]

Would it be preferable and more valuable to invest the same funds to intervene directly with very young children, say, in child-care settings? Both family literacy programs and home visits during the years from birth to age three signify recognition that good programs that start in preschool and run through the third grade are not enough for some youngsters. Something good has to happen from birth to three, too, but the book remains open on the best ways to bring about such improvement. Figuring out how to add value during this early period ought to be within the province and mission of PK–3 education.

3

PREKINDERGARTEN FOR ALL

To walk into a good prekindergarten is to enter a magical world where small people joyously pursue stimulating activities that develop their social, emotional, physical, and cognitive faculties. It is a teeming place where play constitutes the medium of learning and interactions among children and between child and teacher become vehicles for maturation. Numbers and letters adorn walls and may hang from the ceiling as well. Picture books are everywhere. The language-rich environment contains reminders of the tender age of the occupants—stuffed animals, mats for naps, snacks, and, perhaps, even diapers.

Various stations throughout the room offer opportunities to measure out water in containers of various sizes, etch letters of the alphabet in sand, use rudimentary arithmetic to erect structures from blocks, settle into beanbag chairs to peruse picture books, dress in mommy and daddy clothes for pretending, sit at computer monitors responding to instructions dictated through earphones, and putter with pots and plastic dishes to learn cooperation in a tot-sized kitchen. There are routines to follow, queues to form, whole-group activities, small-group activities, and chances to work on one's own. Pre-K teachers want these children to arrive in kindergarten able to follow directions, keep impulses in check, get along with others, and be equipped with pre-academic skills—all of which adds up to "teachability."[1]

Some call preschool the new kindergarten and maybe, to a certain extent, it does fill that role. Concern about asking too much of three- and four-year-olds, however, ignores accumulating evidence that youngsters at these ages can learn far more than educators and parents previously recognized. The linguistic and mathematical potential of children younger than five exceeds what people imagined just a few years ago. Furthermore, early education may prevent or at least mitigate learning problems that might otherwise appear once youngsters enter formal schooling.

Prekindergarten is the essential launching pad of the PK–3 continuum. Children who attend pre-K, as compared with peers who do not, are less apt to enter special education or to be held back, while performing better in school and persisting long enough to get their diplomas. The effects—under the best of circumstances—continue into adulthood, with preschool graduates less likely to get caught up in the justice system and less apt to go on welfare.

Proponents of making preschool more widely available point to the economic benefits that they say will accrue to society. James Heckman, economist and Nobel laureate, argues from the standpoint of productivity that it makes sense to invest in young children from disadvantaged backgrounds.[2] Economists offer wide-ranging estimates of how much the nation could benefit for each dollar spent on prekindergarten—looking, on the one hand, at money saved on such items as prisons and unemployment payments and, on the other hand, at tax revenues reaped from educated adults. Participants in the Perry Preschool Study in Michigan—arguably the most influential look at the impact of preschool—were at age 40 less likely to have broken the law and had higher incomes and more stable lives than similar adults who had not attended the program in the early and middle 1960s.[3]

There are qualifications, though. While the preschool program in Tulsa that is free and open to all income groups—part of a statewide effort—led to gains in letter-word recognition, spelling, and problem solving for all participants,[4] preschool exerts its most profound effect on youngsters from impoverished backgrounds. Affluent children start out ahead and remain ahead of less advantaged youngsters. Jeanne Brooks-Gunn, a scholar of early education, cautioned in testimony to Congress that while high-quality early childhood programs have the potential to alter school outcomes for vulnerable children, there are limitations. "To expect effects to be sustained throughout childhood and adolescence, at their initial high levels, in the absence of continued high quality schooling . . . is to believe in magic," she said.[5]

Some romantics maintain that all children enter school ready to learn, and they criticize the idea that some are readier than others. Surely, many teachers could do more to use what children already know as a prelude to further learning. It is irrefutable, though, that some children are better prepared than others. No one would expect a youngster to play Chopin's études without first taking piano lessons.

Children enjoy an edge when they have a sense of order and understand the routines that often are crucial to learning. Those who begin kindergarten recognizing letters, basic numbers, and shapes, and understanding the concept of relative size, push off more quickly from the starting blocks. In fact, they are ahead of the others in their achievement in reading and math by the spring of their kindergarten year and remain so in the spring of the first grade year.[6] Then, the distance grows wider by the end of third grade.[7] Differing levels of readiness constitute the early warning system of a large and pervasive educational problem—an achievement gap that tends to situate black and Hispanic students on one side and whites and Asian Americans on the other.

Early education can assist in the efforts to overcome disadvantages by making learning part of a continuum, as exemplified by the Chicago Child-Parent Centers (CPC), which provided preschool for both three- and four-year-olds and then supported them through the third grade. Chicago created the centers in 1967 with Title I funding just after the launch of Head Start, both federal programs for poor children, and spread them to 25 sites in high-poverty neighborhoods. CPC stressed early intervention, parent involvement, structured language-based instruction, and program continuity into the primary grades. The guiding premise of the Chicago centers was that a stable and enriched learning environment during early childhood, from ages of three to nine, would build a foundation for success.

A head teacher directed each center, reporting directly to the principal of the affiliated elementary school, not unlike what could happen in a PK–3 approach. The head teacher coordinated instruction, parent involvement, community outreach, and health and nutrition services. Each center also had a parent-resource teacher. Aides and parents supplemented licensed teachers in classrooms. The curriculum emphasized spoken and written language, with the goal of helping children develop basic skills. By 2004, though, the 25 sites had dwindled to 15, only 13 of which continued support through the second or third grade. The home visits that occurred at least once a semester during preschool and kindergarten became less frequent during the first and second grades.

The Chicago Child-Parent Centers were rigorously evaluated. Arthur J. Reynolds studied the program for his doctoral dissertation and continued his investigation as a University of Wisconsin professor, eventually making it his life's work by carrying out a longitudinal study of CPC children who completed kindergarten in 1986. He observed that by the time the children were about 15 years old the "long-term effects of the program occurred primarily because participation promoted early cognitive and scholastic advantages that culminated in better social competence in adolescence."[8]

Children in the program had higher achievements in reading and math and stronger consumer life skills. They had lower grade retention, reduced need for remedial services, and a shorter time in special education for those placed in it. Moreover, participants had a lower incidence of delinquency and were more likely to complete high school. In addition, parents of participants were more involved in the school and had higher expectations for their children. Youngsters fared best the longer they were part of CPC. Those who participated in preschool did better than those who did not, but those who were part of the program through the second or third grade fared better than children whose participation did not extend beyond preschool.[9]

MAKING PRE-K UNIVERSAL

Prekindergarten is not a new idea, having been around since 1903.[10] There are parallels between the movement to offer prekindergarten to all children and the efforts to make kindergarten universal. It took most of the twentieth century for kindergarten to become available in most school districts, and even by 2000 many American children still had only half-day kindergartens to attend. Universal prekindergarten (UPK)—available for every family that wants it but required for no one—can breach walls that would otherwise surround a program often set apart by family income, as was the case in Chicago.

Studies such as one by the National Research Council that praised the merits of high-quality preschools in preparing youngsters to adapt to the demands of formal school programs[11] have nudged the nation toward preschool. Findings from brain research and new insights into cognition have focused further attention on child development. The brain, that great plastic vessel of expanding knowledge, is a wondrous device that undergoes exponential growth in the earliest years at a rate unequalled at any later age. Opportunities not exploited during the preschool years may be lost forever.

Locales that open early childhood programs to all economic groups can capture a constituency that will use its influence to promote and protect pre-K. In North Carolina, for instance, Smart Start was created in 1993 at the instigation of the governor, James B. Hunt Jr., as a public-private partnership to provide child care, health care, and family support. Smart Start was designed to make many of its services available to families of all economic levels, which helped win it extensive support. Similarly, Zell Miller, as governor of Georgia, established universal prekindergarten in 1993 for four-year-olds from all families, regardless of income. He sought to build a wide constituency for the program.

This strategy is not new. Franklin Delano Roosevelt recognized it in 1935 when he included all income groups in the new social security program, and John F. Kennedy in 1963 acknowledged his need to provide programs for the middle class if he hoped to mount a campaign to fight poverty.[12] Today's challenge is to create places in prekindergarten for the children of the vast number of Americans in the economic middle, who struggle to afford private preschools, and especially for the children of low-income families, who don't quite qualify for Head Start. Most of the 39 states that put public funds into pre-K limit their programs to the most impoverished families.

Universal prekindergarten means not having to turn away families, regardless of income. It avoids scandals such as one that arose in San Antonio in 2005, when it became known that three dozen teachers and other school employees had for at least three years been enrolling their own children—in violation of regulations that restricted the program to low-income families—in state-funded preschool classes operated by the school system.

The fact that schooling begins at age five instead of four is arbitrary. Parents must find child care during working hours, often in inadequate facilities that contribute little to the cognitive growth of children. Why not create a voluntary universal system of preschool available to four-year-olds—and, eventually, three-year-olds? It would serve not just the quest for child care, but the developmental needs of children as well. Pre-K is the linchpin of the PK–3 concept, the period in between the nurturing of the home and the formal start of schooling in kindergarten. Furthermore, the gains of preschool are greater for children who start at age three than for those who start later. A study in

California, for example, discovered that those who entered programs at age three ended up ahead of peers who began preschool at four. They had higher cognitive and school readiness gains than youngsters who started the programs a year later.[13]

A main difference between a pre-K program targeted to the neediest pupils and a universal program is the cost. UPK increases the price tag exponentially. The cost for each participating four-year-old in Georgia was $3,871 by 2005, when it had a budget of $271 million and reached into all 159 counties in the state. By that time, however, revenues from a state lottery, the fiscal underpinning for universal prekindergarten, were no longer expanding as hoped. The National Institute for Early Education Research estimates that it would cost about $70 billion, including full-time, year-round, wraparound child care, for pre-K for all of the country's three- and four-year-olds. If states paid for prekindergarten the way they fund the rest of the grades—as an essential part of schooling—all of America's children would have the opportunity for a better start to learning.

Pre-K programs in Georgia and Oklahoma, the most extensive in the country, serve about 70 percent of the four-year-olds in their states. New York State deviated quickly from the aim of reaching all children when it supported only the poorest children despite the legislature's authorization for a universal program. Funding shortfalls and shortages of facilities are key barriers to making programs universal.

Florida's Messy Move into UPK

Passage of a constitutional amendment in Florida in 2002 calling for voluntary prekindergarten for the state's four-year-olds by 2005–06 shows that a well-crafted campaign can capture public support even in a severely stressed fiscal climate. Leaders of the effort crossed party lines in pursuit of backers and ensured that the measure enjoyed wide appeal by seeking preschool for all children, not just for the 26 percent of the state's youngest children living in poverty. The amendment came after several years during which prekindergarten bills failed even to receive hearings in both chambers of the legislature.

The first proposal that the legislature sent to Governor Jeb Bush in response to the amendment was so weak that he vetoed it, saying it would lead to a program of low quality. The *St. Petersburg Times* called it "babysitting" and the *Daytona Beach News-Journal* labeled it "Pretend Pre-K." Finally, the legislature enacted and the governor signed a bill containing a mélange of odd compromises. It did not deal with the uneven quality of private providers, the sector that would provide the bulk of the preschool classes. This failure left many lawmakers and editorial writers wondering if the state would get its money's worth from the program, which received an appropriation of $387 million for the first year.

The struggle in Florida encapsulated the issues involved in creating a preschool system from scratch. The state's Association of Child Care Management, an industry group, lobbied vigorously to ensure that its members would figure prominently in the program. As a result, families receive vouchers that they turn over mostly to private child care centers, including those operated by religious groups, as the public schools have little space to accommodate pre-K classrooms during the regular school year.

The state's investment translated into a $2,500 voucher for each participating child, an amount that allows for a school day of three hours rather than the six hours that an advisory panel had recommended. This means not just fewer hours of substance, but also the need for working families to find and pay for wraparound care the rest of the day. The enrollment of 81,000 of Florida's estimated 220,000 four-year-olds also disappointed supporters, who felt that families did not get enough information about the availability of the program. Some of the lowest enrollments were among the poorest Floridians, whose children most need preschool.

Finally, one of the strangest compromises required public schools to offer pre-K not during the academic year but during the summer, aiming at families that had not sent children to classes during the school year, when, presumably, private providers provided most of the seats. The public school summer prekindergarten assured children, though, of having regular certified teachers with college degrees, not teachers with the child development associate credential held by many working in child care centers. Furthermore, public schools have to offer 300 hours of classes during the summer, a requirement that might mean eight-hour days for the children, given the need to squeeze the time into a foreshortened calendar.

This checkered beginning to pre-K in Florida, while easy to criticize, nonetheless represents a kind of success, placing the state among the handful embracing universality. The law, though flawed, is now on the books and supporters can push to improve it, a more enviable task than still having to campaign for a state-supported universal program, which is the case in most of the country.

Using Diverse Providers

Preschool expansion could follow the route of kindergarten to achieve universality through the public schools. This would require hiring more teachers and building more classrooms. Two obstacles obstruct this path: the cost and the existence of thousands of centers, churches, storefronts in strip malls, and other sites—mostly nonprofit but for-profit as well—that now serve preschoolers, mostly with child care. As illustrated in Florida, this powerful lobby will seek to protect private providers and incorporate them into any system of universal prekindergarten. Paradoxically, many academics and policymakers who support preservation of the private providers and object to public schools assuming total responsibility for prekindergarten also oppose vouchers and even charter schools at the K–12 level. Who says people have to be consistent?

More than half of the prekindergarteners in state-supported programs in Georgia and New Jersey attend classes in private facilities. In creating an infrastructure for its universal system, New York State specifically required that school districts place a minimum of 10 percent of pre-K classes in community settings, outside the public schools. Precedent exists for fashioning an educational infrastructure from a combination of private and public providers. Postsecondary schooling in the United States originated through a private network of colleges founded mostly by religious denominations. Gradually, the public sector of higher education developed and expanded. By and large, though, preschool outside the public schools is a low-budget operation that employs less-qualified teachers (a minority hold bachelor's degrees) and pays them lower salaries.

PRE-K IN ACTION

The spread of prekindergarten does not depend solely on action by states. Individual school systems sometimes act unilaterally to prepare four-year-olds for kindergarten. This occurs especially in districts that recognize the importance of the primary grades in laying a foundation for school success. This can represent tacit endorsement of a PK–3 approach.

Harrisburg: Incorporating Head Start for a Fast Route

Transferring control of the school system from the school board to the mayor was the key to an effort that began in 2001 to improve public education in Harrisburg, the capital of Pennsylvania. The transformation contained a bold plan to implement universal pre-K and to focus on literacy through the third grade. This was a downtrodden school district—where the public schools draw students mainly from poor minority families—that state legislators did all they could to ignore as they went about their business under the Romanesque dome of one of the most beautiful statehouses in the country. Harrisburg's school system ranked last among the 501 in Pennsylvania, so bad that the president of the teachers' union told me it was "a miserable place to be a teacher or a student."

The Republican-dominated legislature turned over the district to the city's mayor of two decades, Stephen R. Reed, a Democrat. He promptly hired a new superintendent, Gerald Kohn, whom he had read about in the *New York Times Magazine*, which lauded him for his work in a mostly poor and working-class school system in southern New Jersey. Kohn, a lean, austere-looking man with a shock of white hair, had instituted a comprehensive preschool program in Vineland that not only gave children a foundation for learning, but also provided a network of social services for them and their families. "That effort was probably the reason the mayor hired me," Kohn said in retrospect. "Preschool and early childhood are the only way you can make a difference."

Presiding from a nondescript school administration building perched near the bank of the Susquehanna River, Kohn at first operated like a triage surgeon in a field hospital. He gave priority to prekindergarten and to the first three grades. Everything was about teaching kids to read and Kohn mounted an ambitious program of professional development to equip teachers and principals with the new skills they would need.

Harrisburg took the fast route into prekindergarten, constructing the infrastructure for what it hoped would grow into a universal system from Head Start centers that the district invited to relocate in public schools. The district mixed in the same classrooms children eligible for Head Start and children from families with incomes too high to qualify. Officials maintained that few families were all that affluent anyway in a school system in which more than 90 percent of the enrollment qualified for federally subsidized meals.

Every classroom had at least two teachers, one provided by Head Start and one from the school district. There was a significant disparity in their pay and the Head Start teachers weren't necessarily college graduates. But the children didn't know the difference and the two teachers seemed to strive for colleagueship. In addition, a foundation grant supported aides who floated among pre-K classrooms. The High Scope curriculum with its centers around the room that use play as a vehicle for learning was the cornerstone of the program. High Scope is based on the historic Perry Preschool approach in Ypsilanti, Michigan, and has been marketed nationally.

It took negotiations and a waiver from Head Start to create this arrangement, which was complicated by the fact that employees of Head Start and the school system did not technically report to the same supervisors. The approach stirred animosity among principals, who were accustomed to taking responsibility for everything within their buildings. The teachers' union objected to the idea of Head Start site monitors having jurisdiction over district employees. Eventually, Harrisburg created a process for site monitors to report to building principals.

The move toward universal pre-K began with Kohn's creation of REACH (Reaching Early Achievement for Children in Harrisburg), an initiative that the W. K. Kellogg Foundation helped fund. The plan included, along with preschool, extended-day child care that used private providers, health care, and social services. Full implementation of UPK in Harrisburg depended on the school system's ability to leverage the prestige conferred by foundation recognition to ferret out additional sources of financial support. Attitudes improved as principals gained jurisdiction over the pre-K classrooms in their buildings.

The effort to give youngsters a better start was evident in a prekindergarten classroom at Harrisburg's Downey Elementary School, where one day children colored and cut out masks that they would don to become characters in *Goldilocks and the Three Bears*. They had already read the story with a teacher, and now, holding extra-thick crayons—all the better to grip them—the preschoolers put the final touches to their project. The youngsters could hardly wait to show off their handiwork.

They rose from their pint-size tables wearing the bear faces and pranced gleefully around the room, masks held firm by bands that fit around their little heads. It was quickly apparent, once they were on their feet, that some children were a full head taller than others, not that any of them appeared to take notice in this combined class of three- and four-year-olds. After frolicking for a while, some children tilted their masks on their foreheads, as a middle-aged person might do with reading glasses, and went to one or another of the room's learning centers.

Montgomery County: Tackling the Weakest Link

The weakest link was the first one tackled when Maryland's Montgomery County Public Schools embarked on its Early Success plan at the end of the 1990s. The idea was to strengthen education in the system by bolstering the years from preschool through second grade, but the district barely offered pre-K. So, it mounted a preschool program by targeting children in its neediest neighborhoods. Montgomery County, like Harrisburg, hastened the process by incorporating Head Start programs into district-sponsored prekindergartens. Thus, the school system offered pre-K to youngsters in 56 of its 125 elementary schools, with classes operating for two and a half to three hours a day. The curriculum framework, aligned with Maryland's content standards, guided the prekindergartens, including those affiliated with Head Start.

Montgomery County added an extra layer of substance to pre-K at five of its elementary schools through an Early Reading First grant from the U.S. Department of Education. This program, funded in conjunction with the federal government's No Child Left Behind Act, sought to intensify early literacy efforts through staff development, extra specialists, a wider array of instructional materials, more work with parents, and enriched child care during the wraparound hours before and after pre-K classes. Principals accepted ownership of the downward expansion of public education. C. Michael Kline, principal of Ronald McNair Elementary, for instance, regarded it as his duty—along with overseeing the school's kindergarten through fifth grade classes—to supervise and evaluate prekindergarten instruction. He even determined who would teach pre-K at McNair, moving one of his outstanding second grade teachers to the position.

That teacher, Natalie Charbonneau, challenges her pupils with high expectations and they respond in kind, as could be seen one day when she sat on a rocker holding up strips of papers for them to see. The children sat on a carpet in front of her, attentive to her every word. "I'm going to show you some patterns I drew," Charbonneau said, displaying a strip on which she had drawn a succession of green and purple boxes. "Hold your thumbs up if you see a pattern. This is tricky. Look carefully."

A child recognized that two purples in a row broke the pattern. "Right, this is not a pattern," Charbonneau confirmed. Then, she held up another strip of paper. Some youngsters recognized that the colored boxes recurred with regularity. "I think this *is* a pattern," the teacher agreed, with great enthusiasm. And so it went, some strips having orange and brown boxes instead of green and purple ones. Regardless of the colors, the children had to look intently to recognize when boxes of the same color appeared where colors should have been alternating. Thumbs up, thumbs down, as Charbonneau solicited their opinions. "Oh, my goodness," she said by way of complimenting a child who noted a broken pattern. Such lessons prepare children for both math and reading. Patterns of numbers help them compute and patterns of words lead them to recognize common phonemes and letter combinations, for example.

Any step that promotes word recognition is important in Charbonneau's class, where 13 of the 22 children arrived speaking little or no English. Only a few days earlier, she had asked pupils to sort objects by size and many of them could not remember what "size" meant. Months into the school year, a number of children continued to speak to each other only in Spanish. Charbonneau thought that having taught first and second grade helped her in pre-K because she knew what awaited her students.

McNair was one of several Montgomery elementary schools piloting the use of an assessment for preschool that aligns with the kindergarten curriculum. This approach allowed McNair to start early to gauge readiness for kindergarten. "We had low expectations for pre-K, but these kids are capable of more than we think," said Principal Kline. He said that youngsters from non-English-speaking backgrounds showed the greatest benefits from preschool. This was especially important as more than 75 percent of the enrollment in the school's pre-K and Head Start classes were English-language learners. Forty-three percent of the district's entire preschool enrollment, including the affiliated Head Start classes, were children from non-English-speaking backgrounds.

New Jersey: Seeking Improvement through Lavish Spending

As the result of orders in 1997 and 1998 by the New Jersey Supreme Court in *Abbott v. Burke*, the state established a universal prekindergarten program to serve the 31 school districts having the lowest socioeconomic status among their school populations. The state pays the entire $440 million annual bill—above and beyond its aid for K–12 education. The cost for the daily six-hour pre-K runs $10,800 per child; the state spends an additional $3,700 per child for court-ordered wraparound services before and after school. It is, in all, a ten-hour day of education and care that continues through the summer. Chances are that no legislature in the country, in New Jersey or anywhere else, would of its own volition have allocated such support for pre-kindergarten. It took a state court to force it to happen.

On the assumption that only early intervention would make a difference in the lives of disadvantaged children, the court directed that all three- and four-year-olds in the 31 Abbott districts have the chance to attend preschool. Cost was no obstacle as the court sought to ensure that all teachers, including those in the private settings that enroll 55 percent of the students, have proper credentials. The court required a certified teacher for every 15 children, gave teachers without bachelor's degrees six years to get them, and helped to pay for their studies.

In turn, the state guarantees that teachers receive salaries on a par with peers in public schools. In addition, every classroom has an aide and there is a family worker for every 45 families. The state also paid for supplies at the outset. New Jersey operates the Rolls-Royce of state-funded preschools.

The state permitted school systems without enough space for the new preschoolers to contract with private child care centers to take the overflow of students. The state education department developed new regulations and standards to upgrade those facilities. When the local school district contracted with the Egenolf Early Childhood Center in Elizabeth, New Jersey, for example, to provide preschool for three-year-olds, Egenolf had been in existence as a private, nonprofit child care center and nursery school since 1890. The city's public schools, which set out to accommodate only four-year-olds, did not have room for the younger children. Moreover, public school teachers, unlike those at Egenolf who were used to toddlers, would likely have balked at changing the soiled clothing of three-year-olds not yet toilet trained.

So, Egenolf—where 95 percent of the youngsters come from Latino families and all the teachers are bilingual—operated seven pre-K classes for three-year-olds during the 2004–05 school year as a result of the Abbott decision. At the age of four, the children would move into prekindergartens in public schools, a practice that Egenolf teachers and many parents deplored as an unnecessary interruption in the children's early schooling. As it was, Egenolf lost several of its credentialed teachers to the school system when the public schools opened their doors to four-year-olds.

With so much fresh money flowing into private centers that previously had little public accountability for their fiscal practices, financial abuses seemed inevitable. *The Record*, Hackensack's daily newspaper, revealed in a series of articles in 2004 that state auditors had uncovered such questionable expenditures as those for wigs, oriental rugs, plus-size clothing, a family cell phone plan, a time share at a vacation hotel, and numerous examples of shoddy bookkeeping. Presumably, time and tighter financial controls ordered by the state have diminished the abuses.

The New Jersey program, which by 2005 reached 80 percent of the eligible youngsters, some 43,000 three- and four-year-olds, made steady progress during its first six years in raising language and literacy levels, but had less impact on math skills. The state education department said in 2005 that the achievement gap had narrowed by the time students completed third grade and that the majority of children in the 31 Abbott districts had passed the state assessment at the end of third grade.

THE PURSUIT OF QUALITY IN PREKINDERGARTEN

Preschool educators differ in their visions for young children. A defining phrase is "developmentally appropriate." Almost everyone with any connection to early childhood education subscribes to the need for approaches suitable to a child's stage of development, but they do not agree on what constitutes appropriateness. This enduring controversy means that sometimes prekindergarten programs, including Head Start, do not sufficiently emphasize literacy. "Programs can be accredited and even rated superior despite failing to provide the kind of rich language and literacy environment researchers have demonstrated to be necessary in order that all children learn to read and write," stated one observer in an American Educational Research Association article.[14]

Richard Lee Colvin, a colleague at Teachers College, Columbia University, saw firsthand how this debate can play out. He visited a preschool in the Bronx that received funding from New York City, the state, and Head Start. He watched such activities as four-year-olds counting sticks from frozen ice cream bars, gluing them to paper, and describing their creations to teachers, who carefully recorded their words. Colvin was surprised to learn, though, that the city's Department of Education did not approve of the school's labeling objects in the classroom with their names or displaying letters of the alphabet low enough on the wall that preschoolers could see them.

Bureaucrats at headquarters told the school that this approach provided inappropriate abstractions. Since the children did not read, according to these enlightened officials, alphabet letters would merely frustrate them and undermine their self-esteem. An inspector from central headquarters ordered the preschool to remove alphabet letters on the wall, as well as the signs with the names of objects. This episode epitomizes an extreme in the battle over developmental appropriateness.

It is not as if most advocates of a more academic approach in pre-K call for lining up little children at desks and lecturing to them. They simply recognize that the surroundings and activities of early education can be laced with the flavor of learning and that schools should permit youngsters to fulfill their potential. Denise Stultz, an administrator in the instructional department in Montgomery County, Maryland, said that if teachers systematically gather information on the progress of prekindergarteners and find that they are reading, "it's malpractice *not* to move them along."

Another dimension of quality involves those who teach in preschool. Salary and benefits in pre-K, which go a long way toward determining the educational background of teachers and administrators, have not increased in step with the rest of the economy in most places in the country. The share of staff at the country's center-based providers with at least a four-year degree was 43 percent in the middle 1980s, but only 30 percent in the early 2000s.[15] Full implementation of PK–3 should require that preschool teachers have proper credentials.

THE UPS AND DOWNS OF HEAD START

Head Start was on the scene long before the states began funding prekindergarten and prior to the movement for universal pre-K. This historic effort to close the achievement gap came before anyone applied that term to the scholastic woes of poor and minority children. President Lyndon B. Johnson unveiled Head Start as a centerpiece in his War on Poverty in 1965. It has grown to a $6.7 billion enterprise enrolling 915,000 preschoolers, which nonetheless fails to serve half of the eligible three- and four-year-olds. Efforts to expand preschool as the first link in the PK–3 progression must take note of Head Start.

Debates about the effects of Head Start date to 1969, when the first large-scale study found that it did not produce lasting IQ gains. Ever since, Head Start has been a statistical soccer ball for researchers. A 1995 study by RAND declared that Head Start had positive and persistent effects on the test scores and achievement of white participants but that large score gains by black children were quickly lost.[16] As recently as 2005, another major research report—part of a congressionally mandated study following thousands of children from their first year in Head Start through the end of the first grade—found the effect was modest. Favorable results on vocabulary knowledge, for instance, showed up for three-year-olds but not for four-year-olds.[17]

An overriding shortcoming of Head Start is that the gains it produces seem to fade despite the expenditure of $86 billion on 25 million children during a period of 40 years. This may say as much about what follows Head Start as about the program itself. A PK–3 approach, for example, would allow each year of early schooling to build on the previous year.

Lurking behind any analysis of Head Start's cognitive effect is the question of the program's purpose. So much has been made of Head Start's promotion of healthy social, emotional, and physical development and its involvement with and employment of parents that critics see an implication that the program has not adequately valued educational growth. The Bush administration, leery of Head Start, called for greater emphasis on literacy and academic skills. It also proposed more assessment of participants, a step that brought down a hail of rebuke.

Disputes over Head Start too often take the form of an either/or argument—the program should lean toward academics or toward physical-social-emotional needs. It is a debate predicated on the false notion that good preschool education cannot fulfill both objectives. The larger issue has to do with identifying the role that Head Start should play in the emerging movement toward UPK and as a first step in PK–3.

Head Start can serve as just one more provider to receive contracts from public school systems to carry some of the preschool load. But

Head Start is more than just another provider. It is an arm of the federal government, not readily monitored or supervised by state or local officials. Sometimes it appears that even federal officials do not hold much sway over Head Start, given recurrent scandals across the country involving excessive salaries and financial irregularities in local programs. Furthermore, many of its teachers do not measure up to standards set for public school faculty.

Maybe Head Start has served its purpose, reaching many of the neediest preschool children during decades when not much else was available for them. Any drastic change, though, ought to include guarantees to absorb qualified Head Start teachers and to provide funds to assist the 70 percent with lesser credentials to upgrade their skills. Several possibilities should be considered for the future as the march toward universal pre-K continues:

- Reconstituting Head Start entirely as Early Head Start to serve children from poor families from birth to age 3
- Using Head Start funds in conjunction with state-financed preschool and spending the money for added special services exclusively for the poorest children
- Continuing Head Start exactly as it is, a federal preschool program alongside locally financed and private preschools.

Whatever role Head Start ends up playing as a part of prekindergarten, the federal program will have to take cognizance of the movement toward universal availability. UPK has momentum and it will figure prominently in bolstering the early education continuum, PK–3, that America needs to strengthen in order to get all children off to a good start.

4

A FULL DAY OF KINDERGARTEN

Laurel Telfer, principal at Rossmoor Elementary School in Los Alamitos, California, speaks from her perspective of 33 years in the school district: "We believe that kindergarten lays the foundation. We don't think that kindergarten is frivolous. It is very serious business. You can't just let kindergarten be graham crackers and cookies." And so it is on a mild, sunny winter day—the kind of weather that once drew Americans to southern California by the carload—that Pam Peters, kindergarten teacher extraordinaire, lets each of her 20 pupils present the class with a scrapbook about his or her family. There are pictures. There are charts. Each child lists a few of the family's favorite things—TV show, dessert, pet, et cetera.

A girl, Hannah, has brought a tin containing a plastic hamburger, exemplifying a favorite family food. Before Hannah opens the tin, Peters, knowing what's inside, asks the class to guess what food it contains. She makes the sound of an H, huffing for emphasis. The tin opened and a plastic hamburger revealed, Peters takes advantage of the teachable moment. "What do you call the bread that goes with a hamburger?" she asks, trying to ensure that they will learn the word *bun* if they don't already know it. Then, an opportunity arises to put more words in play. "What can go on a hamburger?" she asks.

They fire off names of vegetables and condiments: lettuce, tomato, mustard, cheese, pickles, onion, catsup, mayonnaise. Words, words, words. Vocabulary development never stops in kindergarten. Children are continually immersed in language. So many posters and so much pupil work—much of it containing words—adorns the classroom walls that it forms a kind of kindergarten wallpaper. Items containing words hang from the ceiling. Alphabet letters, entire words. Books are ubiquitous, soaking into the very atmosphere of the classroom. All of this conforms with a state requirement of two and a half hours a day of language instruction.

This particular kindergarten class, however, does not regard language as the be-all and end-all. Science looms large. Today, pupils sink and float objects, learning about buoyancy. They hear about Archimedes. Yes, Archimedes. Yesterday, they dissolved items in water, learning about absorption. Last week, they put different liquids into bottles, in layers, and studied density. These words—*buoyancy, absorption, density,* and others associated with experiments—appear regularly so that the children may incorporate them into their ever-expanding vocabularies. Often, Peters asks pupils to predict what will happen next in an experiment. They practice thinking like little scientists. They witness the experiment together and then break into small groups to replicate it.

Math? Of course, there's math. The children in this class constantly make graphs. They graph the months in which their classmates' birthdays fall, showing higher bars for the months with more birthdays and lower bars for the months with fewer birthdays. They make graphs showing which kinds of pets are most popular, the sorts of transportation they like, and so on. Graphing enhances their mathematical thinking and advances their notions about how to convey and display statistical information.

Peters brings parents into the act. Each Monday, the kids take home folders listing the tasks on which they will work that week. Parents then know what's happening at school and they can build on classroom experiences with activities at home. The children bring the folders back to school on Friday, with written comments from their parents. This particular week, parents learned that their children were comparing quantities in math, studying the letter "G" and working on decoding in their workbooks, and talking about the properties of water. Welcome to kindergarten. As Telfer says, it's more than graham crackers and cookies.

Skillful teachers combine play and academics, seeking to hold the attention of their pupils and to entertain them as they learn, much as happens in prekindergarten except with more serious intent. Noel Sauers, for example, another kindergarten teacher at Rossmoor, had her pupils read *The Five Little Snowmen,* and now they are drawing, coloring, cutting out, numbering, and gluing their own five little snowmen. They number them and fold down a flap on each snowman in a way that Sauers demonstrates so as to simulate melting and disappearing. Ergo: A lesson in subtraction.

The children will make a snowman melt to practice subtraction. Sauers and many other teachers favor such manipulative materials as vehicles for helping kids feel and see what they are learning. Adults forget how complicated it was to learn to count, to add, and to subtract. Sauers usually has almost every child in the class counting to 100 by the end of kindergarten. Now, they are ready to sing the song:

Five Little Snowmen Sat
Each with a Funny Hat
Out Came the Sun
And Melted One

"What kind of math is that?" Sauers asks no one in particular. "Subtraction," she says, answering her own question and printing the word on the chalkboard. "You're like first graders today," she says, fortifying their little egos as they tackle the work. Each child folds down a flap covering a snowman. It looks like play, but they are learning the remainder of 5 minus 1, leaving four snowmen fully visible. The task continues, snowman after snowman covered by a flap, ostensibly melting off the page, as the children learn 4 minus 1, 3 minus 1, and 2 minus 1. One snowman remains and Sauers asks what the number will be when that snowman disappears. A few children utter the magic word, zero, the point from which measurement is made, a figure that even the ancient Romans and Greeks did not recognize.

The beat is roughly the same in each of the four kindergarten classrooms at Rossmoor, which has had a full-day program for more than 20 years. The four teachers meet weekly with Telfer to discuss grade-level issues. Each has her own style, from the loosey-goosey approach of Debbie Campbell, who sings and jumps along with her kids as they joyfully belt out "Singing in the Rain" while transitioning from one activity to another, to the more tightly structured methods of Pamela Weaver, who uses Pachelbel's "Canon" as classroom background music and asks the children to "Raise your hand if you heard me say 'Put your name on the paper.'"

And the results from classroom to classroom are roughly the same. Los Alamitos, which begins where Los Angeles County ends and Orange

County starts, hard up against the San Gabriel River, is a place where parents dedicate themselves to their children's education. They readily reinforce in their comfortable homes what Weaver, Campbell, Peters, Sauers, and their teaching colleagues impart in the classrooms at Rossmoor, which has 590 students. Even the school's attractive 12-acre campus, with more than six dozen trees and a straight-on panorama of the San Bernardino Mountains, speaks to the paramount role that Rossmoor plays in its neighborhood. Grassy playing fields surround a series of separate buildings with outdoor covered walkways. The most imposing structure is a sprawling, cathedral-ceilinged library filled with computers.

Kindergarten runs from 8 A.M. to 1:15 P.M. each day, an hour shorter than other grades at the K–5 school, which has two classes of preschoolers and a limited program of child care. In all, Rossmoor has 80 kindergarteners, 20 per class as mandated by the state of California. In the kindergartens, as in the rest of the school, data drives instruction. California has some of the country's strongest standards and teachers try to intervene quickly when students at Rossmoor do not meet those standards. "We ask what happened and make accommodations," Telfer said. "I have a fall planning meeting with each teacher, one on one. We talk about data and about individual students." Intervention for a pupil can take the form of more specific instruction, an after-school clinic, or a review to see if the child needs to be assigned to special education with an individualized education plan.

Kinder Club is the after-school clinic for kindergarteners who need extra help in attaining literacy. The kindergarten teachers observe their pupils through the fall, identifying by Christmas vacation a total of up to a dozen from the four classes who are most in need of attention. Shortly after the children return from their break, Kinder Club begins, running until the end of the school year during the hour following dismissal. How often Kinder Club meets each week depends on the pupils' progress. The kindergarten teachers share the responsibility for running the program.

Educators at Rossmoor hope that prekindergarten will reduce the need that some kindergarteners have for extra attention. Parents of children in one pre-K class pay $660 every four weeks, and parents in the other class pay nothing by virtue of a state grant for children from families who qualify on economic grounds. The prekindergartens—which mix three- and four-year-olds—adhere to standards called Desired Results, which feed into the state standards based on the curriculum that pupils will encounter in kindergarten.

Weaknesses that teachers detected among kindergarteners led to increased emphasis on literacy activities in preschool. "We're bringing more print into their environment," said Barbara Halverson, who oversees the preschool. She and the pre-K teachers keep in regular contact with the kindergarten teachers. "We're looking at the transition from prekindergarten to kindergarten," she said. "We try to take a similar developmental approach. We give them early literacy concepts." The teachers fill out information sheets on each child and pass them along to the kindergarten teachers.

THE GROWTH OF KINDERGARTEN

Full-day kindergarten is not universally available in the United States. Nine states still do not require local school districts to offer kindergarten—half day or full day—and even when states mandate that districts have kindergartens, children must attend in fewer than a dozen states. The compulsory age for starting school is seven in 22 states.[1] Yet, kindergarten is crucial to the PK–3 continuum, the link between the initial exposure to school for four-year-olds and the demands of first grade. It is the year during which children who are barely self-reliant become learners who understand the regimen and demands of the classroom and hone their budding knowledge of words and numbers. The social interaction with classmates that began in preschool takes ever more nuanced forms and play becomes a more complex vehicle for learning.

Marguerita Rudolph and Dorothy H. Cohen, synthesizing the work of others, identified these functions of play: making discoveries; enhancing reasoning and thinking; building bridges to social relations; achieving emotional equilibrium; learning adult roles; expressing needs and releasing otherwise unacceptable impulses; reversing roles usually taken; and working out problems and experimenting with solutions.[2] Thus, it is clear that skillful kindergarten teachers use play as a vehicle for learning in addition to its obvious and necessary role as a source of amusement.

Kindergarten's Evolution

Friederich Froebel founded kindergarten in Germany in the first half of the nineteenth century, following an almost spiritual inspiration. He based his concept on a set of ideas revolving around the connection of individual, God, and nature.[3] These notions led to a structured approach that helped shape the first kindergartens in the United States in the mid-nineteenth century. As kindergartens spread across America, advocates looked to Froebel's precepts for guidance and often sought teachers trained in Germany.[4]

The proliferation of kindergarten—which included children as young as three—during the decades leading up to the twentieth century coincided with the growth of the immigrant population in big cities. In a period somewhat analogous to the early twenty-first century, many Americans recognized (as they increasingly do today in regard to preschool) that kindergarten could facilitate the transition into the mainstream for youngsters from the nation's newest and poorest families. But disagreements, foreshadowing those that exist today over pre-K, were already bubbling up in the early 1900s over how much academic content kindergarten should have.

In those early years, kindergarten stood separate from elementary school, much as preschool does in many places today. As schools absorbed and took control of kindergarten, disputes arose over whether it should be more like the primary grades or the primary grades should be more like kindergarten. In fact, the theme of this book, with its stress on continuity from pre-K through third grade, echoes some of the very same concerns. "[T]here was a growing conviction that the period in a child's life between the ages of four and eight was psychologically one; therefore, no discontinuities in his educational experiences could be condoned,"[5] Evelyn Weber wrote in her history of kindergarten.

Kindergarten received mounting attention during the last two decades of the twentieth century as educators increasingly saw it as vital to children's development, especially when home settings were not adequately enriching. By the 1980s, educators and others spoke of "readiness" for kindergarten and the federal government's National Educational Goals Panel set the objective that "by the year 2000, all children will start school ready to learn." The three main objectives were that children would receive adequate nutrition and health care; parents would be their children's first teachers and devote time each day to helping them learn; and children would have access to high-quality preschool. The goals, of course, remain to be realized.

Kindergarten's Expectations

What do kindergartens reasonably expect of children? They want them to gain control over their small and large muscles so they can perform physical tasks ranging from holding a pencil to jumping on one foot; to follow rules and know the reasons why; to listen during group instruction and become eager learners who develop strategies to solve problems; to begin to observe natural phenomena and draw comparisons among the objects they observe; to use language effectively for communication, retell stories with important details, and read simple words that they often hear; and to sort objects and identify patterns so as to gain a sense of length and weight, up and down, and what pennies, nickels, and dimes represent.

Readiness, of course, is a variable trait. Some children, beneficiaries of enriching experiences, appear at kindergarten doors poised to prosper. Others, whose backgrounds have offered fewer such experiences, already trail their peers. Kindergarten teachers, when they are candid, say they can tell which youngsters will succeed and which ones will struggle in their later schooling. The wish to eliminate—or at least ameliorate—disparities in readiness largely accounts for the push for universal preschool and full-day kindergarten.

Three-quarters of kindergarten teachers consider it important that a child arrives able to count to 20, and fully 85 percent deem it important that a child arrives knowing the letters of the alphabet. At the same time, 86 percent say it is important that a child not disrupt the class, and every kindergarten teacher considers it important that pupils start kindergarten able to get along with other children and show sensitivity to their feelings.[6] Children enter kindergarten differing from one another in ways that go beyond their experiences. They vary in height and weight. Some run faster and some are stronger. Their personalities have already diverged. They are of differing ages—some as young as four and some as old as six, disparities that can represent one-fifth of a lifetime. Some still need stuffed animals to nap, while others have divested themselves of such vestiges of early childhood. One way of teaching will not meet all needs. These variations add to the anxiety of adults who suspect that schools may ask too much of children. Kindergarteners often face tests and get report cards, practices once reserved for pupils in the numbered grades. Journalists, in turn, seem to revel in writing about the disappearance of naptime and how elements of first grade are showing up in kindergarten, exacerbating the unease of parents.

Easing the Transition

The perceived trauma of the occasion leads school systems to try to cushion the transition into kindergarten. This effort during the weeks before the opening of the school year may take the form of a "kindergarten minicamp" in Vero Beach, Florida, or a "kindergarten academy" in Nashville, or eight days of "simulated" kindergarten in Cherry Creek, Colorado. In Hawaii, the youngest kindergarteners—those born closest to the cutoff date for entrance—have "junior kindergarten" once school begins to gain seasoning before moving into regular kindergarten after several weeks or months.

Parents and educators talk about whether some children might be better off remaining in preschool, not starting kindergarten until they are six or nearly six. Pacifica, California, considered a pilot program to set up a kindergarten preparatory class for some five-year-olds who would then not reach kindergarten until the age of six. A state commission in California proposed moving the birthday cutoff date from December 2 to September 1, saying that the younger children would gain maturity by delaying kindergarten entrance. A hole in the plan was the lack of a guarantee of preschool for youngsters held back from kindergarten.

One common strand runs through these endeavors, whatever officials call them: concern over what to do with children deemed unready for kindergarten. Some truly lag and others have no problem except their parents, who think they will give their children an advantage by holding them out of kindergarten, an act akin to red-shirting a college football player who sits out a year of competition to wait until he is bigger and stronger. A PK–3 configuration could help remedy this situation. Think of how unnecessary the various manipulations would be if children entered an educational continuum at either age three or age four and progressed at their own speed without regard to designating their grade level. The need for subterfuges and euphemisms would end.

Kindergarten as a Foundation Stone
in Montgomery County, Maryland

Whatever the disagreements over readiness, it is clear that a solid program in kindergarten can go a long way toward helping children succeed in the primary grades that follow. Montgomery County's school improvement plan for the first several grades, for instance, featured its "kindergarten initiative." The system established full-day kindergartens at 73 schools, with more to come. In addition to a cap of 15 students per teacher in schools serving the lowest-income families, the district put a cap of 22 on other full-day kindergartens. "If children meet benchmarks in kindergarten and first grade, they will score above the 60th percentile in second grade," Denise Stultz, the district's coordinator of special initiatives, said in pointing to the grade-to-grade alignment.

Kindergarten teachers in Montgomery County, with benefit of a more rigorous curriculum and better monitoring of pupil progress, ended up more sharply focused on preparing children for what awaited them in the first grade. They underwent 100 hours of staff development to familiarize themselves with the curriculum and instructional strategies for implementing it. Formerly, as in so many school systems, kindergarten teachers implemented the curriculum as they saw fit—the dinosaur unit one week, the unit on transportation another week—with scant attention to which content would do most to get children ready for the demands of first grade.

Brian Porter, chief of staff to the superintendent, observed: "We found out how deep the problem was when there was a backlash from some teachers who didn't even know we had a kindergarten curriculum. They were teaching whatever they had learned in college and were trying to measure achievement against a standard that was all over the map." Porter said that Jerry Weast, the superintendent, recognized that "if you didn't have early literacy skills in kindergarten, the idea of being a fluent reader by third grade was doomed."

A more prescriptive kindergarten curriculum contained units rich in vocabulary, literacy, and writing. Three times a year, assessments dealing with oral language, letter identification, concepts of print, phonemic awareness, and word recognition revealed students' individual needs. The school system was in the process of expanding full-day kindergartens to all its elementary schools. The superintendent followed the philosophy that "in kindergarten you have to look at what you need to accomplish in the twelfth grade." It is about building a foundation to bear the weight of learning that will be heaped upon it over the years, just as a PK–3 approach advocates.

In just three years, the number of kindergarten students who could read a simple story with familiar content nearly doubled, from 39 percent to 70 percent. As the youngsters, fortified by a stronger kindergarten experience, moved through second and third grades, the schools sustained the improvements. Montgomery County found that students who participated in all three years of the reform effort in early education—especially those from low-income families where English is not the first language—made significant progress in closing achievement gaps.[7]

KINDERGARTEN AT AN EARLY CHILDHOOD CENTER

In an effort to meet similarly diverse needs, the Milford School District in southern Delaware created the Evelyn I. Morris Early Childhood Center in 1993. The school is a hidden gem, tucked so neatly into a semirural area that during recess children on the playground reach through the property-line fence to stroke the friendly horses on the adjoining farm. The school district, which stretches to the shores of Delaware Bay, is a place where many parents are farmers, migrant workers, fishermen, and employees in food processing plants. There is enough poverty for almost half of the pupils at Morris to qualify for federally subsidized meals.

The approach underpinning the school of 630 students would fit comfortably within a PK–3 configuration. Morris houses all of the kindergarteners and first graders in the Milford system and these are essentially its only pupils. "You can focus on early childhood development this way," said Bob Smith, superintendent of the 3,500-student district, which also has a high school, a middle school, and two grade–2-to-grade–5 elementaries. "Instead of three or four first grade classrooms in a building, you have 15 from which to choose in order to match a student with a teacher you think will be good for him." In addition, this little country school boasted four teachers certified by the National Board for Professional Teaching Standards. First grade classrooms filled nearly one entire wing of the one-story school and kindergarten classrooms filled most of the other wing. The exceptions were a few pre-K classes and various rooms for arts and other special activities.

Built as a four-classroom school in 1931, Morris was gradually enlarged by a succession of additions through 2002, when it attained its current size and endured a thorough renovation that tastefully blended the structures of several eras. It got its green metal roof at that time and also received colorful architectural touches like the cheerful yellow, red, and blue arches that gave the building the look of a six-year-old's blocks construction project.

Morris was large enough by 2004–05 to hold 18 separate half-day kindergartens and one full-day kindergarten. The full-day program served children whose screenings during the summer prior to kindergarten showed that their development lagged, making them candidates for extra attention. Moreover, the school assigned a few half-day kindergarteners to attend morning as well as afternoon sessions—an additional boost for those who needed it.

Among the first grades were three "readiness" classes, so named because the kids had struggled in kindergarten the previous year and would not have been promoted without these special "hothouses" to accommodate them. Students still trailing at the end of the year would move to a transitional second grade, giving them a little longer to get up to speed. "This is a smaller class with a bigger dose of literacy," said Nancy Raihall, the teacher.

Raihall's readiness first grade organized itself around the learning centers or stations so common in many prekindergartens and kindergartens, but the work was mainly on a higher level. One day at the math center, for example, Raihall was teaching three boys to solve addition and subtraction word problems by arranging numbers both vertically and horizontally. Nearby, at the computer center, three children wearing earphones manipulated words on monitor screens in response to instructions. Children working with a student teacher at another center cut out words from printed pages and glued them into such sentences as "Are you good at jumping rope?" At a fourth center, a Title I teacher assisted children with crayons and worksheets as they boned up on colors and counting simultaneously, by following such directions as "Color the third fish red."

Two kindergartens and three first grade classes labeled Team Approach to Mastery (TAM) offered another variation on Morris's theme of providing added attention to children who need it. Each class contained special education students whom Morris included in the regular program. Their classmates—the majority of the pupils—in all five rooms were typical students without special needs. The school enticed families of achieving youngsters to enroll their children in these settings by reducing class size and staffing each room with a paraprofessional to assist the teacher. Milford, more than many school systems, recognized that it could best serve its children by giving them assorted routes to make their way through the primary grades, as the ideal PK–3 school should do.

The teachers enjoyed the special colleagueship that comes when all of those working in the building share the same tightly focused concern: early childhood education. "I can't imagine not having daily contact with the kindergarten teachers," said Carol Benner-Chaffinch, one of Morris's preschool teachers. "We ask them questions all the time, especially with our curriculum leading directly into theirs. I ask a question of a kindergarten teacher at least once a day and sometimes four or five times a day. Seeing the kindergartens gives me information to help decide where to recommend that a pre-K child be placed the next year."

The school's kindergarten and pre-K teachers, joined by the principal and assistant principal, meet every Wednesday for up to an hour and usually try to limit their discussion to a single topic. The week I was at the school they were developing a new report card format for kindergarten. It involved a checklist that teachers could send home to let parents know how many more skills their children needed to master to attain satisfactory marks.

Despite its exemplary practices, Morris Early Childhood Center offered most children only a half-day of kindergarten. A teacher of some 30 years like Karen Carey-Wilkerson constantly found herself trying to stuff all that she knew that pupils needed into a two-and-a-half-hour day. Highly efficient and accepting no nonsense, Carey-Wilkerson devoted the brief school day to shoring up lessons that she believed her pupils needed for success in the first grade. She even paused as the children recited the Pledge of Allegiance to remind them that the first word, "I," is always written as a capital letter, allowing no teachable moment to pass unused. Her style delighted parents, who made her the most requested teacher by the families of kindergarteners.

As she spoke to her class, Carey-Wilkerson stressed that the month had three syllables—"No-vem-ber," she had them chanting as they clapped out the syllables. That opened the door to a further explanation of syllables.

"People with two syllables in their names, stand up."

"People with one syllable in their names, stand up." She sent one of the standees to the piano to hit a key as he pronounced the single syllable in his name.

"People with three syllables in their names, stand up."

Back to the calendar. "Today is Friday," she said as she wrote the words on the board. "That's a sentence, but if you just say 'Friday,' that's a word, not a sentence." Carey-Wilkerson would will literacy into these children, even if she had only a half-day each morning to do it. "We need full-day kindergarten badly," she told me. "We could take our time and accomplish more. Creativity is what they need and you need all-day kindergarten and more time for that. We barely get out of our boots and mittens and it's time to scadoo."

MOVING TOWARD FULL-DAY KINDERGARTEN

Full-day kindergarten's advantages are drawing attention across the country, not just at Morris Early Childhood Center. The nation is slowly but inexorably moving in this direction. In Delaware itself, the legislature responded to a proposal by the governor and authorized money to create more full-day kindergartens. Research and common sense indicate that children are better off being in school all day, simply having more time to devote to literacy and math activities.[8] Furthermore, many working parents need their children under supervision for the entire day. As it is, even with full-day kindergarten, families usually still look for before-class and after-class care. Full-day kindergarten expands learning opportunities. There simply is not enough time in the typical half-day program to get much done. The implementation of learning standards around the United States puts pupils coming out of kindergarten in the position of having very rapidly to measure up to first grade standards.

Three separate research teams confirmed in work scheduled for publication in 2006 that children learn more in full-day kindergarten than their counterparts do in half-day programs.[9] WestEd, a major education research group, examined seven studies and found that full-day kindergarten, in contrast to half-day kindergarten, contributes to increased school readiness, higher academic achievement, better attendance through the primary grades, and literacy and language development.[10] The need for full-day classes is so great that some parents, like those in

Seattle, pay extra out of pocket so that their children may attend more than a half-day. Proponents of full-day kindergarten should keep in mind that it also requires more teachers and classroom space.

The favorable results of a full-day program could be seen at Vier's Mill Elementary School in Montgomery County, Maryland, where the longer kindergarten day gives more learning time in a school that has 30 percent of its students living in homes in which adults speak little English. "Those coming with limited literacy and limited vocabulary need extra time and all-day kindergarten provides that," the principal said. First grade teachers, who had previously dealt with children who attended half-day kindergarten, were surprised when they got their first crop of graduates from full-day kindergarten. They discovered that the children exceeded the point that they expected them to reach in the curriculum at any given time during the school year.

Policies to Promote Full-Day Kindergarten

With fewer than two-thirds of kindergarteners in full-day programs, the country needs policy changes to make such classes available to all children. Only nine states require local districts to offer full-day kindergarten, an approach that the Education Commission of the States in 2005 called for all states to take.[11] In the long run, full-day kindergarten can save money if it leads to less remediation and less retention. In the short run, and on a mundane level, it cuts costs by requiring transportation only twice a day instead of the four trips needed to accommodate morning and afternoon sessions.

Walled Lake School District in Michigan, where tax revenues covered only half-day kindergarten, came up with an unusual arrangement to offer a variation on full-day kindergarten. First, rather than having half-day kindergarten five days a week, Walled Lake assigned children in its 14 elementary schools to a full day of kindergarten on either Tuesday and Thursday or Monday and Wednesday. The district offered a half-day on Friday for all children, letting families choose between the morning and afternoon sessions. Voilà: Five half-days became two full days and only one half-day, giving teachers longer blocks of time to perform their magic.

Taking another step, Walled Lake created Kinder Academy to provide a full day of child care and education on the days when children were not scheduled to attend kindergarten. One of every five families opted to enroll their children in Kinder Academy at a cost of $2,700 a year. Paraprofessionals, not the certified teachers who taught in the kindergartens, staffed Kinder Academy, which the district did not call kindergarten because it did not use regular teachers and charged tuition.

The program, which occupied classrooms in the district's school buildings, infused a powerful dose of language into a child care setting. The paraprofessionals read to the children, making time each day for kids to browse the classroom library and look through books on their own. These same paraprofessionals also modeled writing for them, wrote with them, and encouraged them to write in journals in the rudimentary fashion that they could handle. Children spent much of the day moving through centers similar to those in prekindergarten, except most of these dealt with an individual aspect of literacy.

Kinder Academy met the needs of working parents for child care during the hours that their children were not in kindergarten and did so in a more substantive way than the usual child care setting. "When you're only doing literacy, you can do more of it," said Linda Ayres, the administrator who wrote the curriculum and trained the paraprofessionals. Each class had a maximum of 20 children and two paraprofessional teachers for a teacher-to-student ratio of 1 to 10. The paraprofessionals in Kinder Academy could presumably speak with the children's kindergarten teachers about various issues. Even transportation, which often poses a problem for families using child care, was not an obstacle as most youngsters rode the regular school system buses between their homes and the schools that housed the program.

When to Begin Kindergarten

Whether kindergarten is a half day or a full day, there remains the contentious issue of when a child should begin. For years, parents were eager to have youngsters start kindergarten as soon as possible, and cutoff dates late in the calendar year enabled many children who were still age four in September to enter. Increasingly, though, cutoff dates have moved closer to the beginning of the school year so that pupils will be older and more mature. Children must turn five before mid-October to enter kindergarten in 39 states.[12] Indiana, where a cutoff date of July 1 produced the oldest kindergarteners in the country, is in the process of shifting to a September 1 cutoff.

Raising the age for children in kindergarten has been the preference of parents who delay their children's entrance for a year so that they presumably will be higher achievers. Some affluent families see this as a way to boost their children's chances of ultimately getting into selective colleges. But even though delayed entrance may give some children an edge for a few years, evidence of lasting effects is scanty. The National Association for the Education of Young Children (NAEYC) deplores the practice of holding back children from kindergarten for any reason and called on school districts not to counsel or pressure families to delay entrance.

GAINING A COMPETITIVE EDGE IN NEW YORK

The fierce competition to gain admission to the nursery schools and kindergartens of New York's prestigious independent schools—some of which turn away a dozen youngsters for each one they accept—attests to the stakes that parents think are involved in attending the *right* school. The process resembles what the same children and their families will go through a dozen years later in pursuit of a place in the *right* college. Parents of those accepted receive the privilege of paying more than $25,000 a year in kindergarten tuition. The admissions process, even at age four, includes school visits, interviews with admissions directors, testing, voluminous financial aid applications, the mailing of acceptance letters on precise dates with a set number of days to respond, legacies, and wait lists—very much the stuff of higher education.

Thus it was that hundreds of anxious parents, some with children in tow, assembled in the wooden pews of Park Avenue Methodist Church, on Manhattan's tony Upper East Side, one warm fall evening to learn about the application process for independent schools. The weather was so delicious that the church's front doors were thrown open, allowing those strolling along East 86th Street to peer into the nave. What they would have seen straight up the center aisle at a table on the raised area facing the pews, in front of a four-foot-high mosaic cross of gold in a field of green tiles, were the admissions directors of four leading independent schools. The annual event was sponsored by the Parents League of New York.

Parents heard that night that the schools to which they submitted applications would probably consult with their children's nursery schools and might even send observers to watch the tiny applicants in their nursery classes. The admissions directors said that they wanted to know about the social and emotional development of the four-year-olds, as well as their work ethic, citizenship, membership in the community, character, and enthusiasm for learning. Nonetheless, the school representatives said that they sought to put parents at ease and didn't want to feed the admissions hysteria. Fat chance.

Central to the process is the dreaded test administered individually to each child by the Educational Records Bureau (ERB). The organization scores the test on a developmental scale and norms it on a national population, allowing a youngster's performance to be compared with that of peers across the country. Just in case a family wants to delay having a child take the test until he or she is a few months older and presumably a bit more mature, ERB reminds parents that such a step would lead to comparisons with comparably older children. "Remember, the older you are, the more that is expected!" ERB declares in an explanation of its admission testing for prekindergarten and kindergarten.

ERB makes test results available to all of the schools to which the family applies. This is a substantial improvement over the days when a prospective kindergartener had to take a separate entrance test for each school. Parents were cautioned, however, against administering practice tests to their children or having them tutored for the assessment. "Some parents are quiet about having their children tutored," said Joanne Lynch, admissions director at Buckley, a boys' school so elite that it ends at the ninth grades so that graduates can go off to the kinds of boarding schools that George W. Bush and John F. Kerry attended. "But the child may come in and look at the puzzle and say, 'I do that kind of puzzle with my special friend each week.'" Four-year-olds, in other words, can't keep secrets, even to get admitted to the best private schools.

5

BUILDING A NEW STRUCTURE FOR LEARNING

Valerio Primary Center takes education in the early grades very seriously. So much so that the school's only grades are prekindergarten, kindergarten, first grade, and second grade. Valerio is one of 11 schools similarly devoted to early learning that the Los Angeles Unified School District (LAUSD) created, starting in 1987. Few other big-city school systems have made such a commitment in recent years to a configuration featuring the primary grades. This is the sort of school, closely paralleling the PK–3 concept, that ought to be available to every child in every district.

Young children don't have to worry about older students who might bully them. They get all the attention because the school does not have to concern itself with preparing fourth and fifth graders for middle school. Articulation between the grades is stronger and teachers are more aware of the previous progress of individual pupils than in a larger school with a wider range of grades. Professional development focuses exclusively on early development. Moreover, given the school's small size and intimacy, teachers are familiar with each other's work. "Anyone not doing her job sticks out here," says Roberta Barabash, a kindergarten teacher at Valerio.

Yet, these are not the advantages that impelled LAUSD to establish a network of early learning centers. That was a function of enrollment growth and real estate prices. Elementary schools in Los Angeles simply could not accommodate soaring enrollments, driven primarily by immigration, and few affordable sites remained on which to build additional full-scale schools. The answer: small schools that could relieve the enrollment pressure at neighboring full-scale elementaries by siphoning off some children from the lowest grades. Moreover, these new schools could be squeezed onto relatively tiny lots that were not large enough to hold regular schools. Thus, Los Angeles built primary learning centers quickly and at a lower cost than full-size elementary schools.

TIGHTENING THE FOCUS ON THE EARLY YEARS

The small schools also made it possible to avoid some busing, particularly of the youngest children, that Los Angeles had used to redistribute student populations in high-density areas such as those near downtown. The primary centers are not uniform, though, in that some have only kindergarten, others have kindergarten and first grade, and still others, like Valerio, run through the second grade. They also vary in the extent to which they offer prekindergarten.

Cheryl Mueller was the first principal of Valerio when it opened in 1999 and more recently served as coordinator of LAUSD's administrative academy. She conceded that the main motivation behind the early learning centers was not instructional, but maintained that the school system had inadvertently stumbled onto a gem of a solution to relieve overcrowding. "The ideal school organization should be no larger than 500 and consist of prekindergarten through second grade," Mueller says. "The philosophy is different between such a school and a traditional school."

The juxtaposition between Valerio Primary Center and a traditional school could not have been starker. Valerio Elementary School, a gargantuan enterprise with 1,200 students, sits just down the block from the primary center, with a Head Start center tucked in between. The regular elementary school, which runs through fifth grade, duplicates the primary center's grades. Parents can select between the two schools, with the primary center—the more popular alternative—accepting pupils on a first-come, first-served basis. The attraction revolves around not only its smaller size, but also the considerably higher achievement of its pupils, though they came from the same home backgrounds as their peers in Valerio Elementary.

Once Valerio Primary Center fills its slots, families are left with a Hobson's choice of having to send their children to the traditional elementary school. For the most part, the only new pupils at the primary center each year are prekindergarteners and kindergarteners, first and second grade classrooms having filled with pupils who attended the previous year. Joan Blair, principal of the primary center, says that the key to its success is an ability to function as a small learning community, where children and teachers know each other well. "You catch the deficits early, fix the problem, and then they're okay and don't have to sit in special ed classes their whole lives," she says.

A School with Only Pre-K and Kindergarten

Another school in Los Angeles, Stanford Early Learning Center in South Gate, one of the city's most densely populated neighborhoods, does not have Valerio Primary Center's record of accomplishment, having opened only in the fall of 2004. But the kind of alternative it offers is clear. Stanford Elementary School, which Susan Ahern, principal of the early learning center, calls "the mother school," is only three blocks away and has 1,400 students. Another nearby elementary, Miles Avenue, has an enrollment of 2,600. The schools fed into a middle school of 4,000, surely one of the largest in the country, until a new middle school opened in 2004 and absorbed some of their students.

Stanford Early Learning Center contains only 16 classrooms, devoting them entirely to kindergarten and preschool. Even though the school has 302 pupils on its rolls, just 200 attend during any term as the year-round schedule calls for one-third of the children and teachers to be on vacation at any given time. The district put some of its schools on this schedule to reduce overcrowding. Crammed onto an economical one-acre site, Stanford Early Learning Center is customized for its task, comprising a pair of boxy, side-by-side stucco buildings with furniture and accouterments designed especially for tiny bodies. There is a small conference room in which the entire faculty can squeeze around a table, and a library to underscore the primacy of reading.

Given its narrow mission, the learning center can concentrate staff development on what teachers need to help children succeed in kindergarten. The whole staff meets for an hour almost weekly to pursue this agenda. Furthermore, a literacy coach aids teachers in planning lessons and preparing materials. The school's multipurpose room accommodates the entire enrollment during a single lunch period, when all of the teachers in the building eat together. With all the children of about the same age and an enrollment of manageable size, the school evinces a strong sense of community. Field trips, for example, unite everyone in the building in a single outing.

Stanford Early Learning Center was to have included first and second grades, but the district began implementing full-day kindergarten before it opened. So, the school needed twice as much space for kindergarten as originally planned and room did not remain for other grades. Principal Ahern lamented the absence of first and second grades, as having them would extend the time the school has to prepare children for the upper elementary years. Also, kindergarten teachers could collaborate with first and second grade colleagues to strengthen and align the primary continuum. Nonetheless, parents appreciate the specialization embodied in a pre-K and kindergarten school.

"The school can concentrate on the little ones," says Araceli Moreno, whose daughter Giselle attended pre-K. "They can get introduced into the school community slowly. It is a shock sometimes to put them in with older and bigger kids. I think the school is a great idea. The size of the school forces parents to be more involved in their children's education." On Mondays, her day off from work, Moreno volunteered in her daughter's classroom, a practice that the school encourages.

Giselle Moreno's prekindergarten and other pre-K classrooms, just like the kindergartens, infuse almost every aspect of the day with language. The fact that 80 percent of the children live in homes where adults speak to them in Spanish drives this emphasis. Ahern and all but two of the teachers speak Spanish, but instruction is not bilingual, a practice no longer allowed as the result of a California statewide referendum. Ahern launched a program in which adults—using everyone in the school, including the custodian—read to the pupils five times a day. For Ahern, the challenge facing the school was encapsulated one Monday when she asked a kindergartener, "Did you read a book this weekend?" and he responded, "My house is not a library," with no thought that homes as well as libraries might contain books.

The attention to language could be seen one day in Maria Bone's prekindergarten, where she led her pupils through a discussion of how they prepare for school. COMB your hair, BRUSH your teeth, WASH your face. The words tumbled forth, with emphasis on the verbs.

Then, each child spoke, some more distinctly than others, of something that he or she had done to get ready. A boy described the new shoes he had put on that day. Another boy told of sharing a toothbrush with his brother. Each one spoke—Anthony, Sergio, Emily, Alejandra, and the others. Bone occasionally interjected words and phrases in Spanish, sometimes in the same sentence as words in English if she thought it helped to communicate with a particular child. She pointed around the room and, together, the children named what they saw—window, door, table. It was all about language and getting ready for kindergarten.

So keen is the attempt to reach students early to try to mitigate problems that each term the school asks about a dozen kindergarteners—those at highest risk as a result of slow language development—to give up six weeks of their vacation. They attend school daily for a half-day of intensive work in English, leaving them with only two weeks of the normal eight-week vacation. The idea is to keep them from regressing during a time they would have spent away from the classroom and out of contact with stimulation in the development of their English language skills. Federal Title I funds pay for the program.

Advantages of Early Emphasis

American education is a victim of its structure, which usually assigns the primary grades to a school that runs through fifth, sixth, or, increasingly, eighth grade. A place like Valerio Primary Center, on the other hand, has early education as its sole purpose, letting everyone in the school concentrate on building a foundation for learning. A self-contained PK–3 continuum, starting with preschool and continuing through third grade, can alleviate concern about the grade levels of students, who are assigned work according to their achievement levels.

Some main advantages of a PK–3 school are:

1. ALIGNMENT—Curriculum, standards, instruction, and assessment mesh within each grade and across prekindergarten through third grade.
2. LITERACY—A language-rich environment, more at this level of education than at any other, builds the reading, writing, speaking, and listening skills of students.

3. ARTICULATION—Teachers at each level share information about children with teachers at the levels below and above.

4. CONTINUOUS PROGRESS—Students move through the PK–3 continuum at rates that meet their developmental needs, neither rushed nor held back. Multiage and multigrade groupings may aid this process.

5. MORE TIME FOR LEARNING—A longer school day and a longer school year, as well as weekends and summers, expand time for building a foundation for learning.

6. WRAPAROUND SERVICES—Young children and their families need places to make them safe and to reinforce their school experiences before and after the school day. Moreover, the school ideally refers children and families to health and social service agencies for help that they require.

Students advance through the continuum, from preschool through third grade, at rates dictated by their development and their performance. Whether they are in preschool, kindergarten, first grade, second grade, or third grade is incidental. Most will enter the fourth grade at the traditional age of nine, but others may be eight or ten by then.

As in Los Angeles, though, not all school districts recognize the academic advantages of a strong primary focus even though they configure some schools that way.

Sometimes, convenience trumps philosophy. This occurred in Chesapeake, Virginia, where during the 2004–05 academic year the system of 39,000 students included seven K–2 and two K–3 elementary school buildings. One might conclude that Chesapeake created these settings to focus on the primary grades. But this organization was more the product of dealing with rapid population growth than a desire to embrace a PK–3 concept.

Anita B. James, Chesapeake's elementary director, taught in a K–2 school before becoming a principal. She liked the idea that all of the teachers in the building could concentrate on early childhood and also thought it desirable for a principal to narrow her concerns to fewer grades. She felt it was better, though, when children remained in the same building for more years, as in a K–5 school. "When you're trying to impact change or growth in achievement, it is more difficult when you don't have the children for the whole time of their elementary education," James said. "Also, it's more difficult to build a strong, cohesive PTA when the parent group is constantly changing."

This is hardly the opinion, though, in Glen Ridge, New Jersey, where reorganization and space considerations led to the creation of PK–2 schools. "We were at maximum capacity in all of our schools, and we shifted kids to where we had space," said Elisabeth Ginsburg, president of the school board. "But demography turned out to be a gift and we were able to create this environment. We think the good results in our high school have to do with what we do at this [PK–2] level."

An extensive review of the research literature shows a broad empirical base for zeroing in on children from the ages of three to eight to integrate and to align learning during that period, grade by grade, to sustain gains. This review also included studies finding that children need to develop social skills, motivation, sustained attention, and self-regulation during this time. While conceding the limitations of the research to date, the reviewers wrote of the likelihood that children and society will benefit from investments in early education when the components of a high-quality PK–3 program mesh.[1]

COMBINING AGE GROUPS

When the legislature passed the Kentucky Education Reform Act (KERA) in 1990, it called for ungraded primary programs in what had formerly been kindergarten through third grade. Suddenly, elementary schools throughout the bluegrass state faced a future in which they would mix young children of various ages in the same classes with only a pupil's learning progress to determine the level of work he or she did. The idea was, for instance, that if a second grader could read on a third grade level, then the student would have the opportunity to do so. And, conversely, if other second graders still read on a first grade level, they would get work on that level. Individual pupils would advance through the curriculum at rates appropriate to their development.

As a result of KERA, Kentucky converted its elementary schools into places where the primary grades gave more attention to the continuous progress of students and less to whether the work corresponded precisely to their ages. When it works best, this approach means that teachers reassess their pupils' achievement continually, perhaps as often as weekly, in order to assign them new work and to reconfigure reading groups. This philosophy led to creating classrooms that included children six, seven, and eight years old, others with mixes of six- and seven-year-olds, and still other classes of seven- and eight-year-olds.

Kentuckians did not greet the upheaval in the early grades with universal acclaim. Some parents fretted over the idea that classrooms were not clearly separated by grade demarcations. Some teachers, educated to provide instruction in more traditional ways, were uneasy trying to meet so wide a range of needs in a single classroom. Some legislators, besieged by disgruntled parents and anxious educators, had second thoughts about the learning revolution they had unleashed. So, lawmakers eventually muted their intention by giving schools the right to back off from multiage groupings so long as they still used developmentally appropriate practices and allowed for continuous progress. This meant that by the early 2000s half the pupils in primary grades throughout the state were in single-age classrooms.

Nonetheless, what remained of multiage grouping in Kentucky was a model for a practice that could distinguish PK–3 schools. One such place, Kennedy Montessori School in Louisville, organized the primary grades above kindergarten into four classrooms that each housed first, second, and third graders, two other classrooms that put first and second graders together, and three others with second and third grade combinations. A classroom of first graders was the only one at the primary level devoted to a single grade. Above the primary level—and not affected by the mandate—were classrooms solely for fourth graders or solely for fifth graders. With less emphasis on the age at which pupils met specific standards, teachers could concentrate on learning and not care as much about whether it happens, say, at age seven or age eight.

Multiage Classes at Kennedy Montessori

Multiage classes came more naturally to Kennedy Montessori in Louisville than to some other public schools as the Montessori approach calls for placing pupils of different ages in the same classroom. These schools, based on a concept developed by Maria Montessori, an Italian physician, expect that children who have already handled certain tasks will help their younger peers learn the lessons.

The idea of children and teachers spending two or three years together enhances the Montessori notion of building an enduring classroom community. Teachers and students get to know each other better under such an arrangement, sometimes called "looping." In a combined second and third grade class at Kennedy Montessori, for example, the third graders left for the fourth grade at the end of the year, but the second graders remained with the teacher for the third grade and new second graders were added to the mix. Youngsters who have already spent a year in the class help indoctrinate the newcomers to the policies and expectations.

The multiage mix, nevertheless, posed a challenge to some teachers at the next level. Opal Dawson, the principal, said that some fourth and fifth grade teachers complained initially that their lesson plans had been thrown out of kilter by students who emerged from the continuous progress mode of the primary grades. "What will we do with the kids?" Dawson recalled being asked by a fourth grade teacher, who had planned to teach *Charlotte's Web* only to discover that some pupils had read it the previous year. With students already advanced into some of the reading and math that the teachers had expected to offer, these teachers had to revise carefully devised lessons.

Kennedy, which opened in 1963 in one of the city's toughest neighborhoods and was named for the president assassinated that year, did not begin as a Montessori school but later took on that identity as a magnet school. The city eventually bulldozed the troubled housing project adjacent to the two-story tan-brick building and replaced it in the 1990s with streets of attractive new houses. Though Kennedy Montessori continues to draw almost two-thirds of its pupils from families poor enough to qualify for federally subsidized meals, the school's Montessori approach and seriousness of purpose attracts some students from outside the neighborhood. Trophies in a case that greets you on entering the building were awarded not only for athletic prowess, but also for such activities as problem solving and quick recall.

Teaching Teams at Blue Lick Elementary

Some of Kentucky's Jefferson County schools organized teachers into teams so they could collaborate to meet the individual needs of students in the primary grades. I saw how this effort worked at Blue Lick Elementary School, where teachers formed a series of vertical teams consisting of one classroom from each grade—kindergarten through fifth grade. The school also had horizontal or grade-level teams that met weekly for all of the teachers who taught the same grade.

All of the teachers who had first graders gathered one morning for an hour before classes. Teams representing other grade levels tended to meet during the day, but the first grade teachers had made a pact to meet voluntarily each Thursday before the bell to review the curriculum that the school district dictated for the upcoming week. Each teacher took responsibility for burrowing into one part of the curriculum and then shared her observations and ideas. This gave everyone the chance to become a specialist and, at the same time, to benefit from an overview from colleagues who had done the same with other topics. It was like a study group in law school, where students divide up the cases and share the fruits of their labor.

Furthermore, the grade-level team provided a forum for teachers to apportion first grade pupils into reading groups of workable size. Teachers arranged for students to shuttle among classrooms, ensuring workable numbers at various achievement levels, and thereby narrowing the range represented in any one group so that instruction could be targeted. The teachers sometimes used a team meeting to analyze test scores of the students they shared, identifying adjustments they would have to make in instruction.

Being a member of a vertical team also means that each teacher is part of a continuum that involves one group of teachers in a student's education from kindergarten through fifth grade. Members of the team educate the same group of children over a period of years, passing them off from one to the other. Over the duration of a child's years at Blue Lick, as the child moves through the grades, teachers meet regularly with team members to discuss the progress of each child they teach, have taught, or are going to teach. Schools try to group all of the classrooms represented by the vertical team in the same part of the building but are often thwarted by fire regulations that require first-floor space priority for the youngest children. Thus, in violation of good practice, function follows form.

More Multigrade Groupings

Kentucky was unusual in implementing multiage classes on a statewide level, but across the country individual schools and a few entire school districts have adopted the approach. Elm Street School in Mechanic's Falls, Maine, 45 miles north of Portland, for example, has a long history of multiage classes. The availability of such classes depends on the willingness of teachers to accept the assignments. Judy Vaillancourt decided to give it a go after working as a kindergarten teacher. She taught a combined first grade–second grade class for about eight years and then opted to take on a class consisting of second and third graders. "I'm sold on it," she said of the approach.

Vaillancourt found that despite the disparity in ages, children in such settings become close-knit and respect each other. "They can work well independently and in groups," she added. A key to the arrangement is to minimize attention to grade levels. Vaillancourt said there was scant reference in her class to who was in second grade and who was in third grade. "They don't think of grade levels and I don't think that way," she explained.

Dealing with children in a multiage class requires considerable effort simply because they are spread over a wider range of achievement. Vaillancourt found herself devoting great gobs of time to preparing for class, as she had to cover so much more curriculum than the usual teacher. Mary Martin, Elm Street's principal, knew about the extra work as she, too, had taught multiage classes. "It takes a teacher who is really committed to the concept," Martin said, noting that while Vaillancourt retained the commitment, some other teachers in the school gave up trying to teach such classes.

Elsewhere, Ladd School in Fairbanks, Alaska, used multiage grouping for several years. The pre-K to grade six school stands outside the gates of Fort Wainwright Army Post, from which it drew 75 percent of its 500 students. Budget cuts and increases in class sizes led to the demise of several of the merged classes and left only the combined third grade–fourth grade by 2004. Kathie Cook, the principal, bemoaned the loss of the other combined classes. The kindergarten–first grade class, for instance, allowed kindergarteners who were already reading "to be pushed ahead with the first graders," she said. At the same time, several first graders who were slow to read benefited from participating in reading readiness with the kindergarteners.

"The first graders have been excellent peer models for the kindergarteners, helping them to assimilate into the school," Cook said. She also lauded the continuity that enabled the children to have the same teacher for kindergarten and first grade. An advantage of the third grade–fourth grade class, according to Cook, was the opportunity for teachers to develop five levels in reading and three levels in math. "Kids are truly getting instruction at their skill level while being with their peers," she said.

Like educators in Mechanic's Falls, Maine, those in Fairbanks found that multiage grouping required more time and preparation. Cook said: "You need to have teachers who understand and believe in a continuum of instruction. You don't have to do dinosaurs with kindergartens and butterflies with first grades. Teachers have to understand and be comfortable with flexible grouping. They have to know where a child is academically and take them from that point and move them on."

"We never tell parents they have to do multiage," said Alaska's Cook. "They request it. The word gets around and our multiage classes are our most highly requested. The parents of the younger kids buy in quickly because they think their children will get 'advanced' instruction." Cook tried to deal with the concerns of parents by explaining that the curriculum in the early grades spirals, meaning that there is considerable overlap as the weeks, months, and even years pass. "Parents need to trust the teacher that their child will get the curriculum," Cook said.

How well do multiage classes serve students? An extensive research review found no differences more than half the time between multiage and single-age classrooms, and results were inconsistent much of the rest of the time. Gains in multiage classes were most consistently noted for "blacks, boys, underachievers, and students of low socioeconomic status."[2] Teachers in multiage classrooms believe, by and large, that such settings cultivate a familylike climate, create social and academic continuity, promote acceptance of diversity, facilitate a developmentally appropriate learning environment, and lead to improved academic growth.[3] The study that reached these conclusions cautioned, though, that teachers need preparation to work in such settings and that they can feel overwhelmed by the changes required in their practices.

Learning on a Continuum

In the era of the one-room schoolhouse people weren't concerned about seating youngsters of a wide range of ages in the same classroom. Each student moved along at his or her own pace, older ones reinforcing their learning by helping younger ones. Even in the mid-nineteenth century, when schools created grades, a certain degree of looseness remained. "It is important to emphasize that it was the *curriculum* and the work of the teacher that was graded, not the children," write historians.[4]

Thus, students were grouped with peers working on the same level, regardless of age. In many instances, youngsters moved through the curriculum at a rate dictated by their achievement and were reassigned to other classrooms when appropriate. Eventually, though, critics regarded it as a sign of failure for school systems when older children who hadn't been promoted were still in classes with younger students. This concern about "overage" students finally led to separate grades with students of the same age. And so by 1940, automatic promotion was in full bloom,[5] launching a practice that just a generation later would be held in opprobrium as "social promotion." Today, graded elementary schools are the rule, leaving some children to struggle to keep up and others to stifle boredom because the arrangement prevents them from working at full capacity.

Kentucky's Bomkamp family discovered this problem in 2005 when it came time to send five-year-old Alison off to attend River Ridge Elementary in the Kenton County Public Schools, across the Ohio River from Cincinnati. Alison, a bright little girl with hazel eyes, had already begun piano lessons and enjoyed soccer and gymnastics. Separate tests paid for by the family and the school system showed she could do work above the first grade level—no surprise to her parents, who said she counted at a year and a half and read before she was four. They wanted Alison put in at least first grade, not kindergarten, which the school district said her age dictated.

The Kenton County Schools balked. Kentucky's funding statute stated that a five-year-old would receive a state allotment equivalent to half-day support for a kindergarten placement regardless of the grade to which she was assigned. The school system, under pressure from the family, finally admitted Alison Bomkamp into first grade and sought a waiver from the state for full fiscal support. Meanwhile, the district billed the Bomkamps for $3,000, the amount it said it was not receiving in state aid for Alison. The Bomkamps ignored the bill. This was a school's response in a state with a law providing for students to be educated according to their developmental levels. "It should not be such a fight to educate a gifted child," said Shauna Bomkamp, Alison's mother.

Advocates for gifted students want them to advance through the curriculum according to their ability. Yet, misguided policies such as the one that affected Alison Bomkamp often deny America's brightest youngsters this chance. A university research center that studies issues in the education of gifted and talented students felt so strongly about public school betrayal of the gifted that in 2004 it entitled its report "A Nation Deceived."[6] Conversely, if it takes some students longer to do the work, they should be allowed the additional time without penalty. Schools should be about learning, not about cramming every child into a Procrustean bed fitted to one's age. Schools should no more hold back students from work that they can handle than push them into work for which they are not ready.

ANOTHER STRUCTURAL CHANGE: THE CLOCK AND THE CALENDAR

Just as the PK–3 concept aims to overcome an organizational structure that does not work to students' advantage, so should it lead to a reappraisal of the ways in which schools use time. The clock and the calendar—the hours, days, weeks, and months of schooling—hold pupils hostage to schedules not geared to their needs. "Learning in America is a prisoner of time," concluded a commission that examined this issue. "The rule, only rarely voiced, is simple: learn what you can in the time we make available."[7]

The notion of making better use of time should be inherent in any plan that focuses on the period from preschool through third grade. This cannot happen when schools restrict learning to 5.6 hours a day and 180 days a year, putting Saturdays and summers off limits. The U.S. Department of Education virtually invites school systems to extend learning time with allocations they receive through No Child Left Behind. Money from Title I, School Improvement Funds, and a host of other federal programs may be used for after-school and summer activities that can be folded into the primary grades.

Reset the Clock and Lengthen the Calendar

When a blue-ribbon panel in Orange County, Florida, looked at ways to improve schools, it recommended in 2005 that the school system phase in a new schedule over five years at all grade levels to add at least 30 school days. The school board rejected this proposal, agreeing to lengthen the school day only for high school students. The heralded KIPP (Knowledge Is Power Program) academies that operate in conjunction with public school systems in 15 states, often as charter schools, typically begin the day at 7:30 A.M. and conclude between 3 and 5 in the afternoon. In most instances, children have to show up for three or four hours a couple of Saturdays a month and must attend three weeks of classes during the summer.

The legislature in Massachusetts became so convinced of the need for more instructional time that in 2005 it invested in the idea. It allocated $500,000 so that the State Education Department could fund planning grants to some 20 school systems to figure out how to gain as much as 30 percent more time by lengthening the school day or the school year or by using Saturdays or the hours before and after school. Ultimately, the state aims to provide $15 million to implement the best proposals.

Summer punches the largest hole in the school calendar, causing kids to suspend formal learning for almost three months. This made sense in an agrarian society, but defies logic in the twenty-first century. Sandra Feldman, the late president of the American Federation of Teachers, proposed an approach she called Kindergarten-Plus, in which at-risk children would start kindergarten during the summer prior to their official enrollment. The four school systems in New Mexico with the highest percentages of Title I students, aided by a pilot program funded by the legislature, enacted a pilot version of Feldman's Kindergarten-Plus that added 40 days to kindergarten by having children start during the summer and continue into the following summer. Early research attested to the program's positive impact.

In a variation on this plan, Prince George's County in Maryland established a program during the summer *after* kindergarten for children who had fared poorly so that they would not have to be held back. In Peekskill, New York, a Westchester County town that has seen better days, Superintendent Judith Johnson actually mandated summer school for large numbers of students based on their low test scores, a requirement that she conceded was "probably illegal."

Every school year, teachers must devote time in the fall to getting pupils back to the level they had reached at the beginning of summer.[8] Yet, many people take it as a birthright that children should be able to shut down their brains during that season. Objections to using the summer for the purpose of learning reached an extreme in Wisconsin in 2005 when a 17-year-old student and his father filed a lawsuit against the boy's math teacher for requiring homework over the summer.

Schools that assign homework over the summer aim to keep students' minds engaged in academics. Nonetheless, parents with children in the Baltimore County Public School system forced the district to concede in 2004 that summer assignments were voluntary, not mandatory. During the same year, parents in Prince George's County, Maryland, opposed the school system's policy of assigning homework on weekends, presumably another sacrosanct time for putting one's mind on idle.

One of Rudy Crew's first initiatives on becoming superintendent of Miami-Dade Public Schools was to expand summer school. A goal in such instances is to help students catch up or to keep them from falling behind. The effort to end social promotion in both Chicago and New York City included using summer school to let students who might otherwise be held back improve their performance. In fact, in 2004, when New York City didn't have room for all the kids who wanted to attend summer school, the district turned away some high school students and gave preference to third graders who were in jeopardy of having to repeat the grade.

Summertime in Philadelphia

Soon after Paul Vallas assumed leadership of the Philadelphia Public Schools, he instituted Summer Semester, which by its very name implied that a period normally regarded as a vacation would become part of the regular school year. Such an innovation, a sort of third semester, marked a huge step in reconstituting the school calendar. By 2004, Summer Semester enrolled more than 61,000 of Philadelphia's 192,683 students, virtually all of whom attended because they were directed to do so or it was strongly urged upon them.

School officials told 24,587 pupils from first to eighth grades to enroll because their scores fell below the 26th percentile on standardized tests in reading or math, as well as an additional 13,028 who had failed a core course in ninth or tenth grade. In addition, 21,143 English-language learners and special education students enrolled because they were urged, though not required, to do so. The final group included 2,271 five- and six-year-olds—incoming kindergarteners who had not attended any preschool and youngsters who had just completed kindergarten but were deemed to need a boost before starting first grade.

The school system set the stage for Summer Semester in the fall by providing every family with a copy of the district's promotion guidelines. Letters went home during the winter, at the time of the second marking period, to remind parents of the guidelines and to tell them that students who did not measure up would have to attend school during the summer. The schools sent letters again in early June and phoned the homes of students for whom Summer Semester would be mandatory. The strongest weapon to compel attendance was the promotion policy. Students in the benchmark grades—third, fifth, and eighth—had to meet criteria to advance to the next grade.

Naomi Gubernick, the administrator responsible for Summer Semester, joked that the school system must have purchased every industrial-type standing fan in Philadelphia in the summer of 2004 to help make classrooms tolerable. Classes met four days a week for six weeks, from 9 A.M. to 1 P.M., avoiding the hours when temperatures were highest. There were also some air-conditioned buildings among the 115 schools opened for Summer Semester. Apparently, the fans, the air conditioning, and the threat of retention induced an 80 percent attendance rate in summer classes. Philadelphia cobbled together its $18 million summer budget from a grant from the William Penn Foundation specifically for children entering kindergarten and first grade, a federal Title V grant for educational improvement, assorted other grants, and regular school funds.

Schools everywhere could enhance learning opportunities by adding time to the school calendar immediately after the end of the spring term and still leave weeks for summer vacation in most of August. One can hardly talk of the continuous progress that ought to characterize PK–3 education without noting that a three-month summer interruption represents a huge impediment. It is not a matter of expecting students to absorb in six weeks what they did not take in during the previous nine months as much as simply giving them more time to learn it.

LITERACY

What young children need most during their early years of schooling is a sturdy foundation upon which to construct the ability to read. The failure to help all children put such a framework in place has been the greatest failing of America's schools. It is no wonder that so many pupils find their house of reading in splinters by the time they reach the fourth grade. In most cases, patch-up jobs just won't work and young children who struggle to read become teenagers whose learning falters and then adults whose futures are compromised. Children need extensive exposure to rich language in a multitude of forms to become strong, swift readers who glide across a page like a graceful swimmer cutting through water.

One cannot stress enough, especially to parents, the trouble that lies ahead for youngsters who lag in reading when they reach fourth grade. Their problems multiply as they cannot identify words by sight, as their delayed development of reading skills affects their vocabulary growth and alters their attitudes and motivation toward reading, and as they miss chances to cultivate comprehension strategies. After the first three grades of elementary school, mired in this quicksand of reading dysfunction, they may never gain the footing to acquire average levels of reading fluency.[1]

The PK–3 school should exist, if for no other reason than to be a place to underscore the primacy of reading. In the middle elementary grades, the emphasis shifts from learning to read to reading to learn, sealing the fate of children not ready to make this transition. Harvard University's Catherine Snow points out that literacy is a "prerequisite to the acquisition of new information and the formulation of new ideas,"[2] which, in effect, is what happens to the curriculum after third grade. Snow headed the National Reading Panel, created in 1997 at the behest of Congress to assess the effectiveness of different approaches for teaching reading. Its report in 2000, "Teaching Children to Read," identifies five essential components of reading instruction: phonemic awareness, phonics, vocabulary development, fluency, and comprehension.

In the wake of the release of the panel's report, the U.S. Department of Education issued "Reading Tips for Parents," encouraging parents to read to babies starting at six months; to use sounds, songs, and gestures to help babies learn about language; to talk to infants and toddlers to help them speak and understand the meaning of words; to take books and writing materials for youngsters on outings away from home; and to limit the amount and type of television programs that their children watch.[3]

The role of parents in encouraging literacy is no less important once children enter school. They enjoy having adults read to them and welcome opportunities to read to adults as they gain the incipient ability to do so. Rich conversation between parents and children continues to expand literacy as pupils make their way through the early grades. Furthermore, adults who read books, magazines, and newspapers demonstrate that they value the printed word. Parents must be vigilant to discern the shoals and reefs as their children navigate through the difficult straits of learning to read. The good news for parents is that they can help head off perils by surrounding their children with rich language experiences from infancy onward.

ONE DISTRICT'S EFFORT TO BOLSTER READING

And so it is that in the month of July, an air-conditioned wing at James Monroe, one of 11 elementary schools in Edison, New Jersey, contains 78 pupils from throughout the system who just finished first or second grade but trail their classmates in reading. Now, in six classes with at least two master teachers per room, the children get intense exposure to all aspects of language each morning in small groups and individually. Above all, teachers try to arm them with strategies to make sense of the printed page. "Look at the picture," a teacher urges a small group of children in one of the classrooms, prodding them to seek clues to meaning in the illustrations accompanying the words. Remember, these are pupils young enough to have pictures on virtually every page they encounter.

"Sound out the first letter," a teacher reminds the children, hoping to make phonics a first step in solving the puzzle. "Look for a little word in the big word," a teacher says, imploring kids who had completed first grade to recognize the word "it" inside "sit." "Break the word apart and find a word you know." Finally, a teacher urges, "Skip the word, read the rest," trying to keep children from bogging down when they do not recognize words, hoping they might figure them out from their context in sentences. There is seriousness of purpose despite the seasonal allure of playgrounds and swimming pools; only snack time interrupts the daily three-hour sessions. Some of the district's best primary teachers have been hand-selected for this task.

Edison, a 45-minute commuter train ride from Manhattan, is a town of 100,000, where one out of five of its 13,713 students is of East Asian or South Asian descent. In May, the district sent letters to pupils' homes to inform parents that their children "met the requirements" to attend the Summer Literacy Academy—casting participation as a privilege. Kim Duhamel, the supervising teacher, telephones homes when children miss two consecutive days, asking why and imploring parents to get their children onto the buses that pick them up each morning.

The scene is similar in each classroom this particular summer at James Monroe. Children cut pictures from sheets of paper and arrange them according to the beginning sounds of the pictured objects—pictures of chickens and cheese under "ch," pictures of a thermometer and a thimble under "th," for instance. Other children sort words by the sounds of their vowels—sat, slap, and jack together; nail, fail, and pail together. Yet another group rattles off words beginning with the "cl" sound—clean, cloud, clam, clap, closet—calling out the words as the teacher prints them on a chalkboard. Books, read together and read alone, offset the isolated phonics and put words into the context of sentences and stories.

Eight incipient third graders, having just finished reading a storybook about a mouse named Owen who persists in carrying his yellow blanket with him wherever he goes, prepare to identify the main character, the problem, and the solution. In another classroom, children who have completed a nonfiction book about the environment discuss what they have learned about pollution. Elsewhere, children sit on a green rug, looking at a huge "Good Morning" letter on a poster mounted on an easel, trying to identify mistakes in punctuation and capitalization. "Why does the 'W' have to be capitalized?" a teacher asks about the first letter in a sentence. "A capital letter," the teacher says, answering her own question, as so many teachers are wont to do. "What else does a sentence need?" she asks, inviting someone, anyone, to say "A period."

The children—mostly clad in shorts, tee-shirts, and sneakers—listen raptly, evincing the sort of interest one might not expect amid the distractions of summer. This could be the regular school year except that the rest of the building is empty, furniture stacked against the walls in the corridors as the floors of classrooms await waxing by the custodian. Disruptions are few, but not overlooked. "I know it's hard to be here in summer, but you are lucky to be here," Duhamel scolds two sheepish-looking boys whom she has taken into the hall after they told their teacher that they did not want to do the work. "Do you have to practice for soccer?" she asks one who she knows plays the sport. "You have to practice to read, too. Instead of being at soccer camp, you're at learning camp. Now, go in there and learn."

The emphasis on strategies for decoding and comprehending is firm and unremitting. A teacher in a white tee-shirt, khaki Capri pants, and sandals pulls down a screen and wheels an overhead projector into place. Sentences appear on a screen. "What do you do when you meet a reading roadblock?" she asks. "Cover the word and keep your place—Stop, Think, Look, Listen," she continues, repeating an adage that the teachers drill into the kids. "What word makes sense in the sentence?" She blocks a word from the screen by putting her finger over it and asks the children to figure out the missing word.

At some point every day, each child reads individually with a teacher, a luxury that the program's six-to-one pupil-teacher ratio makes possible. "How does he feel about Binnie?" a teacher asks a child sitting next to her on a couch. They just finished reading *The Greatest Binnie in the World* together and now the teacher prods the youngster to think about the story and a character's reaction to the title character. "Did he show her how to climb down? Did Binnie change at the end? Does your brother ever save you or protect you?" She tries to gauge his comprehension as she fires one question after another and discusses his responses with him. The teachers use such one-on-one sessions to assess progress in order to give pupils books at appropriate levels.

Teachers also encourage children to memorize *sight* words, common words like "see," "must," and "big" that they will recognize immediately, as adult readers do, and not have to bother to stop and sound out during their reading. Some sight words—"would," "through," "because," "thought," and "light," for example—have irregular spellings that defy phonic strategies. Ideally, pupils will know at least 300 such sight words by third grade so as to make their reading more fluent.

Writing, too, is part of the program, which deals with all aspects of language and literacy. Each day, kids write in journals. "They have ideas, but writing's a big challenge for them," says Maryann Powers, a teacher who tries to get a group of four pupils to think about the beginning, middle, and end of their writing entries. These master teachers realize that a summer session of less than a month is hardly long enough to ensure that children will return in the fall able to keep up with their peers. Most will probably remain weak in vocabulary and phonics.

"The other day," says Tracey Stricker, another teacher, "I asked them to cut up words and sort them by their sounds. Some of them did not know the word 'sort.' Why do we have kids who still have never heard the word 'sort'?" The teachers hope but have no guarantee that parents will continue working with their children during August. "The home situation contributes to why they are here in the first place," observes one teacher.

Under the best circumstances, these children would advance smoothly through the stages of the early reading process from kindergarten through second grade. It is a process—if all goes well—that starts with kindergarteners as *emergent readers*, growing ever more aware of print, enjoying listening to stories, and beginning to understand differences in syntax and vocabulary likely to appear in written language. As *early readers*, they recognize words they encounter most frequently and know many letter-sound relationships as they start to wean themselves from relying on pictures to make sense of what they read.

Then, as *transitional readers*, they mostly read silently and, when reading aloud, do so with fluency and phrasing, possessing a large core of words that they recognize by sight without having to sound them out. Finally, as *self-extending readers* by the end of second grade, they ideally integrate word structure, syntax, and meaning. They handle longer texts that they read over several days or weeks and make strong attempts to attack new, multisyllable words. This is what teachers hope their students will do.

RENEWED EMPHASIS ON LITERACY IN THE PRIMARY GRADES

Literacy education has assumed a more prominent position in the nation's schools, as indeed it should. It's not as if elementary schools in the United States ever stopped trying to teach students to read. Rather, the nation began to take reading instruction for granted and tended to overlook the failures. Now, there is fresh determination and the spotlight shines brightly on children from prekindergarten through third grade, reading's make-or-break period.

Louisiana, for instance, recognized the crucial nature of the primary grades when it established its K–3 Reading and Math Initiative in 1997. State officials wanted, optimistically, to head off the need for intervention after the third grade. This sort of attention to the early grades is what the PK–3 school would automatically provide. Louisiana allocated funds, which were to reach the $12 million level in 2005, to school systems on the basis of their K–3 enrollment and encouraged—but did not require—them to spend the money on lower-performing students. One need not look far to find such youngsters in Louisiana, where 54.4 percent of the students attend Title I schools and 52.7 percent of households have annual incomes of less than $35,000.

The initiative led to steady progress in raising scores on reading tests. The percentage of students across the state reading at or above grade level rose for second graders from 43.6 percent to 69.9 percent and for third graders from 65.5 percent to 80.8 percent. Gains in New Orleans, which had the state's largest school system, were more modest. Moreover, New Orleans, plagued by budget problems and central office turnover, substituted its own assessment program for the one used in the statewide initiative. Now, after Katrina's lethal visit, the program is in disarray.

As reading has gotten more attention throughout the country, many school districts have dedicated blocks of time for reading and, sometimes, even more than one block per day. Specialists help teachers design reading instruction and provide them with staff development in more and more schools. Other specialists intervene directly with children whose reading lags, not an entirely new development given that such intervention has existed since the advent of Title I of the Elementary and Secondary Education Act in 1965. Now, though, with the prod of No Child Left Behind and the federal government's Reading First grants, there seems to be renewed vigor and perhaps more underlying knowledge behind such efforts.

Classroom visitors find *word walls* to which teachers regularly add new words, listed alphabetically, that youngsters frequently encounter and should learn to recognize by sight. (Wouldn't it be good if schools shared these expanding lists of words with parents so that the words could be reinforced in the home?) Teachers increasingly understand and have the ability to determine children's reading levels. Reading takes many forms through the typical day. There are times when the teacher reads to the whole class, children read to each other, the teacher guides small reading groups, pupils read alone, and youngsters meet in one-on-one sessions with the teacher to discuss what they have read so that she can diagnose their progress.

Students in primary classrooms also write more today, tacit acknowledgment that writing and reading tap into the same sources and reinforce each other. Spelling bees, which faded into obscurity in many places, are making a bit of a comeback, and even penmanship, which the word processor appeared to render obsolete, commands some fresh respect. Schools continue to have libraries, but a growing number of classrooms house their own libraries, with books designated by levels so that each student can find something appropriate to read. Basal reading series remain dominant, but districts increasingly encourage teachers to use *real* books in addition to, or, perhaps, in place of traditional reading texts. Thus, young readers encounter various genres of children's literature, including poetry and more nonfiction.

Words, Words . . .

The primary grades are devoted to enriching language so that children will recognize words and know what they mean. In a first grade classroom in Lincoln, Delaware, for example, Donna Hutchins leads her pupils through a lesson in homonyms. Seated cross-legged on a large carpet, they arc around the teacher, who sits next to a table with a chart filled with words: *blue-blew, week-weak, tale-tail, be-bee, so-sew, would-wood,* and lots more combinations.

"Do they sound exactly the same?" she asks no one in particular. As each child, 21 in all, deals with a combination of homonyms, the youngster not only has to pronounce the identical-sounding words, but also has to define them, use them in sentences, and provide words that are their opposites. It is a thoroughgoing bout with language. "That's what homonyms are, sound the same and spelled different," she periodically reminds her charges as she uses a pointer—reminiscent of teachers of a bygone age—to single out words for attention.

Elsewhere, at a school in Montgomery County, Maryland, children sit together on a rug, facing the teacher who looks at them from a chair next to an easel with a large book perched on it. The book is open to a poem, "Wind Song," by Lillian Moore. "Grasses swish, treetops sigh, flags slap and snap at the sky," says the teacher, Carrie Frankel, paraphrasing the poem that she and her third graders have just read. "Where is something not live but acting like a person?"

"Flags snap," a child responds.

"So, it's acting like a person," the teacher says, using her pointer to draw attention to the passage. "The poet's giving the flag human qualities. The poet's giving an idea of what's happening that way—wires on poles whistle and hum, ash cans roll. The author gives these nonliving things real-life characteristics." She invites the pupils to make the noises of the words that the poet used. "What does swishing look like? We worked on that when we did onomatopoeia. This is an example of personification." Together, the students make the sounds—whistling, swishing, sighing, slapping, and snapping, all with great expression. "Lillian Moore is talking about all those things," Frankel says, trying to get her class to identify the characteristics of the poem and to understand and explain it.

. . . and More Words

Vocabulary is crucial to comprehension. The concern in the lower grades for ensuring that students build their vocabularies is evident one morning at the monthly team meeting of pre-K and kindergarten teachers at Broad Acres Elementary in Montgomery County. It is just before 8 A.M. and the 13 teachers have assembled in a classroom, sitting in seats that in about a half-hour children will occupy. "Think of some of the creative ways to get language into use," suggests Mary Iannicelli, who chairs the meeting. Iannicelli, then a reading teacher and more recently the school's staff development leader, doesn't have to mention the challenge the teachers face at Broad Acres, where 75 percent of the 500 students live in homes in which parents speak a language other than English.

A teacher tells of how she tries to build vocabulary around transportation and vehicles. She holds a model truck in her lap. "I have them label and talk about what a bulldozer does, for example," she explains. "Otherwise, they miss the whole point of the story. Food is another big one. Mushrooms or whatever they don't get. We read 'Honey for Baby Bear.' They don't know what honey is. So, they don't get the story. Bring in objects for your lesson so it will make sense to them."

The principal, who has joined the gathering, urges the teachers to "define words when you use them. It's not just that they are English-language learners. Poverty also is a cause. They aren't read to."

Iannicelli amplifies this point: "Our parents—even the ones who are involved and volunteering—I've noticed do not get into the give-and-take of conversation with their children."

The teachers discuss how they can guide children during their play in the various classroom centers to help them develop stronger vocabularies. One teacher speaks about using the "pretend" kitchen to help them expand their knowledge of words. "In a refrigerator," she says, "you can talk about juice and different kinds of containers. You can talk about such foods as lettuce. They don't know lettuce; they just call it salad."

A teacher mentions using the area where children play house in much the same way, introducing pupils to such words as "living room." Someone agrees, pointing out that probably few of the pupils know what a living room is. She recently visited a youngster's home, an apartment that was basically one large room with four foldaway beds. The child had no idea of a home with a living room and probably couldn't relate to the word unless someone explained it to him, the teacher surmises.

Another teacher, still searching for creative ways to introduce vocabulary into lessons, says that she sometimes uses hand puppets in a unit on firefighters. One of the puppets introduces cards with the names of objects—helmet, hose, ladder, air tank. "None of them knew ladder," she says. As the meeting closes, the principal says, "The vocabulary has to be all the time, not isolated to 30 minutes at the end of the day."

EVERY 1 READS IN
JEFFERSON COUNTY, KENTUCKY

Many of the same emphases showed up in Kentucky's Jefferson County Public Schools, serving Louisville and the rest of the county. The district launched an initiative in 2001 to have every student in the school system reading on grade level by 2008. Every 1 Reads concerns students in all grades, but the strongest focus is on the elementary level and the earliest grades.

Primary grade classrooms in Jefferson County were consumed by the pursuit of literacy. Students spent a minimum of two and a half hours a day on reading and writing, alone and in groups. On top of this, those who trailed their classmates received an added 30 to 90 minutes a day.

Many of the worst readers in the first grade got intensive one-on-one instruction from a specialist for 12 to 20 weeks through the Reading Recovery approach. The Reading Recovery teacher visited first grade classrooms each morning to work in small groups with children reading below grade level. In the afternoon, she provided individual lessons for about a half-hour each to the same students. As some of them increased their achievement, exceeding others, her attention shifted to those they had passed. "I help them reach average or a little above average," said the Reading Recovery teacher at one school. "I try to help them become independent readers."

Central to the process is an attempt to equip children with strategies and skills by which to make sense of words, sentences, paragraphs, and stories. Teachers monitor, support, and coach pupils throughout this effort. Small reading groups are continually in flux as teachers rearrange students according to their changing achievement levels. Most elementary schools create repositories of books designated and organized on 44 different reading levels to ensure that all children can have books to read as close to their levels as possible. In one elementary school, where no other space existed for this library of level-arranged books, stacks of books and materials fill the stage in the auditorium.

Teachers continually assess students to monitor their progress and ensure that they receive books on their reading levels. Unlike tests that a student takes by writing answers or checking off items, teachers themselves fill out the assessments as they listen to youngsters read and ask them questions about it. Two diagnostic instruments mainly serve this purpose. One, Dynamic Indicators of Basic Early Literacy Skills, known as DIBELS, consists of one-minute tests to probe competency in letters of the alphabet and sounds, as well as oral reading fluency. The other, known as DRA, Developmental Reading Assessment, uses text on a child's level of achievement to determine accuracy, fluency, and comprehension.

DIBELS and the DRA are ubiquitous in primary grade classrooms across the country these days as schools try to take a more analytical approach to reading instruction. Assessment and instruction have become two sides of the same coin, creating a symbiotic relationship that demands that teachers in the early grades be as conversant in diagnostic testing as in pedagogy.

Ultimately, Every 1 Reads and most other approaches to reading instruction seek to prepare students for the standardized reading tests by which the outside world will judge them, their classes, their schools, and their school districts. Jefferson County projected its goals for students, grade by grade, and extrapolated from the goals to determine the skills and performance that the children were expected to attain during each year of elementary school. Classroom teachers administered assessments in fall, winter, and spring to monitor the progress and to diagnose instructional needs of individual pupils at these points.

For example, by the end of the second grade a child in Jefferson County should, among other achievements, be able to read regularly spelled one- and two-syllable words; accurately decode multisyllable words; use cues to identify unknown words and construct meaning; use basic phonic elements to identify unknown words; read at least 90 words per minute aloud; incorporate new vocabulary and grammatical constructions into his or her speech; read and comprehend both fiction and nonfiction appropriate to the grade level; discuss motives of characters; figure out how earlier and later parts of a text make sense together; and give reactions to a book by referring to parts of the text when presenting or defending a claim.

LITERACY INCLUDES WRITING

Good literacy programs in the early grades incorporate writing, too. The idea at the beginning, even in preschool and kindergarten, is for kids to get familiar with putting letters and words on paper, to recognize that no one can read unless someone else has written something. Writing in these grades takes many forms: modeled writing, shared writing, interactive writing, guided writing, and independent writing. Teachers, for instance, write down sentences dictated by children still too young to write themselves and thereby model writing as a step toward helping students to write on their own. They strive to transform youngsters into confident writers who will reach the middle and upper grades of elementary school able to express themselves with accuracy, clarity, and verve—just as should happen at every PK–3 school.

How the Process Begins

"We're going to write to our friends today," Kelly Herzing, a kindergarten teacher at Ronald McNair Elementary in Montgomery County, Maryland, announces nonchalantly to her kindergarteners one day, as if they had been writing all their lives. They had recently composed letters to their parents. Herzing takes them through the drill. "What's the first thing?" she asks, immediately answering her question by saying, "What's the date and number?"

"Two-ten–05," responds a student, never bothering to mention that "two" is February and "ten" is the day of the month. Then, Herzing, working at an easel as the kindergarteners sit on the floor in front of her, starts writing, "Dear . . ." and asks what part of the letter that is.

"The greeting," volunteers one of the kindergarteners.

"I'm going to write 'Dear Joseph' because he's not here today since he's sick. What should I write to him?"

"I hope you feel better," suggests a student.

"Do we miss him?" the teacher asks, offering a hint of what the children might write. "At the end, I need to put my name. And on the back, you can draw a fabulous picture."

The children return to their seats, where each receives a fresh sheet of paper with "Dear" at the top and "Love" at the bottom along with a card bearing the name of a classmate to whom to address the letter. They work from what they know, printing the classmate's name after "Dear" and their own names after "Love." They copy the date from the board on which it has been printed and other words from the word wall, where frequently used words are posted as the children encounter them over and over.

"I don't know what to write," says one.

"How do you spell 'like'?" asks another.

Herzing and an aide circulate among the children, lending assistance. The five-year-olds actually begin writing letters—

"I love you."

"I will giv yiu a fott."

"You are mi favrate. I love."

"I wish your my frend."

Some have nothing on the paper except the name of the classmate that they have copied from the card. Others, unable to write much of anything, have turned over their papers and are drawing their "fabulous" pictures. Herzing is pleased. She has seen a lot of growth during the first half of the school year.

The Process Continues

One day at Jefferson County's Norton Elementary, a school that draws from one of the district's most affluent neighborhoods, in a combined fourth grade–fifth grade class of high achievers, Sue Levy is trying to get her students to be careful observers as a step toward incorporating rich description in their writing. They had drawn pictures of the subjects about which they proposed to write. "The reason I had you draw the pictures of your subject was so that you had clear pictures in mind of what the person or event would look like," Levy tells the attentive students. "Now, I want you to write a physical description of your subject, not a story." Before turning them loose to write, however, she asks a girl to come to the front of the class. "Let's give a physical description of Jessica," Levy says.

"Brown hair," says someone.

"Give me more," the teacher urges.

"Long brown hair in a pony tail," comes a more detailed response.

"More."

"Wispy bangs," adds a student.

"Blonde highlights," says another.

Then, a student says something about what Jessica must be thinking as she stands in front of her classmates. Levy will have none of that. "It has to be part of a physical description," she tells the students. "You have to be able to see it."

Eliza offers additional description: "She is about 50 inches tall. She has light blue eyes. Her ears are pierced. She has a nice little bracelet. She has a pretty smile."

The teacher asks no one in particular, "What do you think highlights her eyes? She has dark eyelashes. Can we say she's wearing a red, short-sleeve top? Can you give more description?"

"The top has two stripes," says one.

"She has jeans with pockets," says another.

"Could we say that she is petite?" asks the teacher. "What does petite mean?"

"Small."

Levy asks, "Can we say she is an all-A student?"

"No," intone several youngsters in unison, indicating that they understand what physical description would mean in writing about Jessica.

"Right, it's not part of a physical description," the teacher explains with satisfaction. "Now, do you understand what you are supposed to write? You have 10 minutes of absolutely no talking, no walking around the room, to write."

These are the ideal students that a solid literacy program through the early grades can produce. How many of the children in Jefferson

County will perform at this level by 2008, the year when the district wants every student working on grade level, remains problematic despite the concerted campaign. According to Levy, her students are self-starters and her job is to nurture their motivation to make them independent learners. She says: "We ban boring learning. I don't stand in front and tell them what they need to know. They have ownership. I want them to investigate. They want to learn. I try to use every technique I would use to motivate gifted children. I try to get them to take responsibility for their own learning. They go for the gold. When I get them in my class, a lot hate school. I don't set rules. We talk about respect and responsibility. If we have a problem, we have a class meeting and discuss it."

BALANCED LITERACY

The No Child Left Behind Act, passed by Congress in 2002, led to the creation of Reading First, a program that aims to ensure that every child can read at or above grade level by the end of the third grade. The U.S. Department of Education set out to distribute almost $1 billion annually to school systems under Reading First, promoting the idea that programs to teach pupils to read should rely on scientifically based findings.

For decades, reading experts have argued over the best way to teach reading, debating how much to emphasize phonics on the one hand, or whole language on the other hand. Phonics stresses sounds of letters and parts of words, while whole language involves figuring out words from the context in which they appear rather than from their sounds. This book will not try to resolve this disagreement, which has been the subject of dozens of previous books. Rather, one can only hope that educators will abandon ideology and use instructional methods that have proven effective. The truth is that neither approach ought to exist in isolation from the other. "There is substantial evidence that phonics and whole language can coexist and complement each other," write Yange Xue and Samuel J. Meisels.[4]

The school systems in Jefferson County, Kentucky, and Edison, New Jersey, are among many that refer to their reading instruction as *balanced literacy*, a term that came into wide use in this new century as educators sought to satisfy requirements for federal funding. In writing this book, I visited a number of districts that professed to pursue balanced literacy, a philosophy, not a program. School systems use the term as they wish, though, and what passes as balanced literacy varies from place to place.

While phonics figures strongly in the balanced literacy of some school systems, phonics is less evident in the versions of balanced literacy employed elsewhere.

Much that happens under the aegis of balanced literacy leads to encouraging youngsters to appreciate the written word in all its forms. They begin by learning the rudiments of a book and the habits of readers—title page, author's name, words running from left to right and top to bottom; how to recognize and predict a story line; clues and strategies for deriving meaning from text.

Sometimes, though, this approach seems a far cry from actual reading. Students may be asked to visualize the story, getting the picture in mind, as I observed one day in a Harrisburg, Pennsylvania, elementary school. The teacher read a poem, "School Bus," and then worked with the children on visualization, a skill that he was introducing. "A yellow box on wheels, stuffed with kids," he repeated the line he had just read, asking them to shut their eyes and visualize the scene. Then he asked the children, who were sitting cross-legged on a large carpet, to turn to a partner so that each could tell the other what he or she visualized. Some grew animated as they described the mental images they had formed; others hardly knew what to say.

"What did you see?" the teacher prodded them, slowly drawing out the word "stuffed" as if to paint a picture. "What does it look like inside the school bus if it is *stuffed* with kids? How would that make you feel? How would it sound in a school bus if it was stuffed with kids?" He held flash cards in his hands, each with the name of one of the children in the class printed on it. He turned one over from the top, held it up so everyone could see how the child's name was spelled, and asked that child to respond.

"I want to talk about a couple of words," the teacher said. "Why do you think the author said that the bus was open and shut? What about when he said the bus would stop and start a lot?" The teacher never wrote on the board or showed the words to which he referred. This was a literacy lesson without reference to the sounds of letters or combinations of letters. The teacher cited potential vocabulary words without writing down any of them for the children to see or to try to sound out.

Principals and, in turn, teachers were under pressure from the central administration in Harrisburg to follow the version of balanced literacy laid down by headquarters even if some of the city's educators did not think it gave sufficient attention to phonics. Top administrators referred to their approach as "constructivist," by which educators usually mean that students are supposed to build their knowledge from clues and from what they already know. "We haven't eliminated phonics," said Winston Cleland, the assistant superintendent for curriculum and instruction, who has since retired. He explained that the district had created a pacing guide, which was "like a curriculum guide, to help teachers on how to use phonics." He continued: "We're definitely trying to make sure skill development of phonics is there. It isn't whole language."

◻ ◻

The decades-old dispute over the best way to teach reading to children continues, fueled by adults who believe with all their hearts that they act in the best interests of young learners. Some students emerge from the primary years as sure and confident readers, while others come out faltering and, in the worst cases, hardly reading at all. The situation grows more complicated by the day as increasing numbers of children of parents who speak no English enter the schools of the United States. One can find hope, perhaps, in the fact that the schools give more attention than ever to reading. Furthermore, if the PK–3 concept takes hold, it may ensure that language development becomes the lodestar by which all of primary education sets its compass.

NUMERACY

They are only second graders, but their teacher, Nancy Gregg, wants them to solve the problems without writing down anything. "Which ones can you do in your head?" she asks as she stands next to a sheet of poster board containing the problems on an easel:

36	200+17+300	182	645–224	596	392	99+57	353	7
+24		–69		–185	+385		+404	4
								+7

"If this were a test," says Gregg, "which ones would you do first?"

"The easy ones," say several of the children, showing that they are already savvy to the ways of timed tests.

She reminds them before taking a stab, first, to identify the problem as addition or subtraction, in order to avoid an error that children in the primary grades sometimes make as they tackle math problems. Gregg calls on Matthew D., as she identifies him to differentiate him from the other Matthew in the class, to solve one of the easiest problems, the sum of 36 and 24. Matthew D. doesn't venture an answer and hands shoot up around him as classmates seek the opportunity to produce the right answer. The teacher encourages him to try a different problem if he doesn't care to answer the one that she has offered. Matthew provides 757 as the sum of 353 and 404.

Then, another boy, Tyler, adds 7 and 4 and 7. "It's easy for me," he says, explaining that all he had to do was add 7 and 7 to get 14 and then add 4 to get 18. "Addition is easier than subtraction," he says.

"How many of you think addition is easier?" Gregg asks the class. Most raise their hands. "So, what should you practice more, addition or subtraction?"

Courtney adds 36 and 24 in her head and gives the correct answer. Gregg speaks with the class about the methods Courtney and others have used to solve the problems. Using Courtney's problem, they talk about the number of tens in 36 and the number of tens in 24, as well as the six ones left over from 36 and the four ones left over from 24. Voilà. Five tens and 10 ones equal 60. One by one, using mental math, the students solve each problem that Gregg has presented, bringing to bear the strategies that are the hallmark of their North Middlesex Regional School District in north central Massachusetts, abutting the New Hampshire border.

At Spaulding Memorial School, a prekindergarten to second grade school where Gregg teaches, as well as at the other schools in the 4,800-student system, dedication to problem solving in mathematics stems from the importation of the teaching approach used in Singapore. That small country, only three and a half times the size of Washington, D.C., regularly ranks near the top on international comparisons of math achievement and leads the World Economic Forum's index of economies that make the best use of information and communications technology. Singapore Math, as it is known, influences the way that North Middlesex exposes its students to the subject as early as preschool. By the time they reach the early primary grades, pupils break down problems using models of thinking borrowed from the Singapore approach, readily recognizing the inverse relationships between addition and subtraction and between multiplication and division.

Students need to build a foundation for mathematics in the early years or they will flounder in high school, avoid math in college, and cut themselves off from careers in fields demanding knowledge of math. "We have lots of kids coming into high schools who are not yet ready to take rigorous math coursework," says Michael Cohen, president of Achieve, an organization that helps states raise education standards.[1] He offers this observation in commenting on a study showing that a majority of high school dropouts said that difficulties with math caused them to quit school.

SINGAPORE MATH— FROM MYSTERY TO MASTERY

The transformation in North Middlesex began in 1999, triggered by the district's dissatisfaction with its dismal math test scores, particularly at the secondary level. Fortuitously, during the same period, the state education department gave the district the chance to send some teachers to an institute on math content, where they learned about the syllabus issued by Singapore's Ministry of Education. Ultimately, three of the school system's teachers and a professor from nearby Fitchburg State College agreed to plan a program in 2000 to prepare a small number of North Middlesex teachers to use Singapore Math. The school system focused initially on the middle school grades, but it quickly became clear that for higher math achievement to bloom in secondary schools, North Middlesex would have to plant the seeds during the early primary years.

One of the teachers who formulated the district's plan for Singapore Math was Bob Hogan, who taught fifth grade at Ashby Elementary School. Hogan, who graduated from Fitchburg in 1996, grew up and attended public schools in Brockton, Massachusetts, a city best known for producing shoes and Rocky Marciano, the late heavyweight boxing champion. Math always came easy to Hogan; his epiphany came in the seventh grade, when his math teacher, a Mr. Kelly, motivated him with a tough, challenging approach to the subject.

Hogan, like many teachers, was frustrated by the district's difficulties as it tried to boost math achievement. He wondered whether the problem was with the kids or with the teachers. Looking back on those days, Hogan recalled that he, as a former double major in math and education, worried that perhaps other teachers simply did not have adequate content knowledge of the subject. He also noticed some major differences when he compared the North Middlesex curriculum with Singapore Math. "In America, we race through concept after concept, skill after skill, and kids don't master the 500 pages," said Hogan. "Students go through their books at a rapid pace, just being exposed to math."

By contrast, Singapore Math uses thin booklets that present students with far fewer topics but treat those topics in depth to help youngsters reach mastery. Singapore Math eliminates much of the duplication that often characterizes American curriculums. Moreover, Singapore Math presents students with more multistep, multiconcept problems that require higher levels of thinking. The approach provides students with strategies, frequently using algebraic concepts to solve problems.

"It promotes understanding," said Kathie Maher, a second grade teacher who is a colleague of Nancy Gregg's at North Middlesex's Spaulding Memorial. With Singapore Math, "You have them putting numbers together and taking them apart before asking them to memorize the multiplication tables. You spend a great deal of time slowing things down, exploring, and manipulating. Now, we not only introduce the concept of multiplication, but the reciprocal, division." The Hoover Institution at Stanford University, which studied the beginning period of North Middlesex's implementation of Singapore Math, concluded that students' experience in the program had a positive impact on their test scores.[2] Efforts by the state to improve math instruction led eventually to Massachusetts's ranking in 2005, along with California and Indiana, as one of the top three states in the rigor of its math standards.[3]

North Middlesex: Math Instruction by Deconstruction

From the beginning, North Middlesex not only provided its teachers with an annual summer program on how to teach Singapore Math, but also worked with them to improve their own knowledge of math. The district aimed to give elementary school teachers a good grasp of the work at least two grade levels above the ones in which they taught. This way they could see how the curriculum and instruction aligned from grade to grade. It was not easy. The teachers struggled to learn and struggled to teach what they had learned. Claire Landry, a first grade teacher with 22 years' experience at that point, said she was enthusiastic, but several months into the term nothing that she had learned seemed to work. "Then, all of a sudden," she recalled, "everything snapped into place." That was back in 2000.

The lesson from North Middlesex Regional School District—which serves the three small towns of Ashby, Pepperell, and Townsend—is not so much a testimonial for Singapore Math as a statement that American schoolchildren can perform much better in math than they do now, and that they can end up actually liking math and feeling confident about their abilities instead of feeling intimidated, as are most Americans of all ages.

On the other hand, the virtues of Singapore Math do not resonate with everyone. The method is not a perfect match with many parents, who regard it with a mix of awe and suspicion. The terminology baffles some and, most important, they are exasperated by their inability to help with homework that they do not understand. When an educator from Singapore visited Massachusetts to discuss the program with educators in the North Middlesex district, she advised them simply to tell parents "what we tell them in Singapore"—that it's between the teacher and the child and the parents should stay out of it. The Americans did not find this advice helpful.

In any event, the improvements that Singapore Math helped produce occurred in a school district in a semirural part of Massachusetts that is turning increasingly suburban. It has typical youngsters, not a hand-selected group, and is an area with few poor families and so few minority families that they border on the invisible. Yet, student demographics do not seem to be the issue. The content of the curriculum, the pedagogy, and the increased knowledge of the teachers are what set North Middlesex apart when it comes to math instruction.

When youngsters solve math problems in North Middlesex—where the first, second, and third grades have a minimum of an hour of math a day—they literally take apart the numbers and reassemble them to gain insights into the process. One morning in Cathrine Johnson's second grade class at Ashby Elementary, for example, the youngsters were in their second week of unraveling the mysteries of multiplication. The problem: "There are 2 flowers in each jar. There are 5 jars. How many flowers are there altogether?"

"What is one thing you need to do?" Johnson asked no one in particular.

"Write a word sentence," said Alex.

"What else?" she continued, trying to get them to think about the steps she had taught them—write a word sentence, label, draw bars, solve, write a number sentence. "Let's look at our problem, but don't start trying to solve it. You have to think about it. What do we know? Two flowers, five jars. What do we need to know?"

"The total," blurted Sean.

And so they began, writing and drawing on the ubiquitous personal white erasable boards that are de rigueur in the system's elementary schools. Each student drew a horizontal bar, dividing it into five sections—a section representing each of the jars. Then, the student would write a "2" in each section. Suddenly, two times five came alive as students could visualize the problem. They wrote the appropriate number sentence under the bar: "$2 \times 5 = 10$." Each student completed the exercise with the word sentence: "There are 10 flowers altogether." One child, Dakota, went even further. After drawing the bar and dividing it into five sections and writing a "2" in each section, he wrote several solutions on his slate, each one representing another way of attacking the problem:

$$2+2+2+2+2=10 \qquad\qquad 2\times5=10 \qquad\qquad 5\times2=10$$

"Yes," Johnson responded, seeing what Dakota and some other students had done with the multiplication problem. "You can add to solve that." Satisfied that the youngsters understood the solution, Johnson asked them to erase their personal slates. "Who can remember from yesterday what we learned that's the opposite of multiplication?" she asked.

"Division," Nate said without hesitation.

"What do you do when you divide?" Johnson asked.

"We split," another child said.

"I'll give you a word problem and see how we'd illustrate it," Johnson said. "Jeff has 18 crayons. He divided them up evenly into two boxes. How many crayons are in each box? Draw a bar. Let's think about the problem. We know how many crayons he has. We know the total. So, what goes on top of your bar?"

Each student first drew a horizontal bar and then drew a vertical line to divide the bar in half, making it easier to visualize the two boxes into which the crayons would go. Then, the students wrote an "18" above the bar, signifying the total number of crayons in the two sides of the bar. "What do we need to add to the problem?" Johnson asked. "What will we put in each box? We don't know. So, how will we solve the problem?"

"You could draw 18 dots and split them," John suggested.

"You could do it backwards," Heather said. "Nine times two is 18."

"Do it backward with multiplication to check your division," the teacher suggested.

A Fresh Way to See Math Problems

Primary grade teachers in the elementary schools of North Middlesex Regional frequently use manipulable materials to help pupils visualize math problems, a step that clearly makes it easier for them to find solutions. Kathie Maher, the second grade teacher at Spaulding Memorial School, one day asked two boys in her class to pass out cubes made of colored plastic. The cubes come in strips of 10 that, something like Lego blocks, a child can break apart to make 10 individual units. Maher asked the students to see how many different ways they could divide up the cubes while making sure that they used all 30 and that they kept each group of cubes equal. She checked to assure that the second graders understood the meaning of equal. Using their individual white slate boards, students described the arrangement they created in number sentences.

They assembled the cubes and described the various combinations—5 sets of 6, 6 sets of 5, 10 sets of 3, 3 sets of 10. Finally, one girl, Anna, came up with 15 rows of two, which she wrote in a number sentence as $2+2+2+2+2+2+2+2+2+2+2+2+2+2+2=30$. "What's an easier way to write that?" Maher asked.

"15×2," said Anna.

"Why would we want to use multiplication as a quicker way of addition?" Maher continued, trying to help the children understand that they could take apart numbers and put them back together in lots of different ways.

"Not as many numbers," said one little boy, referring to the row of 2's that Anna had strung together.

"Yes, it's shorter," Maher agreed. "And what happens sometimes when you add a long string of numbers? Is it easy to make a mistake?"

Another way that Singapore Math encourages children to visualize a problem is by having them draw a number bond. Asked to subtract 13 from 83, a student will draw a box and write 83 in it, representing the known sum of 13 and the unknown number. Then, the student draws two lines coming off the bottom corners of the box, each line leading to another box. The student writes 13 in one of the two boxes and leaves the other box blank. The student knows this is the number to determine. By reducing the two known numbers to units of tens and ones, the student determines how many more tens are needed and solves the problem by reversing it and turning it into an addition problem.

Mary M. Waight, associate superintendent for instruction in North Middlesex Regional, had a firsthand experience in what visualization can do when she visited a classroom where the teacher had asked students to solve this problem: "There are 250 students in tenth grade at Northgate High School. All tenth graders must take French or Spanish, but not both. If the ratio of males to females in tenth grade is 2 to 3, and 80 of the 100 French students are male, how many females take Spanish?"

Waight proceeded to set up an algebraic equation with "x's" for the unknowns and was laboring, painstakingly, step by step toward a solution. Meanwhile, the students raced to the answer by constructing two bar models, one split into two boxes of 50 each for the males and the other split into three boxes of 50 each for the females. They subtracted 80 (the number of male French students) from the total of 100 boys and then subtracted the remainder, 20, from the 150 girls and determined that 130 females took Spanish. Waight was still working through the problem as the students arrived at their answer: 130 girls.

North Middlesex's implementation of Singapore Math continued apace each year, reaching into all of the school system's first through sixth grade classrooms by 2005. In addition, a smattering of kindergarten teachers and even some pre-K teachers adapted the approach to their classrooms. The fallout from the change in the elementary grades could be seen in the middle school grades, when the district enrolled all of its seventh graders in pre-algebra and all of the eighth graders in algebra, setting the stage for about half the students to move into Algebra II in high school.

CHANGING ATTITUDES ABOUT MATH

The venture in North Middlesex represents an important counterattack on the belief that mathematics is not a subject for everyone. The attitude has historic roots. As long ago as 1838, Benjamin Peirce, chair of the math department at Harvard, less than an hour's drive from the towns that comprise the North Middlesex Regional School District, campaigned successfully to drop the college's math requirement after the freshman year on the grounds that the discipline was accessible only to the few.[4]

Such beliefs stubbornly persist and, worst of all, it does not embarrass otherwise educated people to be dimwits about math. Adults who would be aghast to learn that a peer knows nothing about art or lacks basic information on world events dismiss ignorance of math as inconsequential. This condition owes its provenance to ill-taught math in the early grades, a situation that often leaves students bereft of a foundation or of a desire for further study. Math achievement across the United States tumbles after the middle elementary grades. Just as with reading, the early grades ought to provide a foundation for mathematics that extends through high school. A PK–3 orientation that values math can make a major difference.

Speaking about Numbers

One change in math instruction, in keeping with the approach taken by Singapore Math, would be for teachers to encourage more talking about math while pupils do math. That's right: having kids speak at length in class—about what they do as they solve problems and carry out computations. Too frequently, the only talk in math involves giving the right answer. In elementary schools in China studied by American researchers and a Chinese colleague, however, an answer serves as the start of an extended discourse about algorithms, and the mathematical rules and reasoning needed to find the answer. Discussions of this sort, guided by skilled teachers, help Chinese students absorb mathematical knowledge as they discuss how they carried out calculations, applied rules, and reasoned their way to answers. Furthermore, the conversation reveals a great deal to the teacher about students' thinking processes. "[D]ifferences between the U.S. and Chinese classrooms in terms of the quantity and quality of extended discourse are striking," the researchers found.[5] The discourse is important not only to confirm the correct answer, but to explain how the computation could be used in other situations.

A new focus on early learning, as this book proposes, must include fresh approaches to teaching math by teachers well versed in the subject, teachers who hone their ability to impart their knowledge to children in engaging and rewarding ways. This will not happen, though, without professional development for veteran teachers and different ways of preparing new teachers. Researchers at the University of Michigan, for instance, are trying to discover just what mathematics elementary school teachers need to know to teach the subject effectively. They have found in more than ten years of research that teachers of young children must be able to explain problem solving, listen to students' explanations, and examine students' work. They need the ability to analyze the sources of their pupils' errors and they ought to speak to them in proper mathematical language.[6] In other words, teachers should not only know math content, but how to teach it to young students.

One step toward producing teachers for the first three grades who can more readily meet such demands would be to let them gain expertise in a narrower range of subjects instead of the broad command that the typical elementary teacher is supposed to have over every subject. At Broad Acres Elementary in Montgomery County, Maryland, for instance, teachers in every grade specialize, assuming responsibility for only math and science or for only language arts and social studies. The school calls them "specialists" in recognition of this arrangement. In addition, as at other Title I schools in the district, Broad Acres has a math content coach to provide direct instructional support to teachers.

A Singapore-Style Approach

The principles underlying Singapore Math are not unique to that approach. Mickey Garrison, the principal of Fullerton IV Elementary School in Roseburg, Oregon, for instance, arrived on her own at a way of teaching the subject that has much in common with practices in North Middlesex, Massachusetts. It too involves helping children see that there may be several different ways to solve a problem and encouraging them to take the numbers apart. Children use manipulable materials and models. She combined several different commercial curriculums and continues to add other materials.

At Fullerton IV, those teachers most amenable to change were the first to receive professional development training, as their counterparts in Massachusetts did, to deepen their understanding of mathematics and to learn about the appropriate representation of mathematical ideas. They learned and then taught their students mathematical language and precise mathematical vocabulary for discussing problems. Educators in these two places at opposite ends of the country concluded that an approach geared to problem solving can engage young children if only teachers will take the time to learn more about mathematics than their peers in most elementary classrooms ever bother to do. Teachers and students in both places have been imbued with a mathematics that involves risk taking, and they recognize that the subject has more to it than calculations that produce the *right* answer.

Roseburg, like North Middlesex, is not the sort of place in which one expects to encounter breakthroughs in curriculum and instruction. Its out-of-the-way locale in the Hundred Valleys region of southwest Oregon features an outdoors lifestyle of hunting, fishing, and boating that attracts tourists. Parents scrape by with low-paying seasonal jobs and half of the youngsters in Fullerton IV's more-than–90-percent-white enrollment qualify for federally subsidized meals. "If we don't give them a solid foundation during the early years," Garrison said, "they will be at a great disadvantage in the fourth grade and lose ground in subsequent grades after that."

CONTROVERSIES OVER MATH

Something like the debate over reading instruction rages in math. In both subjects, the controversy has to do with the extent to which teachers should expect students to "construct" their own knowledge. Thus, in reading, constructivists argue that a strong dose of phonics is unnecessary, as students will figure out words from the context in which they appear. In math, constructivists want to let students "discover" concepts; they tend to oppose drills, memorization, and grounding students in too many basic facts.

Differences of philosophy in how to teach math to children seem ongoing. Instruction in elementary schools during the last half of the twentieth century was dominated, first, by the so-called New Math that derived from a logic that proved incomprehensible to students as well as to many teachers. Since the late 1980s, the predominant approach has stemmed from standards promulgated by the National Council of Teachers of Mathematics, which encourages teaching that cultivates students' abilities to make discoveries in mathematics.

The National Science Foundation (NSF) has tried to put its imprint on math in elementary schools, funding several projects that led to the creation of widely used curriculums. Math Trailblazers, Everyday Math, and TERC all evolved with NSF support. These programs share attributes with Singapore Math, focus on problem solving, and use applications to real-life situations and hands-on activities. Another program, Saxon, takes a somewhat more traditional approach to math instruction with its emphasis on concepts.

Almost every approach to math instruction in the primary grades, Singapore Math included, has at one time or another been the subject of dispute. Issues arise—almost none ever fully resolved—over whether one or another program is too prescriptive, lacking in rigor, unable to engage small children, too tolerant of calculators, or incomprehensibly bad. Overlaid on this debate is the fact that competing publishers seek to reap substantial profits from these programs. What seldom gets enough attention, though, is the need to assure that teachers in the lower grades understand math and have the preparation to convey that knowledge, whatever program they use.

Sometimes the math debates get cast in political terms, with those advocating a constructive approach portrayed as progressives and those opting for more work on concepts and basic facts regarded as traditionalists. The lone consideration should be what's best for kids. Math, on the one hand, will inevitably invite students to make discoveries, but it is folly, on the other hand, to believe that schools should banish instruction in basic facts and shy away from well-conceived drill. It will always be better to have memorized the multiplication tables than not to have done so.

During the past half-century, math achievement in American schools has suffered in comparison with results in other countries. A report sponsored by the U.S. Department of Education to see what the nation can learn from Singapore Math points toward some of the explanations for this development. The study, carried out by the American Institutes for Research, compared key features of Singapore and American math in the primary grades. It found Singapore's textbooks richer in abstract concepts, its tests more challenging, and its teachers better prepared in math content and pedagogy.[7] The experience in North Middlesex illustrates that attention to the knowledge and instructional skill of teachers is essential to any attempt to improve. Altering the curriculum alone will not suffice.

This is not to say that math has been an unmitigated disaster in American schools. Students in this country—at least at fourth grade—showed steady improvement from 1990 through 2004 on examinations administered by the National Assessment of Education Progress (NAEP), the federal government's testing program. The percent of fourth graders scoring below the basic level on the NAEP math test declined by half since 1990 and the percent at the proficient level more than doubled. Even this outcome, though, has been called into question by a Brookings Institution study that found the questions too easy and challenged the notion of progress.[8]

Little things matter. Letting children in primary classrooms rely on calculators, for instance, is a sure route to depriving them of thorough knowledge of basic concepts. They don't have to think through a solution if they can just press buttons and get an answer. They should compute by hand, which, after all, is a form of discovery. Similarly, a student who has committed the multiplication tables to memory has acquired a tool of immense value.

How much do students really know if they haven't had to perform the calculations? One scholar who compared the performance of nine-year-olds with and without calculators discovered that calculators change everything. Calculators made the least difference in addition, but the differences in arriving at correct answers with calculators vs. paper and pencil were 89.2 percent vs. 59.7 percent in subtraction, 87.9 percent vs. 42.5 percent in multiplication, and 77.1 percent vs. 48.3 percent in division.[9]

There are certain constants in math to which schools should expose young children in each generation. In building a foundation for competence, they should learn by the third grade to perform basic arithmetical functions. They should conquer the intricacies of telling time, determining dates, and handling money. They should acquire the basics of linear and liquid measure. All of this ought to amount to an introduction to algebra even though teachers do not refer to the work as such. Let's take a look at how this plays out.

LAYING FOUNDATIONS: ABSTRACT CONCEPTS AND FRACTIONS

As in reading, a portion of a child's development in math occurs outside the classroom. Informal experiences play a large role as youngsters grow aware of numbers and strive to learn the rudiments of counting. Young children, after all, exist in a universe of out-of-school math where they try to make sense of numbers and their meaning, gradually becoming aware that order reigns and that rules dictate what is right and what is wrong. Imagine a child's struggle to come to terms with the basic concept that to count properly he or she must take note of each object and do so once and only once. And think of the feeling of power that comes with the realization that after he or she can count to 20, the other numbers merely follow the pattern of one through nine.

Children come to understand that numbers have names and, gradually, they recognize a sense of order—4 follows 3, for instance, and 4 never comes before 3. Adding to a child's initial confusion, on the other hand, is the fact that the order in which one counts a particular object usually doesn't matter. They also must learn that the same number doesn't necessarily have to be ascribed to an object each time they count it. Children develop strategies for counting just as they do for figuring out words. Counting and numbers may mean something altogether different to children and adults.[10]

One-to-one correspondence, for instance, is an abstract concept that kindergarteners need time to grasp. Joyce Goubeaud tried to use concrete methods to instill this notion in the minds of her children in North Middlesex's Ashby Elementary School. She asked five of the kindergarteners to sit in front of her on a rug in a corner of the classroom, the first step in introducing them to different combinations of the number 5.

"How many people do we have here?" asked Goubead. They counted off from left to right, one to five. With that notion firmly established, she asked how many boys there were, four, and how many girls, one. Then came the hard stuff. "Can I make a number sentence?" she asked, using the terminology that they would need to solve math problems in the primary grades. "Four plus one equals five," she said by way of answering her own question. "How many girls and how many boys? One plus four equals five. Four plus one equals five."

"Do we use the same number?" she inquired, hoping that they were getting the idea that different combinations could add up to the same sum. "What if Jake left? Now, what would the math problem say?" she asked as she traded places with Jake and sat with the other four children. "Now, how many girls and how many boys? Two plus three equals five. So are those different ways to make five?"

Goubeaud unrolled a long sheet of paper numbered from 1 to 5 on the floor in front of the children. She placed little plastic kittens next to each number. "What if we did this?" she asked after having put down three yellow kittens and two blue ones. "We still have five. Three plus two equals five."

She turned toward a slate that she had placed on an easel, low and close to the children. "Five on the floor, five on the board," she said as she wrote "3+2=5" on the slate. "What if we switch?" she asked, trading a blue kitten for a yellow one. "2+3=5," she wrote on the slate. She changed the number of blue kittens and yellow kittens several more times, showing the children that various combinations could total five. She showed them that even if all of the kittens were of the same color the total (5+0) could still add up to five. "So, there are lots of different ways to make five." They were getting it. One of the boys, Spencer, mentioned a combination that even Goubeaud had overlooked—1+1+1+1+1=5.

◘ ◘

The primary grades are also the place to lay a foundation for fractions, possibly following a path similar to that taken by Joanne DiNatale in her second grade class at North Middlesex's Peter Fitzpatrick School, likely one of the few in the country named in memory of a former custodian. The pupils gathered around DiNatale one day as she sat in front of an easel with a book open to a page with a picture of a delicious-looking bright yellow banana. On the next page, the picture showed that someone had sliced the banana near its middle. DiNatale congratulated the youngster who said the banana had been "cut in half." That was the word she was trying to elicit—"half." And off they journeyed, into the fascinating world of fractions.

"Let's think about what 'in half' might mean," DiNatale suggested.

A boy named Cameron said that "it's something that's the same as the other half." So far, so good.

"Why do you think this person cut the banana in half?' asked DiNatale, seeking further elaboration on her students' comprehension of what two halves constitute.

Blair had an answer so good that the teacher could have kissed her. "I think so each kid will have an equal piece." There it was, that word "equal," without which it would be impossible to have halves. "The banana's been cut into two equal pieces and each child gets the same amount," DiNatale said, writing "½" to label each amount. "So a fraction is a piece of a whole thing," she added. "There's that word again: 'Whole.'"

Turning the page, DiNatale came to a large picture of a muffin, viewed from above so that it was clear that someone had cut the muffin into three equal parts. Later came a picture from above of a pizza that someone had sliced into four equal parts. There was talk of "one-third" and "one-fourth." From there, the discussion verged into mention of "symmetry." "These are lines of symmetry," DiNatale said, stressing that there were four equal pieces, cut down the middle and across the middle.

"Are you noticing," she asked the class, "that when the bottom number of your fraction gets higher, what happens to the pieces?" Yes, they seemed to realize that a larger number on the bottom of the fraction meant more pieces in the whole. They recapitulated—a banana sliced into two equal pieces, a muffin sliced into three equal pieces, a pizza sliced into four equal pieces. "If you divide a pizza into four pieces, how many pieces can each child have?" DiNatale asked with the book open to a picture of two smiling boys.

"Two," one of the students said without hesitation.

"Which is the same as what?" asked DiNatale.

"Half." the student replied. So, there it was. Two-fourths and one-half were the same thing. And just to make sure that they got it, the book continued with an ear of corn that someone broke in half, a pear salad that was divided into three equal portions, and a pie sliced into fourths. Finally, DiNatale closed the large book on the easel and announced that they would review words about fractions.

8

A FULL COMPLEMENT OF SUBJECTS

Children lack sufficient intellectual nutrition during the early years of their schooling if they must subsist solely on a diet of reading and math, as essential as those staples may be. A full menu of subjects is appropriate throughout schooling. A problem, though, is that efforts to show progress under the No Child Left Behind act have induced schools to limit the intake of social studies and science, not to mention music, art, and other subjects that even in the best of times do not always get the attention they should.

Maryland's Montgomery County Public Schools, a district adjacent to Washington, D.C., exemplifies the situation by which elementary schools relegate social studies and science—major subjects in the secondary curriculum—to minor status, especially in the earliest grades. Children each day spend anywhere from an hour and a half to three hours in reading and at least 45 minutes in math in the system's lowest grades. In Montgomery and elsewhere much of social studies gets taught through reading and a bit of science gets taught through math.

In an ideal curriculum, social studies and science would play a bigger role during the years from preschool through third grade. But time is a precious commodity in the primary classroom. Teachers dole it out sparingly, bound by priorities. The Montgomery County schools paired social studies specialists with language specialists in fashioning the district's literacy curriculum. "If you're choosing a topic for reading," asked

Bill McDonald, a now-retired administrator in the district's curriculum department, "why not one that supports concepts of social studies and science?" The district's instruction guides keyed specific lessons to science and social studies during the literacy block. At the second grade, for example, a lesson called for students to read a nonfiction account about butterflies and insects.

The National Science Resources Center, an affiliate of the Smithsonian Institution that produces science materials used by about 15 percent of the country's elementary schools, says that it built its Science and Technology for Children program so that teachers could integrate it with reading, writing, math, and social studies. The center, for instance, asserts that "children develop their reading, writing, speaking, and listening skills as they complete record sheets, maintain science notebooks, read stories about topics that they are studying in science class, and share findings in both formal and informal settings."[1]

THE PLIGHT OF SOCIAL STUDIES

Even before the No Child Left Behind legislation, social studies was a poor cousin in the curriculum of the primary grades. Some teachers do not value the subject and, moreover, consensus about what to teach in social studies and how to teach it is not readily attained. These are some of the main problems in social studies in the primary grades:

- Poor textbooks and a lack of good materials
- Insufficient teacher knowledge and interest
- Limited professional development opportunities for teachers
- Inadequate attention to making social studies age-appropriate
- Overreliance on holidays and heroes
- Limited research on how best to teach social studies in the primary grades

Elementary teachers, like so many Americans, tend to possess scant knowledge of history and a not particularly strong interest in the field, an indifference that stems from the childhood boredom that they—and most of the rest of the class—felt when the subject was taught to them. The cycle, unfortunately, remains unbroken. Teacher education in many colleges offers only a minimum grounding in social studies and it may stress methodology over content.

Heroes and Holidays

Left on their own, elementary teachers may be uncertain as to which ideas and concepts in social studies to convey grade by grade. To simplify matters, they often approach social studies through holidays and heroes. A visit to a school during a holiday period provides a glimpse of the extent to which the calendar exerts its influence on the tone of the entire building.

It's the Friday before Thanksgiving at the Morris Early Childhood Center, for instance, and social studies reigns supreme in the guise of Indians, Pilgrims, turkeys, and pumpkins. Indian music, with chants and the light beat of tom-toms, plays softly in the background in some classrooms. As Morris offers only prekindergarten through first grade classes, the levels at which a holiday may be most palpable, it seems that every teacher has incorporated Thanksgiving into the lessons and the décor.

The school, in semirural southern Delaware, enhances the seasonal aura by sending classes on field trips to nearby Abbott's Mill Nature Center, with its acres of pine woods and a grist mill dating to 1802. There, the natural scene becomes an alfresco classroom in which to impart lessons on the ways and customs of the Lenni Lenape Indians, whose trails and portage paths once crisscrossed the mid-Atlantic region. Children examine various artifacts and reproductions of the items that characterized life centuries earlier. Once back at the school, Ellen Morton talks to her kindergarteners about arrowheads and points out to the children that "Native Americans in Delaware lived in longhouses, not tepees."

In another wing of the school, Chrissy Meszaros has gathered her first graders into a tight circle to discuss how they expect to spend the holiday. She takes advantage of the seasonal motif to create bar graphs during a math lesson as the children enumerate the number of celebrants they expect at their Thanksgiving tables. Thus, Thanksgiving becomes a demarcation in the school year, and Meszaros explains that after the holiday the class will use dominoes to learn to add numbers totaling more than 10.

In another classroom, Karen Carey-Wilkerson asks the children, who sit at desks and tables for a whole-class discussion, "What did we go to Abbott's Mill for?" The question triggers a conversation about how the Indians lived. This is social studies, kindergarten style. The teacher directs a pupil to retrieve two arrowheads from a box. "Real Lenni

Lanape held these in their hands hundreds of years ago," Carey-Wilkerson declares with awe. "Where are the Lenni Lenapes now?" she asks.

"Dead," one of the five-year-old boys says irreverently, without the least bit of wonderment.

"Stones are nonliving," the teacher responds, not missing a beat in referring to the flint from which Indians carved their arrowheads. "They can sit there forever."

Carey-Wilkerson, clearly an enemy of idle time, quickly segues into a lesson on Squanto, supposedly an English-speaking Indian who helped the Pilgrims. She draws a circle on a sheet of paper and tapes the paper to a board on an easel so everyone can see what she is doing. This will be Squanto's face. She demonstrates each step of the project—drawing, cutting, gluing. Carey-Wilkerson and an aide distribute paper and glue sticks; the children get markers from a nearby table. "Draw your Native American," Carey-Wilkerson says, carefully dispensing the instructions that kindergarteners need. "Draw a circle for the Native American's face. It doesn't matter what kind of face you're drawing. It has to have eyes, a nose, and a mouth. Then, cut out feathers and glue them to the paper." Social studies and art merge.

Jeff Tolbert, another kindergarten teacher at Morris, uses the Thanksgiving theme to promote math by having the children connect numbers on worksheets on which the lines eventually form a picture of a Pilgrim whom they can color. Tolbert also plays pretend with the children, spreading an imaginary Indian blanket and acting out the ritual of grinding corn against the hollowed-out portion of a stone, all the while describing the actions of Native Americans of many years ago.

Sharon Bailey uses the holiday as a backdrop against which to teach her kindergarteners a lesson that runs from social studies into science and then into math and, finally, into language and writing. She begins by discussing the first Thanksgiving and the food at the feast. Bailey shows the children some cranberries and asks what use they may have had, other than as food. "Squish them. What can you do with the juice?" she says, encouraging a possible response, eventually having to explain that one could use the juice as a kind of ink. Bailey circulates among the children, cranberries in hand, so that each can have a closer look. She asks whether they think the raw fruit is sweet or sour, a science lesson if ever there was one. The children vote: 14 for sweet, 4 for sour. She employs the tally as a brief math lesson.

Then, Bailey hands out sheets of papers with turkey stickers in the upper corners. "Today," Bailey announces, "I want you to think about turkeys. We see them at farms. They can fly. They can walk. What kind of an animal is a turkey?" What she wants, of course, is for someone to say "A bird," but no one does. "Think about it," she continues, prodding them. "It flies and has feathers." This kindergarten class contains some of the school's most at-risk pupils, most of whom can barely print their names.

"Today, we want to write facts about turkeys," Bailey continues. "Do you see the word 'turkey' anywhere in the room?" she asks. She had printed the word on the board, pointing out that "T" was capitalized, coming at the beginning of a sentence. She tries to get the class to print "fly" on their papers, as in "Turkeys fly." "Put a meatball in between," she urges, injecting the notion that a "meatball"—the kindergarten equivalent of a space—is required between words. "And put a period at the end." Next, the class takes on another sentence: "Turkeys look fat."

"We can see one of our sight words, 'look,'" she says enthusiastically, drawing the attention of the class to the list of sight words—those they are learning to recognize without having to sound them out—on the Word Wall on one side of the room. Other words on the wall, all in alphabetical order, include *a, blue, can, like, me, red, see, the, yellow, yes,* and *you.*

Make no mistake. Thanksgiving is big in elementary school, particularly in the primary grades, where it gives teachers a hitching post to which to tie a good deal of instruction for several weeks every fall. The use of holidays as a vehicle of instruction is so pervasive that sometimes it takes an unusual twist, as in a third grade classroom at Zavala Elementary School in Austin, Texas, one December morning, in a class of bilingual children whose parents are mostly immigrants from rural Mexico. "Why do they celebrate Hanukkah?" the teacher asks after reading a story to the students. She tells the fidgety children about dreidels, latkes, and Maccabees. "Why do they light eight candles?" she asks, hoping someone would remember from the story that the oil in the desecrated temple was expected to last only one day. "Because they want presents," says one of the boys.

Heroes function in much the same way as holidays. Washington and Lincoln are front and center in February. (After all, each lost his individual holiday to create the strange amalgamation known as Presidents' Day.) Schools have injected Betsy Ross, Crispus Attucks, and other female and minority fringe figures into the curriculum to achieve a bit more balance as they salute heroes. But whether the subject is female, black, or a traditional white man, social studies still shines its light through this prism.

Hero worship has its shortcomings, though. Christopher Columbus, once a giant in the elementary social studies curriculum, totters on his pedestal these days. Most schools continue to teach about him on Columbus Day, but a small number of schools use the occasion to tell of his excesses against Native Americans and an equally small number of schools simply ignore him, consigning the tarnished hero to Trotsky's dustbin of history.

Critics contend that a focus on holidays and heroes trivializes lessons. Try telling this to a six- or seven-year-old. Thanksgiving and some other holidays give them an anchor for their learning. There is time enough, when children grow older, to discover that turkeys can be foul beasts, pumpkins are simply overgrown squash, and Pilgrims could be intolerant and downright deadly to Indians. And Indians, well, students may eventually learn that there were good ones and bad ones, and almost all of them suffered at the hands of European newcomers.

Perhaps the situation could change if more research showed what works and what does not, what is most appropriate and what is not. Certainly, some distinguished professors conduct research on social studies in the primary grades, but, by and large, secondary school social studies appeals far more to scholars. They find it infinitely more fascinating to find out how many 17-year-olds, on the verge of voting, cannot name the sitting vice president than to find out how many 7-year-olds don't know the name of their state capital.

Attitudes, Politics, and Building Community

At one time, geography figured prominently in the social studies curriculum of the primary grades. But it has been eclipsed. Maps and globes have disappeared from many classrooms, having been rendered nonessential by the Internet and unfashionable by those who disparage rote knowledge of capitals—as if that were all that geography constituted. History itself lacks even the modest status formerly accorded it. Today's elementary teachers, products of an ahistorical society that celebrated relevance during the schooling of many of them, tend to shy away from imparting history lessons in the primary grades. This attitude persists despite research showing that history is not too abstract for young children to understand.[2]

Then, there is the dispute among academicians, unknown to the general public, about whether modern social studies undermines the pursuit of history and of the social sciences as individual disciplines. Social studies, after all, stems from what was once largely the study of history to now encompass a conglomeration of geography, government, sociology, economics, anthropology, psychology, anthropology, and other social sciences. For children in the primary grades, these various fields often combine in the blender of a social studies curriculum centered on self, family, and neighborhood. This curriculum expands in concentric circles in some schools so that by the third grade it may include the country and the world, mostly from an egocentric perspective.

Is this good or bad? Are schools short-changing little children or are they providing salience that makes social studies more visible to the untrained eye? Stephen J. Thornton attempts to frame the debate. He sees, on the one hand, critics who contend that social studies is "a mishmash of information and skills, lacking in substance," with no indication of how the subjects relate to the academic disciplines. On the other hand, according to Thornton, defenders say that social studies is "a logical arrangement of subject matter, thus making the material more learnable" and letting students experience the subjects "in a broad, meaningful context."[3]

As Americans grow more polarized in their political attitudes, the outlook for social studies grows more grim, perhaps most so for the youngest children who are the most impressionable. The country could gravitate toward social studies for the blue states and another version for the red states. (Aren't we already moving in this direction in science with the split over evolution?) A furor that occurred in the 1990s over history standards does not bode well for trying to formulate meaningful and substantial curriculum for the primary grades. Pressure from the right to preserve tradition and from the left for political correctness may compel schools and teachers to resort to an innocuous approach that offends no one.

Part of social studies in some elementary schools is an effort to build community in individual classrooms and in the school at large. Children learn to follow rules and discover the penalties for deviating. Visit an elementary school in most locales and you will see lines everywhere, as students queue up to walk through the hallways to bathrooms, to lunch-rooms, to playgrounds, and to dismissal. Often, this involves keeping close to the wall, holding down voices, proceeding at an orderly pace without running, and maintaining a set distance between children.

Some deride such procedures as unconnected to real citizenship. But getting children to understand the need for rules in their little society makes for a smooth-functioning classroom where pupils pick up after ac-tivities, do not fight with each other, and defer to someone who is already speaking. Such conduct forms the kind of social compact that makes community possible at the PK–3 level. And how different, after all, are these behaviors from those that enable the larger society to operate—waiting for a red light to turn green, standing in line at the bank, not walking out of the restaurant without paying? Does it not make sense to regard the socialization that helps build community as part of the tacit social studies curriculum?

SCIENCE IN THE EARLY GRADES

Unlike social studies, science will be subject to testing under the No Child Left Behind law, beginning in the 2007–08 school year. Presum-ably, this will force elementary schools, including the lowest grades, to take science more seriously. A major problem, though, even when ele-mentary schools make time available for science, is that many teachers feel unqualified to teach the subject.

Typically, elementary school teachers are expected to know and be able to teach every subject. The children may be only six or seven years old, but teaching the fundamentals of physical, chemical, and biological phenomena still poses a substantial undertaking. Deans of colleges of education and the elementary school teachers whom they train agree that preparation for teaching science is not as thorough as for other sub-jects. Thus, science has had second-rank standing in the elementary cur-riculum, both because schools do not consider it important and because many teachers lack the knowledge and confidence to teach it well. Ele-mentary school teachers say that they are three times more likely to teach English and math each day than science and social studies. Only 31 percent of education deans think that elementary teachers are very comfortable answering pupils' questions about science and only 7 per-cent of deans feel very confident that today's K–5 students get a good science education.[4]

Science and technology are essential to America's place in the world. Yet, many students feel negatively about these subjects by the time they complete high school. Moreover, they lack a grounding to pursue the disciplines in higher education, ending up with little comprehension as adults of some of the most important issues that affect them—molecular biology, nuclear energy, telecommunications. Equally important, they cut themselves off from a host of career possibilities. The nation could alter this egregious situation by reformulating approaches to science in the earliest years of education, from preschool to third grade, when students are building their foundation and their attitudes. Improving the education of teachers for the earliest grades, in both the quality and the amount of preparation they receive for teaching science, would be a first step in this process.

Doing Science with Stories

Renee G. O'Leary has tried single-handedly to change some of the ways that young children learn science and to have a positive impact on their attitudes about the subject. A retired public school kindergarten teacher with a Ph.D., O'Leary embarked on a second career as a science specialist for 317 children in kindergarten through third grade at Caravel Academy, an independent K–12 school in Bear, Delaware. She found this age group a natural audience for science, eager to discover how the world around them functions.

At the heart of her approach were age-appropriate lessons that she prepared on two levels, one more complex than the other. Experiments delved into such phenomena as absorption, density, the five senses, surface tension, camouflage, static electricity and simple circuits, reflective surfaces, and rock and soil properties. Typically, the lessons built on such children's stories as Cinderella, The Golden Goose, Snow White, and The Little Engine That Could, seizing on aspects of the tales to develop themes for experiments. What about all those sweets, for example, that Little Red Riding Hood took to Grandma? Couldn't she have found something more nutritious for the old lady?

O'Leary linked home and school through her Portable Affordable Simple Science program, which she copyrighted as P.A.S.S. Children took home materials in clear, plastic kitchen bags that, instead of food stuffs, contained rocks, magnets, and other inexpensive items that they could use to demonstrate for their parents the experiments that they had carried out in school. O'Leary sent home a sheet with the final lesson, asking parents to submit comments about the year's work.

"I like the fact that parents were included in each project, which gave me additional quality time with my son," a kindergarten mother responded to O'Leary and continued: "We had a lot of fun on projects that asked us to mix something or needed water. My favorite projects were the five senses and the mixing of powder to make colors." The mother of a first grader wrote: "The lessons were the first steps toward observation and critical thinking. At home, explaining the projects to parents and writing about simple topics allowed them to take their first step in both oral and written communication. I am very pleased by these 'seeds' in forming Erin's future not only in science but in other areas as well."

National Science Resources Center

On a much larger scale, the National Science Resources Center was created in 1985 to serve elementary and middle schools in the wake of the federal government's *A Nation at Risk* report, which deplored the condition of American education. The center has the advantages of working under the aegis of the Smithsonian and the National Academy of Sciences and tapping expertise outside the government in science, engineering, and medicine. Its Science and Technology for Children program has produced curricula and materials tailored to specific grades so that pupils can investigate scientific phenomena.

The investigative cycle—which lasts for six to eight weeks for each of the 24 units that span the elementary school years—has four steps: children focus on what they already know, carry out an experiment as an inquiry into the new, reflect on what they've observed, and apply the knowledge to real-life situations. This approach aims to teach skills that lend themselves to all kinds of problem solving. Children typically complete the first two units in kindergarten and then three or four units a year in each grade thereafter. Most teachers offer lessons of 30 to 45 minutes each about twice a week as they move through a unit.

In life and earth sciences, for instance, kindergarteners and first graders learn about organisms and weather, while second and third graders learn about the life cycle of butterflies, soils, plant growth, and rocks and minerals. In physical sciences and technology, kindergarteners and first graders study solids and liquids and comparing and measuring; second and third graders study solids, liquids, and gases; balancing and weighing; chemical tests; and sound.

Central to each lesson is a kit that contains all the materials that children need to conduct experiments. The National Science Resources Center licensed a commercial firm, Carolina Biological Supply Company, to sell the kits, which can run from less than $200 to more than $1,000 per unit for an entire classroom. The center, a not-for-profit organization, uses its share of the revenues to develop new materials. Kits sold by Carolina Biological Supply and its competitors reach as many as one in four of the country's elementary pupils. This science-in-a-box approach means that classroom teachers without a background in science can lead lessons and that schools do not have to scrounge around for materials.

Even the living organisms needed for the experiments—frogs, crabs, millipedes, crickets, snails, beetles, seeds and moss, worms—accompany the various kits. A teacher's manual includes instructions for habitat requirements and temperature ranges appropriate to the particular organism. Imagine how first graders would feel to arrive in their classroom one morning to find all the crickets dead because the environment had not been properly maintained! Teachers receive such detailed information as how to place butterfly eggs on leaves and the number of hours it will take for them to hatch.

Maryland's Montgomery County district stored its science kits at a central materials center and circulated them among the schools according to a schedule. Teachers in the elementary grades received some training to use kits, but there was no assurance that a teacher would, in fact, use it. Sometimes, teachers returned kits unopened. The district's science supervisor saw a slight increase in the number of kits that came back to the center apparently unused after implementation of No Child Left Behind, perhaps reflecting pressure on teachers to increase time devoted to reading and math. This is not the only problem that sometimes arises with kits. In a third grade class at Norton Elementary in Louisville, for example, teacher Cindy Young told me one day, "Science is at a standstill because our life specimens were lost in shipment."

While kits facilitate the teaching, critics charge that they become a crutch for both student and teacher; they provide a way to observe science in action but make it possible for youngsters to avoid independent investigations and for teachers to use only the kit instead of becoming conversant with science. Such reservations seem short-sighted given the time pressure on elementary teachers. A kit—in the hands of a good teacher—can be a basis for learning the scientific method and for launching independent investigations of the child's own design. Furthermore, when teachers use instructional guides and prepare themselves properly, lessons can build on discoveries students make using kits to impart scientific facts in the context of the experiment.

Science and Technology for Children uses no formal textbooks, making science very much a hands-on subject. The National Science Resources Center maintains that when teachers have textbooks, they overemphasize vocabulary and facts, and that when children *do* science, they examine objects, observe phenomena, design experiments, collect data, and discuss their ideas.[5] The program has materials for students to read but tries to engage their interests through activities, an especially important goal in the primary grades, when children have short attention spans and limited reading abilities.

OTHER SHORT-CHANGED SUBJECTS

After literacy and math on the one hand and social studies and science on the other, additional subjects appear in the curriculum of the primary grades even less regularly. Schools vary in the amount of time, if any, that they give to the arts, foreign languages, and physical education, for instance. This is particularly lamentable in the case of the arts. Young children, not yet fully able to express themselves in writing and still reading without fluency, crave such outlets for expression as painting, music, dance, and drama.

The Arts

Increasingly, though, the arts have to justify whatever time and expenditures they receive. Thus, detailed studies have examined the role of the arts on learning to read, on creative thinking, on dropout prevention, on SAT scores, and on other school factors,[6] as well as the extent to which intrinsic benefits of arts education spill over into the public good.[7] The arts, like social studies, now often have their best chance of attaining a spot in the curriculum when teachers can integrate them with other subjects. The arts are not expendable everywhere, however. Arkansas, for instance, is one of the few states to require elementary schools to offer 40 minutes of art *and* 40 minutes of music every week.

New Mexico has a special affinity for the arts. Such towns as Santa Fe and Taos have long attracted visual and performing artists as residents and regular visitors. And, a committee chairman in New Mexico's House of Representatives, whose wife owned a gallery, provided built-in support for the Elementary Arts Act that the state legislature passed in 2003 to bolster arts education in elementary schools. Passage of the bill meant $20 million extra for schools in 2005–06. Districts used the funds to add arts teachers and supervisors, to hire artists-in-residence, and for materials and equipment. Only two of New Mexico's school districts previously had arts coordinators; afterward, almost all districts had such a position. One of the most intriguing expenditures involved the widespread use of physical education in elementary schools as a vehicle for teaching dance and creative movement. For all its benefits to the arts, though, the law had a weakness. It distributed money as part of the state's general funding for schools, not as a separate category of support. Therefore, nothing but conscience and good will precluded educators from using the money simply for general operations if budgets tightened.

Arts and physical education were integral to the mission of the Children's Academy of New Albany, which opened in 2005 in southern Indiana as a PK–3 school, succeeding the failing school that had occupied the building for many years. Other than stripping away the fourth and fifth grade, the enrollment remained essentially the same—the poorest, lowest-achieving students of New Albany's 13 elementary schools. Sheila Rohr, the principal, and others who planned the new school felt that one way to boost the confidence of students unaccustomed to success was through the arts. Thus, the school became the only one in the district with full-time teachers in art, music, and physical education, assuring each child of two hours a week in each of these subjects. Much of the work in the subjects for a portion of the year was geared toward preparing for performances. A different grade level performed for the school every nine weeks and drew on singing learned in music class, sets designed in art class, and dance learned in physical education. Students in the other grades and parents watched the performances that school officials hoped would increase the self-esteem of the youngsters, who invested themselves in preparation. "The act of getting up in front of peers and family will be good for them," said Susan Topping, the art teacher.

Students at the Children's Academy would literally have a stage on which to display their talents. An alumnus anonymously donated $350,000 for the school to renovate an expansive space that, with an air wall, had served as both a gym and a cafeteria. The redesigned area would include the stage that teachers hoped would be an important platform for a school at which in the past, despite their tender years, students displayed an abundance of anger and a lack of self-control. Art teacher Topping and Summers Montgomery, the physical education teacher, thought that their subjects, along with music, might teach youngsters subtle lessons in perseverance and persistence. For some, it could be a chance to shine at school even if they struggled in the main subjects.

Foreign Languages

The PK–3 years are also a prime time period to introduce students to a foreign language. By the beginning of this decade, an estimated one-third of the country's elementary schools, taking advantage of children's inquisitiveness, offered such instruction. Most study of foreign languages in elementary schools, though, is hardly substantial. Only 7 percent of all elementary schools offer instruction in which students are likely to attain high proficiency.[8] The most intensive programs use immersion, an approach in which a youngster's entire day is spent in another language. There is also dual immersion in which the class mixes students from, say, Spanish-speaking backgrounds and English-speaking backgrounds, and pupils spend half the day in each language.

More typically, though, elementary schools merely introduce pupils to a foreign language—80 percent of the time it's Spanish—and provide some cultural context with a short lesson once or twice a week. This approach, called FLEX for Foreign Language Experience program, cannot lead to fluency but may inspire students eventually to enroll in full-blown courses. The next most frequent approach, FLES, or Foreign Language in Elementary School, strives to convey some speaking and listening skills, with instruction from two to five times a week for 20 to 40 minutes each session. These two methods, FLEX and FLES, account for four out of five programs.

The pressure to find time for subjects tested in conjunction with the No Child Left Behind act diminishes chances that foreign languages will play a larger role in the curriculum of the primary grades any time soon.

Furthermore, qualified teachers of foreign languages for elementary schools are in short supply. What passes for foreign language study at the elementary level will in all likelihood, sadly, continue to be of slight consequence at a time when the United States could gain mightily by giving students substantial early exposure to other languages.

Young children develop along many dimensions. Their incipient interests and talents need stimulation in order to emerge. They should learn very early that education is not restricted to learning to read or to computing numbers. If one values the whole person, then even the PK–3 progression should offer the opportunity for fully rounded experiences. One subject reinforces others. The overlap and integration of subjects offer far more avenues for inclusiveness than many acknowledge when they argue that there is not enough time to cover everything. The span from preschool through third grade can provide children with a taste of the smorgasbord of knowledge that awaits them in the years ahead. They should enter the intermediate grades of elementary school yearning for more, wanting to partake of the richness of the curriculum through which each will find the passion that becomes his or her métier.

9

SE HABLA ESPAÑOL . . .
AND 86 OTHER LANGUAGES

My father was in America nine years alone. He came back to Honduras to get us. He paid the coyote to bring him, my mother, my little brother, and me. We traveled by many buses. In Mexico, the driver told us to pretend to sleep when the police came to check our papers. Two times the police took my father off of the bus and he had to pay them money to get back on. Many people got left behind because they didn't have money. We had to hide the money carefully because the police would take it all. We finally got off the bus and walked an hour until we got to the line. We stayed in a house for two weeks. We paid $30 a week.

A guide took us on horses to another house. It took us five hours. We passed many people walking. The new house was made of mud. We rested five hours and then walked for four more hours. My dad carried my little brother and our luggage. We were still in Mexico and my father had to pay more money to the police. A man took us across the river. Men carried the children. Some ladies got on a car tire and were pulled across by ropes. After we crossed the river, border police stopped us but let us go. We hid in a grass field. The police came and put my father in handcuffs. They took us to the police station. My father had pay stubs and the police let us go.

—a description of his arrival in America by a
student at Broad Acres Elementary School,
Montgomery County, Maryland

In the late nineteenth and early twentieth centuries, when immigrants flooded into the United States at Ellis Island and other ports of entry, the character of the nation was irrevocably altered. Children who barely spoke English crowded into classrooms, and parents who felt estranged from an incomprehensible culture sought to help their children make a transition with which they themselves struggled. Today, the situation repeats itself and the immigration surge shows no sign of slowing during the first decade of the twenty-first century. The 34.2 million immigrants and their children in the United States in 2004 made up 11.9 percent of the population, just below the peak of 14.8 percent of a century ago.[1]

Schools face enormous challenges in trying to accommodate these new students, who account for 21 percent of American kindergarteners.[2] When Americans think of school systems with large numbers of immigrant children, ports of entry and border towns come to mind first— schools in such states as Florida, New York, New Jersey, Texas, Arizona, and California. In fact, more than 25 percent of the elementary-age pupils in each of these states have foreign-born parents.[3] One of the most surprising developments since the early 1990s, though, has been the spread of families who speak little or no English into the country's heartland. In Denver, for example, once a quintessential center of white hippie culture, the number of students of Latino background has gradually risen to the point that they now comprise 57 percent of an enrollment of 62,000.

Increasingly, pockets of settlements of immigrant families show up in such states as Iowa, Nebraska, Kansas, North Carolina, and Georgia—all of which the U.S. Department of Education said had increases of more than 200 percent during the 1990s in the number of English-language learners in their schools. Not only must the youngest ones learn to separate from their families, they also must cope with the regulations and expectations of schools, an adjustment for any child, native or foreign born. They have to accomplish all of this at the same time that they learn English and hurry to keep up in their academic subjects. All the while, they and their often impoverished families live in circumstances with all of the problems that accompany poverty.

Tension often surrounds attempts by schools to deal with the needs of students whose parents were born abroad. Issues of race, ethnicity, language, and immigration intrude on discussions of English-language learners, which end with one seminal question: What does it mean to be an American? Programs for students from non-English-speaking backgrounds place schools squarely in the middle of these controversies. The arrival of an estimated 10 to 14 million undocumented aliens since 1990 magnifies the squabbles. In 1982, the U.S. Supreme Court ruled that public schools must enroll all children living in the United States, regardless of immigration status, though this decision does not apply to higher education.

Educating the children of immigrants has indeed been costly for the country's taxpayers, but some of these students, in turn, have also enriched the schools. They now make up 50 percent of the finalists for the U.S. Math Olympiad team, 38 percent of the U.S. Physics team, and 25 percent of the Intel Science Talent Search finalists.[4] In central New Jersey's Middlesex County, for instance, some of the public high school valedictorians in 2005 were MaryCarmen Daza of New Brunswick, born in Mexico and on her way to Rutgers to study biomedical engineering; Patrick Pangan of Dunellen, born of Filipino parents and on his way to Brown to study mathematics; Prasad Tare of South Brunswick, born in Bombay and on his way to Cooper Union to study electrical engineering; Hussein Rahim, born in Kenya and on his way to Rutgers to major in biology and genetics; and Vanessa Rivera of Perth Amboy, of Puerto Rican extraction and on her way to Wellesley as the first step toward either law or medical school.[5]

The years from pre-K through third grade loom as a proving ground for the ability of schools to absorb immigrant children and provide them with a worthy education. Carried out successfully, this mission could equip these students to navigate their way through high school and college with distinction. And, if the schools fail in this awesome task, the American dream may be little more than a nightmare for this segment of the population.

Public schools have no choice about their part in this scenario, a role that is bound to continue for years to come as children of immigrants are more than one out of five of the nation's youngsters under the age of six. One cannot talk about PK–3 without taking the implications of this fact into consideration. Almost 70 percent of these students will be concentrated in 10 percent of the country's elementary schools—buildings with bigger enrollments, larger class sizes, and higher incidences of poverty than other schools—mostly in urban centers where they will make up almost half of the entire enrollment.[6] More than half of the youngsters under the age of seven in New York City are growing up in immigrant families, one-third of them from Latin America and the Caribbean. Yet, many people who criticize achievement levels never bother to acknowledge the difficulties of what schools must accomplish, particularly for immigrants.

Lest anyone think that educating the children of recent arrivals to the United States is the sole challenge facing schools, I pause to point out some of the others. Unwed mothers bear one-third of the nation's children; 29 percent of white children and 52 percent of black and Hispanic children with single mothers grow up in poverty; and more than one of five children under five moves to another home each year, breaking the continuity of services they *may* be receiving.[7] In other words, in discussing the difficulties of building a foundation for learning in today's public schools, and setting aside the immigrant children, we are not talking about the schools of yesterday.

Still, no discussion of the education of children in the primary grades can be complete these days without acknowledging the impact of immigration and recognizing that English-language learners are disproportionately concentrated in the earliest years of schooling, which has implications for a PK–3 configuration.

MEETING NEEDS OF IMMIGRANTS: MONTGOMERY COUNTY, MARYLAND

The needs of some immigrant students can be especially severe. The Montgomery County School District in Maryland identified a small group of youngsters who entered the system not only lacking a command of English, but having been out of school for at least two years in their native countries. Some of the younger ones had not previously lived in a stable environment, accustomed perhaps only to life in a war zone. Besides needing to learn English, they had to become familiar with the culture of school—how to conduct themselves in a classroom, what it means to do homework, to attend school every day and on time. For such children, the school district set up its METS program, Multidisciplinary Education, Training and Support.

Altogether, the school system had 318 students in the METS program in 2005, most from Latin America and Africa. Most were of high school age, the point at which the transition is most wrenching. There were 61 children of elementary school age in the program, and the district grouped them together, in three classrooms in two different schools. Almost all would remain in the program for at least two years, many even longer. "The first year is just adapting to the country and the culture," said Leonor Guillen, an instructional specialist in Montgomery County. "It takes a long time for them to adjust. School behavior is difficult for them. They never learned it." Teachers assigned to METS classes are certified to teach English as a second language (ESL) and have specialties in reading and special education. Although some children in the program are classified for special education afterward, there are, too, successes such as the Cambodian boy who entered METS as an elementary school student and eventually became a high school honors student.

Schools in Montgomery County illustrate the changing composition of American elementary and secondary education and the implications for English-language learning. A school system that barely had any non-white, English-language learners in 1968 was more than 19 percent Hispanic by 2004. Moreover, the white segment of the enrollment had shrunk to 43 percent as the representation of black and Asian students had increased along with the Hispanic enrollment. In the early grades, with which this book is most concerned, it was not unusual for prekindergartens and kindergartens at some of Montgomery County's Title I schools to have a majority of Hispanic children.

The school system in 2004 had 12,762 students in the English as a second language program and at least as many who were formerly enrolled and had moved into the regular program. Those enrolled came from 159 countries, the 1,340 children from El Salvador comprising the largest contingent. Peru held second place with 479 students. The country with the largest contingent was from none other than the United States, where 5,219 children—fully 41 percent of the total—had been born.

The 2000 census of Montgomery County revealed that English was not spoken in 31 percent of the households. The absence of English in so many homes meant that the school system had to find new ways to reach this part of its constituency with information. In some homes, parents also lacked fluency in reading and writing in their native language. The school system took to producing videos to distribute to homes. In addition, the system began advertising on Spanish-language radio stations in search of candidates for its prekindergarten program, which it vowed to extend to all needy four-year-olds.

Two streams of students flowed into English as a second language, one carrying youngsters who were born abroad, and the other, those born in the United States. A proficiency test determined their placement; those with the least command of English were rated as Level I and those with the greatest command of English as Level IV. Children were assigned to sessions of English as a second language with peers of the same level; most started at Level I. For every 41 students eligible for ESL sessions, the school was assigned an ESL-certified teacher. The heaviest concentration of such pupils, almost two-thirds, was in preschool through second grade.

TRANSITION TO ENGLISH

On top of everything else, Americans do not agree on the language of instruction for immigrant students or on how long schools should wait before expecting them to function fully in English. Meanwhile, the vast majority of these children return each day to homes in which English may not be spoken except by someone on a television set.

Progression into English: Austin, Texas

On paper, Latino bilingual education students in Austin follow a steady progression in a curriculum that increases English-language content by 10 percent a year—from preschool classes that are 90 percent in Spanish and 10 percent in English to 50 percent in each language during the third grade, and predominantly in English thereafter. Matters do not work so neatly in practice, though. Families emigrate when children are of various ages and some pupils begin school in Austin at grades later than prekindergarten, and even among those who start in pre-K, many simply don't reach parity in third grade.

A visitor to some third grade bilingual classrooms throughout Austin Independent School District may hear little English even though many of the students have attended the city's schools since they were four years old. Sometimes all of the listings of frequently encountered words on the word walls are in Spanish. English may appear on few of the signs and posters around the classroom. When teachers ask questions in English, the children, lacking confidence, may answer in Spanish, contrary to the usual expectation that they will respond in the language that the teacher uses. In one building, a third grade teacher and her principal conceded that the school had not been sufficiently systematic in earlier grades about making certain that kids received the increasing portion of instruction in English they should have.

Other obstacles loom as well. At another school, the teacher of a bilingual fourth grade, a level at which the school system's framework calls for 60 percent of the work to be in English, instructed in Spanish on Mondays, Wednesdays, and Fridays—60 percent of the time—and in English only 40 percent of the time, on Tuesdays and Thursdays. Paradoxically, the Texas Assessment of Knowledge and Skills, the statewide test that was supposed to ensure rigor, played a role in this. The teacher, concerned about how the youngsters would perform on the dreaded assessment, took advantage of the option of administering it in Spanish, hoping that would mean higher scores. Therefore, she taught predominantly in Spanish to prepare students for the test.

Bilingual education in Austin and most other school districts in the United States is a work in progress even decades after programs began. The transition that students supposedly make from bilingual programs after four, five, or six years may be no smoother than a ride on a poorly paved Texas country road. A teacher in Austin of a regular fifth grade class, almost half of whose students had been in bilingual classes through the third or fourth grades, said that "something is wrong" if youngsters start bilingual classes in preschool or kindergarten and still need them after third grade. She said she had to battle to get some of the students in her school's bilingual fifth grade class to join her students for math instruction, which she thought they could handle in English. Finally, the other teacher relented; the students took math in English and did just fine.

Despite such challenges, Austin may be doing a better job than many other districts in educating students who enter the schools from homes where parents speak little or no English. A study of 11 urban school systems in connection with the performance of fourth and eighth graders on the National Assessment of Educational Progress showed Austin and Charlotte-Mecklenburg outranking the other nine districts. Furthermore, scores by Austin students, including subgroups of Hispanics and African Americans, steadily improved in 2004 and 2005 on the state assessment, even as the number of immigrants in Austin schools tripled over a period of five years.

Pascal (Pat) D. Forgione, a northeasterner, was Austin's seventh superintendent in ten years when he took the job in 1999. He worked to implement a standards-based program that was the same for students in the early grades whether they were enrolled in regular or bilingual classes. In addition, Austin supplemented the state-funded, half-day preschool for four-year-olds from impoverished and non-English-speaking families by offering a full-day program. In 2005, Forgione put one of his best principals, Martha Garcia, in charge of bilingual education. She had led Ortega School, where 93 percent of the students lived in poverty and 40 percent were English-language learners, to the point at which it was one of the five of Austin's 74 elementary schools in which 100 percent of the third graders passed the state test. Garcia was living the dream, having grown up in a west Texas family headed by immigrant parents from Mexico who had never attended a day of school and yet raised five children who all earned graduate degrees.

Learning English in Denver

Unlike some locales, where students come from a wide mix of foreign-language backgrounds, 92 percent of Denver's English-language learners speak Spanish. The remaining 8 percent speak 86 other languages, with Vietnamese and Arabic the only two of those languages with more than 100 speakers in the public schools. (Mexico is the birthplace of 10 times as many students in American elementary schools as any other foreign country.)[8]

In 1999, a U.S. District Court approved what Denver's school system calls its English-language acquisition program (ELA) in which the average student spends almost five years. The heart of the program is the transitional native-language instructional model, which for a child in the primary grades typically begins with virtually the entire curriculum—except for 45 minutes daily of English-language development—taught in Spanish. The program, as in Austin, aims to increase the portion of instruction in English each year. Public schools in Denver offer an entire program in Spanish for kindergarteners only.

Students in Denver are eligible for ELA if they predominantly speak languages other than English or if a language other than English is regularly used in their homes, regardless of birthplace. Altogether, 20,000 of Denver's 62,000 students fall into one of these two categories, but parents may choose whether to let their children receive program services and so 15,000 youngsters are in the program. The parents of 13 percent of the eligible pupils in elementary schools request waivers to keep their children out of the program, and far higher portions opt out in the secondary grades. The district uses two assessments in addition to the statewide tests to monitor the achievement of English-language learners while they are in the program and after they have exited. One test assesses oral proficiency in English and the other measures progress in reading and writing in Spanish.

In its effort to have enough Spanish-speaking teachers, Denver—in addition to a vigorous staff development program—has sponsored visa applications of teachers recruited from Spanish-speaking countries, paired itself with the Mexican city of Cuernavaca to bring in teachers under an educator exchange program, and instituted an additional salary stipend of up to $800 annually for its ELA teachers.

Schools in Denver with fewer than 60 English-language learners offer English as a second language rather than the Transitional Native Language program. In ESL, children who speak various languages gather in a small group for at least 45 minutes each day to be taught in English by a teacher who very likely speaks none of the languages of the children. They spend the remainder of the school day in the regular program with a class of English speakers. The goal, especially in the primary grades, is for pupils to gain facility rapidly in English.

Denver's Southmoor Elementary School, for example, serves an upscale neighborhood at the city's edge that has so few English-language learners, it did not offer the transitional native language program. As only four youngsters of some 50 in the school's two full-day kindergartens qualified as non-English speakers, Southmoor provided them with English as a second language. The four were boys from India and Algeria and girls from Venezuela and Korea. The two boys arrived at the school with some English, but neither girl understood English at the outset.

The first semester, the two girls went to the separate instruction for 45 minutes each day after lunch, meeting with a trained teacher who used only English to help them make the transition to their new language. English was not spoken in either of their homes (both mothers were unable to speak English, though their fathers knew some English). The boy from India did not go to ESL class until the second semester as he was finding it difficult simply to adjust to being in school. The boy from Algeria qualified for the program but refused to go and threw tantrums in resistance. He was the youngest kindergartener in the school, having made the cutoff by just a few days, and a kindergarten teacher, specially trained in English-language acquisition so that she could provide support in a regular class, agreed to let him stay with her.

By the end of the school year, three of the four children were emergent readers, still at the bottom of their class in English literacy in this high-performing school but at a level that would have put them closer to the mainstream in a more typical Denver elementary school. They understood the reading process, recognized 30 to 50 words by sight, had some of the phonemic skills to decode unknown words, and were ready to move on to more fluent reading. Their teacher, Lee Betz, did not consider them at risk. "They have made tremendous gains in their understanding of how the English language works, the structure of written language, and how to use it both as a reader and a writer," said Betz. "I believe that they will be successful readers in first grade and beyond."

The girl from Korea ranked among the strongest readers in Southmoor's two kindergartens and quite likely would qualify for a highly gifted program in the first grade, achieving what Betz described as a "phenomenal" level of advancement. All four pupils were scheduled to continue meeting with the ESL teacher for 45 minutes a day as first graders to further help them make the transition. Denver's school system portrays English as a second language as part of its effort to close the achievement gap in a school system in which four out of five students are not white.

It remains to be seen, though, whether ESL and the English-language acquisition program will help solve the problems of Denver's public schools. Only 25 percent of Latinos and 40 percent of African American ninth graders, compared with 71 percent of white students, reached proficiency on state tests in 2004. Graduation rates were 62 percent for Latinos, 73 percent for African Americans, and 80 percent for whites. "Denver's public high schools are failing," the city's Commission on Secondary School Reform concluded in 2005. Later in the year, a new superintendent called for a reorganization of the district's English language acquisition program.

THE DUAL LANGUAGE DILEMMA: A NATIONAL DEBATE

More than three decades after the U.S. Supreme Court in 1974 declared in the Lau case, which had originated with Chinese American students in San Francisco, that public schools must accommodate the needs of English-language learners, too many students do not become proficient in English—in Denver and around the country. One can more readily understand this failing in the case of teenagers who enter American schools at an age when learning to function at a high level in a new language is a daunting task. Surely, though, one might expect better results for pupils in kindergarten and the primary grades. The Supreme Court did not order any particular approach for educating English-language learners other than to direct the schools to give them some kind of help. All too frequently in the years since then, children have been held captive to the battles of adults who argue about educational methods for those of non-English-speaking backgrounds.

Latinos sunk roots in Denver at least three or four generations ago and so much time has passed that some students with Spanish surnames speak no Spanish. Thus, those deemed eligible for the school system's English language acquisition program are a mix of children born outside the United States, born in the United States to recent immigrants, and American-born to parents who are longtime residents. Across the country, almost 20 percent of elementary-age pupils judged to have limited English proficiency are third-generation Americans, the children of parents born in the United States.[9]

Most English-language learners—in schools in Denver and elsewhere—are not immigrants at all. They were born in the United States to immigrant parents, both legal and illegal residents, and are therefore citizens, according to the Constitution. I found the same pattern in school systems everywhere. Many observers and policymakers do not realize that debates over how to educate English-language learners are to a great degree about Americans. Though Americans by virtue of their birthplace, the children are growing up in homes where the adults may speak little, if any, English.

Across the country, three-quarters of the children of immigrants hold U.S. citizenship, as does an even higher portion of those under the age of six,[10] probably including at least 3 million whose parents entered the country illegally. The principal at an elementary school in Los Angeles, for instance, found that though 80 percent of her pupils came from homes where little if any English was spoken, only nine children in the school building were born outside the United States. She said that she had registered every pupil in the school and knew the numbers well.

The country continues to argue over the best way to educate English-language learners, weighing the merits of bilingual education versus immersion in English or some middle ground such as English as a second language or dual immersion (partly English and partly some other language). Harvard's Timothy A. Hacsi, in a tour de force history of the bilingual wars, points out that a wealth of research data does not "present compelling evidence one way or the other on what kind of program will help children learn English and be successful students" except to make it clear that "submersion classes where only English is spoken do not work."[11] Moreover, the quality of the program is probably far more important than its philosophy.

The American Educational Research Association, in a policy paper that sought to go beyond the debate, wrestled with fundamental questions involving the best ways to make English-language learners literate and what rates of achievement in English to expect. The paper stated that English learners, starting in kindergarten, can gain word-reading and spelling skills equal to those of native speakers in two years through training to distinguish and manipulate sounds, lots of practice, explicit instruction in the sounds of letters and how they combine to form words, and assessments to monitor their progress. Even with excellent oral language support in the primary grades, though, it takes longer than two years for English-language learners to become as fluent as native speakers and to acquire the broad vocabulary and reading comprehension skills needed for sustained academic achievement, according to the paper. In addition to acquiring the vocabulary to engage in class discussions about academic content, the youngsters need to learn word order, grammar, and other elements of phrase and sentence structure to strengthen their comprehension of what they read.[12]

I saw this difficulty, as it affects the ability to write in English, up close in schools in Austin, where bilingual students who could read and do math in English struggled with composition. It is clearly the last and most challenging piece of the bilingual puzzle to put in place even for youngsters who function reasonably well in oral English. "Half the class has been here since prekindergarten, but they're not highly proficient in English," said Olga Rowehl, a third grade teacher at Cook Elementary School. "The only English they get is in school. There are no books in English for them to see at home." When Rowehl, a product of schools in Puerto Rico, introduced the students to newspapers, she discovered "they had no idea what a newspaper was—in English or Spanish."

Numbers, on the other hand, are numbers whether children manipulate them in Spanish or English. Her students' growing understanding of arithmetic was evident in Olga Milk's first grade class at Austin's Sanchez Elementary at the outset of the school day as the pupils went through the ritual common to primary grades everywhere—the morning circle devoted to the calendar. They used mostly Spanish but English, too, as they counted the number of days since the term began, took time to go through the 100s chart, and added the day's temperature to a graph they kept, engaging in a whole-group discussion about whether 68 degrees was closer to 70 or to 60. Then it was time for "which number is bigger," followed by some counting by 5's in Spanish and by 2's in English. They used ersatz coins to "buy" pumpkins and decided that 9+0 was the same as 0+9.

A measure of how schools are doing in educating English-language learners is the requirement of the No Child Left Behind act that educators chart the gains of such pupils separately and face penalties if the students do not make adequate yearly progress. No state met all of its academic goals for these children when the U.S. Department of Education issued its first report on state-by-state findings for English-language learners in 2005.

THE ROLE OF PARENTS

Whatever one thinks about the responsibility of immigrants for learning to function in English, the reality is that the parents of many students in the public schools don't speak English. This makes it incumbent upon the schools to find ways to reach out and engage those parents so that they will reinforce their children's education. In New York City, a central office translates school information into eight languages. Schools ought to find ways to help even parents who have not lived in the United States very long and have limited command of English to better support their children's education.

Joanie Grace, a prekindergarten teacher in Austin who is so good at what she does that the district has her provide professional development to colleagues, began 15 years ago to invite parents into her classroom at the start of the day to help children, not just their own, put letters and words on paper. If the parents are illiterate, Grace asks them to help children draw pictures of subjects about which they would like to write. She even brews coffee for them.

One morning in Grace's classroom at Sanchez School, a building with Aztec-inspired architecture that echoes the heritage of many of the 447 students, eight parents—one with an infant in her lap—had squeezed into the small seats at the tot-size tables to guide youngsters in their discovery of the miracle of inscribing sounds and meaning on paper. Grace moved from table to table, advising and assisting, confident that the parents would take such experiences back into their homes to reinforce the work of the school. "I come to help and, personally, I'm surprised by how much they've learned," Hector Hernandez said in Spanish about the children he had observed and helped. He worked as a cook and his schedule allowed him to take his daughter Lixy to school every day and stay with her for the writing period. At one point that morning, Grace could not contain her joy when a little girl at another table who wanted to write the word *iman*, Spanish for magnet, grasped a stubby crayon and, on her own, printed an I and an M, followed by a row of squiggles.

Outreach to parents holds promise for all schools serving the children of immigrants. A four-year study of a family literacy program in Santa Barbara, California, found that the program increased the literacy levels of immigrant parents, their ability to help their children with homework, and their favorable attitudes toward their children's education.[13]

The average participant in the Santa Barbara program had been in the United States for seven to nine years. These parents tended to view teachers as the educational experts on whom their children should rely and deferred to the teachers, according to the team of researchers from the University of California at Santa Barbara. The researchers said that before the program began, the families wanted to assist their children but didn't know how. By the third year of the program, according to the researchers, pupils from participating families had higher scores in reading comprehension and math than peers from nonparticipating families. In turn, the research showed that parents put a greater emphasis on having their children speak, read, and write in English so that they would do well in school. Homework had become a collective family activity.

The soaring growth in the immigrant population of the United States underscores the importance of such programs, which seek to make the family a resource for the academic development of their children. It is a practice that should be a part of each PK–3 school that serves an immigrant community.

INSTILLING HABITS AND DISPOSITIONS

Habits and dispositions that will last a lifetime take form during the pre-school years and the primary grades of elementary school. Increasingly, schools recognize the crucial nature of these years and try to shape the attitudes and social and emotional behavior of young children. Any school focusing on children during the period from prekindergarten through third grade would be remiss in not acknowledging habits and dispositions as a proper concern. A country like Japan, for example, recognizes "the moral and academic formation of children as the fundamental act of social survival, economic investment, and even national defense."[1]

Concerns should range from the work habits of children to their values to their classroom conduct. Youngsters must learn, for example, that effort leads to achievement. Similarly, they must come to understand that their acts have consequences and that they are part of a society whose proper functioning depends on their good behavior.

The daily instruction in reading at Pershing East Elementary, a PK–3 school in Chicago, for instance, was the setting one morning for just such a discussion in a second grade classroom. It flowed out of a book entitled *The Green Frogs: A Korean Folk Tale*. "This is about why we have rules in societies," explained the teacher as he held the book open wide so that the children could see the pictures along with the text on the facing pages. "They're doing the opposite of what their mother told them. Was that nice?"

"No," the children intoned in unison. It was clear that the naughty young frogs were not obeying their mother, who was trying to teach them to croak. Their disrespect knew no bounds.

"Don't get dirty," the mother admonished the young frogs, who promptly jumped into a puddle, continuing to do the opposite of what they were told.

"She was old and sick and told her sons where she wants to be buried," the teacher read as the tale took a morbid turn. After their mother died, the remorseful offspring changed their ways and buried her near the spring as she had asked, ruing their refusal to heed their mother during her lifetime. "It rained for days and nights," the teacher read, explaining that the young frogs worried that their mother's grave would wash away. "Ever since," he continued the story, "when it rains, green frogs sit by streams and cry."

"Take out a paper," the teacher requested as he wrote three questions on the white board at the front of the room:

Why is it important to follow rules?

What would happen if you don't follow rules?

List three things you enjoyed about the story.

HOW TO MOTIVATE CHILDREN

The idea that schools should begin inculcating habits of the mind before the first grade underscores the goal of reinforcing work habits throughout the PK–3 years. The first grade offers an opportunity to put good habits to the single-minded service of learning to read and write. By the second grade, certainly, pupils are no longer "babies" and should possess a sound work ethic and tackle all subjects with zeal. Second graders in many locales take statewide tests and in third grade the children face tests that figure in No Child Left Behind. All of this, whatever adults may feel about testing, is dead serious business. After third grade, unfortunately, much of the individual attention melts away as academic demands harden. Those who have acquired habits of diligence will fare best when they reach the middle elementary grades and beyond.

Students need to become self-motivated during this period. All too many American children consider achievement the result solely of brains, not understanding that effort yields rewards. Nor do they value delayed gratification. Many give up too easily—"The teacher doesn't like me," "I don't want to get another low score on a test," "I studied and I still didn't get a good grade." Schools and homes should do all they can to encourage and bolster resiliency in children during the primary grades so that they believe in their abilities and cultivate the habit of reaching into themselves to attain goals.

There is a package of traits that schools—and, ideally, families—can help young children acquire. Researchers go so far as to claim that "much of the effectiveness of early childhood interventions comes from boosting non-cognitive skills and fostering motivation."[2] These same researchers call these traits self-reinforcing, asserting that self-control and emotional security, for example, may bolster intellectual curiosity and promote more vigorous learning.[3]

A school serving children from pre-K through third grade should organize itself around researcher Lauren B. Resnick's notion that effort can actually create ability. Resnick urges schools to dismiss the notion that achievement is a function primarily of aptitude. She believes that effort-oriented education should have clear expectations, giving as much time as necessary to meet those expectations; fair and credible evaluations; celebration and payoff for success; and expert instruction.[4]

From the beginning of their school days, children need teachers who encourage them to concentrate on tasks and to practice. Before completing third grade, for example, they should have learned to draft and redraft what they write. They should come to recognize that the first words they put to paper—or onto a computer screen—are not necessarily the best. Eventually, finding success, pupils will have more confidence in their abilities. Their beliefs about whether they expect their efforts to lead to success are at least as important as their actual competence.[5]

For these reasons, it would be good if every PK–3 program allowed kids to pick projects in which to become *primary experts*. The school would allot a portion of time in the primary grades—first, second, and third—for children to delve into topics in depth, periodically reporting to the class and/or exhibiting the fruits of their labor. One student, for instance, might become a primary expert on the Boston Red Sox; another, on the planet Mars; and still another, on the history of dollhouses. Another student might try to learn all she could about Louisa May Alcott and still another might delve more deeply into dinosaurs than almost anyone else in the class.

Teachers could guide these individual investigations in ways that lead students to integrate literacy, numeracy, science, social studies, the arts, and other subjects in their quest for information. Imagine what it would do for confidence and motivation for a young child to possess such special knowledge! A youngster might pursue one topic over the three-year period or a different one each year. Students would learn research skills and persistence and gain pride in accomplishment. This is the stuff of which genuine self-esteem is made. Forest Avenue, a PK–2 school in Glen Ridge, New Jersey, tells parents in a handbook that while the school considers development of self-image an important part of its educational program, it is best achieved through successful accomplishment in school. Amen.

Children need to learn the kind of persistence that these primary-expert projects would produce. If teachers in the primary grades insert such lessons into their instruction, they will equip students for the demands that follow. Schools should reward persistence during the early grades as a way of encouraging children to strive in this direction. Students are bound to discover, with each passing year, that success in education requires an increasing amount of diligence. From such an approach comes an academic work ethic. Ideally, this feeling will pervade the school. Teachers in the primary grades should gird students to withstand the ravages of negativism that might later besiege them.

Allan Alson, superintendent of the Evanston Township High School District in Illinois, sees each day the long-term results of the best and worst that occur during the first few years of schooling. "A student who reaches high school with well-established skills and a love of learning," said Alson, "is very likely to know how to be organized, how to study, how to seek assistance when necessary, and to be more certain of how to pursue his or her interests. Students who are lacking in academic skills and are seemingly unmotivated have not developed powers of self-advocacy and are likely missing the habits of the mind to approach learning in a successful manner."

Deborah Stipek, the education dean at Stanford University and an expert on motivation, points to the importance of what happens to youngsters in the very earliest grades—kindergarten and first grade—in affecting everything that comes later. Their experiences can "put them on a pathway that becomes increasingly difficult to change" and can have "serious and lifelong implications" for motivation. She maintains that students may, under certain circumstances, lose self-confidence and become anxious about learning by second or third grade.[6]

Teachers certainly affect the degree to which youngsters exert themselves. They send signals, knowingly and unknowingly, to students by their facial expressions, body language, and verbal feedback. Children can interpret too much sympathy when they fail, too much praise when they succeed, and unsolicited help as signs of a lack of confidence in their ability. "Even in the first grade," said a report from the federal government on motivating students, "children believe that teachers are likely to watch low achievers more closely" and expect less from them.[7] The report urged teachers to create conditions in which low-achieving pupils do not give up but keep trying.

We cannot forget, though, that responsibility for instilling these habits and attitudes in children does not rest solely with schools. Parents must not abdicate their role. Research attests to the positive influence that parents can have by talking with their children about school, checking homework and helping with it, rewarding children for schoolwork, and providing support such as trips to the library and playing thinking games with them. In fact, family involvement of this sort is especially meaningful for kids' academic expectations and self-esteem, according to a survey of thousands of students in elementary schools, regardless of gender, ethnicity, or economic circumstances.[8]

Furthermore, beyond school and home, a whole range of places, experiences, and people can help set children on the road to educational success. You can often see this effect among youngsters who live in homes filled with books and magazines, travel with their parents, start lessons of one sort or another (a sport or music, for example) even before kindergarten, and benefit from a network of caring relatives, neighbors, and friends. Collectively, these linkages, norms, and support systems provide the social capital that enhances a child's possibilities.[9]

STRIVING FOR GOOD CONDUCT

Students who begin to regulate their behavior at an early age learn to conduct themselves in ways that do not disrupt their classrooms. This is no small matter. Patterns form as early as preschool and kindergarten. The vast majority of teachers and even parents say that a few chronic offenders can spoil the school experience of classmates. Seventy-seven percent of teachers say that they could teach more effectively if they did not have to spend so much time dealing with disruptive students.[10] Ross A. Thompson, a specialist on brain development, wrote: "Promoting school readiness is not simply a matter of encouraging literacy and number skills. It must also incorporate concern for enhancing the social and emotional qualities that underline curiosity, self-confidence, eagerness to learn, cooperation, and self-control."[11]

While disruption in the primary grades seldom takes the almost lethal form that it can assume among older students, misconduct should nonetheless be addressed early, when youngsters do not yet have the size and wiles to inflict greater harm. Similarly, primary students—just a few years away from being recruited—should come to understand the dark side of gang membership. One of the goals of the PK–3 progression ought to be to make everyone a good citizen of the classroom, as corny as that may sound. That is why socialization ranks so high among the purposes of pre-K and kindergarten.

Teachers in first, second, and third grades can borrow a page from the manual on good preschool teaching, emulating what their colleagues teach the youngest pupils about respecting each other. Rules and routines loom large during the years from preschool through third grade. Children line up at the door to leave the classroom. They move through the corridors in single file. They are reminded to say "please" and "thank you."

Elena Bodrova maintains that self-regulation should be instilled in preschool children so that they will control aggressive behavior and use positive strategies in interacting with others. She is a senior researcher with Mid-continent Research for Education and Learning. Bodrova has found that this ability, more than cognitive skills and family background, predicts academic performance in the first grade. We may quibble about the division of responsibility between home and school, but certainly foul-mouthed, aggressive, disruptive pupils in the primary grades have not benefited sufficiently from self-control lessons in either place.

Young children may kick, bite, and push. Socialization at home and in preschool is supposed to relieve youngsters of such habits, which can develop into full-fledged aggression in the upper elementary grades. An eight-year-old at a Las Vegas elementary school was arrested, handcuffed, and taken to jail in 2005 after allegedly biting an assistant principal.[12] Homes, far more than schools, are responsible for producing such youngsters. Paul Vallas, chief school officer in Philadelphia, observed: "When you have kindergarten, first and second grade children engaging in behavior you would expect from much older children, that reflects problems in the home, not the school." One indication of the prevalence of misconduct and the exasperation of educators is the fact that schools suspend and expel children as early as prekindergarten.

A report from the Child Study Center at Yale University brought unprecedented attention to this problem in 2005, when it found that preschools expelled children at a rate three times that of K–12 education.[13] This mind-boggling statistic was widely reported in major media outlets throughout the United States. The Yale study found the highest rates of expulsion in faith-affiliated and for-profit centers and the lowest rates in public school prekindergarten classrooms and Head Start programs.

While the study did not explore the reasons for this phenomenon, it did indicate that expulsions occurred less frequently when preschool teachers and their pupils had access to psychologists and other trained personnel. I suspect that better-prepared teachers are more able to cope with acts of severe misconduct by very young children. For-profit settings and those unaffiliated with the government can more readily dismiss children who are difficult to handle, much as private and parochial elementary and secondary schools may do.

HOW SOME SCHOOLS DEAL WITH BEHAVIOR PROBLEMS

Some problems with behavior are inevitable in the primary grades. The question becomes how schools cope with these situations. Social workers and psychologists serve on the front lines—usually circulating among several schools—and tend to have too many cases and not enough hours to meet all the needs. Nurses constitute an early warning system for impending problems. Janice Loschiavo, a registered nurse with a certificate in school nursing who shuttles between two PK–2 schools in Glen Ridge, New Jersey, says that she sees "the same 10 percent" of kids most of the time. Usually, they have no physical maladies; they are simply sad. Observers, even parents, tend to overlook the fact that little children have the same emotions as adults. Anger and rage are sometimes their only outlets. Four separate approaches illustrate some of the ways that schools handle these various problems.

Chilling Out Instead of Acting Out

At Evelyn I. Morris Early Childhood Center in Lincoln, Delaware, a "behavior coach" tries to keep misconduct to a minimum. Simply called "coach" and dressed in attire resembling that worn by a gym teacher, Christine Bailey deals with inappropriate behavior in the building and on the buses that serve the 150-square-mile school district in southern Delaware. Referrals from teachers and bus drivers and complaints by parents and students prompt her interventions. The behavior coach, the school counselor, and the school social worker stand in the lobby each morning greeting children as they arrive at school and help monitor their behavior at lunch, two of the times most susceptible to disruption. The oldest pupils are only first graders, but the school created Bailey's position out of concern over what to do about youngsters who are repeatedly disruptive—diminutive recidivists, so to speak.

Bailey and Elizabeth Carlson, the principal, said that misconduct does not occur in a "social vacuum" and that usually the anger of four-, five-, and six-year-olds stems from "mental health issues" that afflict them and their families. Children use aggression to send messages that they don't possess the verbal skills to articulate, according to the two educators. It's difficult to sit in class and cut and paste or focus on leaving spaces between words they print, Bailey and Carlson said, "when your attention is consumed with the memory that the police had to come over last night and break up a fight between mom and dad." Among the problems that Bailey and Carlson see bringing out the worst in some pupils are poverty, homelessness, life in foster care, deaths of parents and siblings, incarcerated parents, and bitter divorces. "All of these social issues impact on their behaviors, attitudes, and ability to trust adults," they said.

Schools have more measures to deal with the misconduct of secondary school students and older elementary children than with the infractions of those in the lowest grades. After all, students are not only more apt to misbehave as they get older, stronger, and more self-reliant but also to do so in ways more threatening, more violent, and more dangerous to others. Schools even have the option of steering teenagers into alternative programs to remove them from the mainstream. Options are fewer when pupils act out at younger ages. "We often ignore the fact that many children lead very troubled lives, and we speak of their resiliency and ability to go with the flow," Carlson said of the younger pupils. "We forget that children feel as deeply as adults do and that they then act on those feelings."

Morris has children who spit, throw furniture, and hit teachers when they grow angry. This is where the behavior coach steps in, first deescalating the situation, then striving to understand the child and, if possible, to help the child understand himself or herself. Action Central is an un-furnished room, almost a padded cell without the padding, that goes by many names—the time-out room, the behavior room, the behavior coach's room, Coach Bailey's room. Whatever people call it, she uses the room whenever she needs a quiet, peaceful space for a child to chill out.

Bailey keeps the room free of adornment because she learned through experience that an angry child will pick up almost anything and fling it during a crisis. Posters that the coach hung on the wall got torn down regularly by children having tantrums. With nothing left to grab, some children remove their shoes and throw those. Sometimes a recalci-trant child will flee into the adjoining rest room. A kindergartener who did just that scooped up handfuls of toilet paper and stuffed them into her mouth. Once they became wet wads, she threw them at Bailey.

Taking Time to Consider One's Actions

Elementary school pupils in Harrisburg, Pennsylvania, learn to deal with situations fraught with conflict by "doing turtle," that is, pulling back into their figurative shells. This gives them time to think over the situa-tion and let strong emotions pass. Such restraint was the result of a pro-gram, Promoting Alternative Thinking Strategies (PATHS), that taught them to regulate impulses. One principal told of his conversation with a kindergartener who had lost his temper and erupted in the classroom. "He looked up at me afterward," the principal described the child, "and said, 'I didn't stop and think. I didn't use turtle.'" Harrisburg offers PATHS in all 12 of its elementary schools and includes preschoolers in the seven buildings in which they are taught.

A little green turtle became the symbol of the program, developed by researchers at Pennsylvania State University, which uses stories to teach kids ways to modify their own behavior. One series of lessons tells the story of an aggressive young turtle who experiences both behavioral and academic difficulties because it does not stop to think before acting. The turtle, beset by numerous uncomfortable feelings, eventually takes the advice of a wise older turtle to "do turtle"—use self-control to pull back into his shell until negative feelings subside.

Harrisburg received funding of more than $3 million from two fed-eral sources—a Safe Schools/Healthy Students grant to the school sys-tem and a HOPE grant to the Dauphin County Mental Health and

Retardation program. Experts designed the program specifically for children from kindergarten through fifth grade to promote social and emotional competence and to prevent or reduce violence and negative behaviors. While six- and seven-year-olds, for instance, are unlikely to engage in the kinds of acts that led Congress to enact the Safe Schools legislation in the wake of the 1995 shootings at Colorado's Columbine High School, elementary school is not too early to show concern for their emotional problems.

A look at one troubled family in Harrisburg illustrates this point. Charlayne Thomas, not her real name, spilled out her problems one day during a visit by a school system social worker, Eugenia Smith. Sitting in her tiny living room, Thomas, 34, whose three children appeared in enlarged photographs hanging on the wall behind her, said that her nine-year-old son had already spent a month in a residential facility for emotionally disturbed children in Gettysburg to which the school system had sent him. Moreover, just two days earlier her other son, 13, was led away from school in handcuffs and banished to an alternative school after attacking a teacher. "He was having a lot of problems with teachers and other kids," the mother said of her older son. Only her eight-year-old daughter remained regularly enrolled in school.

The family's simple apartment was across the street from a Brethren church, which provided living units in the building on a temporary basis for families like the Thomases, who had been homeless. Thomas moved to Harrisburg from Williamsport, where she had spent ten years living with her children and the father of two of them, after relocating there from Philadelphia. Now, there was apparently no man in her life. Thomas said that her children received few social services when they were younger and that the boys were now "out of control," having missed a lot in terms of learning how to behave. "Maybe they wouldn't be the way they are now," she said. "I worry about their future." She theorized that her older son was a negative influence on the younger one.

"Do you think anger management would have helped?" asked Smith. Thomas did not respond directly, instead pointing out that the boys had suffered verbal and physical abuse at the hands of the man who had lived with the family and that she thought such experiences had a lot to do with their recent misconduct. Smith theorized that having lived with an abusive adult in the household, the boys now seemed to be acting out their aggression.

"I just go day to day," Thomas said, occasionally turning her head to look at the television set, which she kept on during Smith's visit. She continued: "My daughter's doing good. She seems to be the only one not in trouble. The school system might have done more for the boys. I tried to teach them right from wrong. They should know better." She said it was "hard, very hard" dealing with her older son and that her younger son was "oppositional, defiant."

Experiences like these have prompted schools to want to instill a sense of self-regulation in students while they are still very young. PATHS proceeds on the principle that school can be a setting in which to focus on changing behavior. The ability to discuss emotions, under this theory, helps children to control their own behavior. Ideally, they will reflect on their emotions and solve their problems. The program addresses these principles in lessons organized around three main units: self-control; feelings and relationships; and interpersonal problem solving.

Trainers from PATHS provide workshops for teachers as well as a one-day refresher workshop in the middle of the school year. The program also makes available consultants and materials. Teachers present the program's curriculum to their students three times a week for a minimum of 20 to 30 minutes a session. The program comprises 150 lessons with age-appropriate material designed for teachers to use over a five-year period throughout elementary school. In addition, Harrisburg schools use therapists for early intervention and treatment services for students who need closer attention.

The school system—in partnership with the county library system, the YMCA, the local housing authority, and a health care provider—made Little Turtle Family Activity Kits available to parents to use with their children. Materials carrying pictures of the familiar green turtle, the symbol of PATHS, provide information on social and emotional learning and tell parents how to promote their children's development—for example, by teaching their children acceptable ways to express feelings, by examining their own problem-solving skills, and by disciplining their children constructively.

Creating an Academy for Behavior

Taking another approach, springing from different needs, Turie T. Small Elementary School in Daytona Beach formed a Behavioral Academy as a response to the problem of children roaming the open-style campus and misbehaving in the morning, after the free breakfast and before classes began. Based on an analysis by a consultant, the school confined students to the school's multipurpose room and teachers monitored the room, handing out reading materials to youngsters who weren't in the cafeteria eating breakfast. The school also established a weekly behavioral class, but the intervention did not end there.

An ongoing feature of Turie T. Small's effort at behavior modification was the distribution of Bulldog Bucks, named in honor of the school's mascot. The school emphasized group behavior by awarding Bulldog Bucks to entire classes. A class might win awards for not acting up when a substitute teacher filled in or by keeping in line when walking from one activity to another.

An entire class could redeem Bulldog Bucks for rewards—$35 for popcorn and a movie for the class, $25 for a special Friday recess, $10 for a book reading by the principal or some other school dignitary, for example. The pupils most readily motivated toward good conduct by the program were those in the primary grades; Bulldog Bucks did not so easily persuade those in the upper elementary grades that they should behave.

Building Character

Concern about safety at its schools in the spring of 2003 gave rise to an interest in character education in Austin Independent School District. In addition to the security issue, misbehavior cost the school system money as the absence of suspended students reduced the average daily attendance on which the state bases its aid. The character education plan, aimed at all grade levels, was introduced in the middle of the 2004–05 school year and each principal designated two staff members to attend training workshops.

Austin linked character to scholastic achievement by taking the position that acquisition of character skills would lead to students putting forth sustained effort in the classroom and having the resiliency to achieve. This idea of casting character education in terms of its connection to scholastic achievement, not just in terms of morality, fits into a new national trend.[14] Promoting character can be part of education reform in that it affects academic aspects of the school.

In Austin, the campaign means highlighting a different character aspect each two-month period, starting with the opening of the 2005–06 school year and continuing through the 2006–07 school year. These character traits are respect, courage, caring, honesty, perseverance, responsibility, integrity, fairness, self-discipline, and trustworthiness. Students receive laminated palm cards, one side in English and the other in Spanish, in conjunction with each featured trait. For respect or *respeto*, for example, students were asked on the card to strive "always to be courteous with others and tolerant of personal differences." Given the concern of young people these days about not being "dissed," respect is clearly a trait worthy of attention. Three items for discussion are listed on the card as bulleted questions:

Who do you respect and why?

What does respect mean to you?

How do you show respect for others and the environment?

THE RESPONSIBILITIES OF SCHOOLS

Just as schools expect students to adopt habits and attitudes favorable to learning, families may reasonably expect schools to reciprocate by creating a climate that supports learning. Students will believe in their own efficacy and probably achieve most when they have classrooms in which they feel safe, disruption is minimal, and they relate well to peers. They also want supportive teachers who like them. Negativity, harshness, and unpredictability undermine achievement. Stephen Brand and colleagues at the University of Rhode Island gathered data from first through third grade classrooms throughout their state that pointed to links among school climate, behavioral adjustment, and academic competency.[15] Their findings confirmed what they had learned earlier about the effects of school climate on older students.

In the earliest grades children may lose confidence in themselves, in school, and in teachers if the climate for learning does not allow them to thrive. Their attendance and behavior may suffer. This does not mean that teachers should coddle youngsters. It does, however, underscore the need for teachers, especially in the lowest grades, who understand development and educational psychology. For their part, principals in elementary schools should be vigilant to the needs of children and teachers and head off forces of turbulence. A principal unable to counter adverse learning conditions belongs in some other kind of job.

An extensive study of first grade classrooms showed that students' engagement in academic activities and their positive behaviors were more prevalent when classrooms provided more instructional and emotional support.[16] In other words, youngsters—especially from preschool through third grade—need a classroom environment structured to support success. Schools are not consistent in this regard; studies have found wide variability in the school experiences of young children. Surely more can be done during teacher preparation and staff development to try to raise the capability of teachers to provide this sort of support to students.

ADJUSTING THE SCHOOL TO THE STUDENTS

Some schools try harder than others to adjust to student needs. Norton Elementary School in Jefferson County, Kentucky, organized each of its teacher teams, regardless of whether teachers taught one grade or a combination of grades, around instructional methods that recognized the learning styles of pupils. The teams ranged from the traditional approach to what Norton labeled a developmental approach, and various teams took approaches in between, combining elements of the traditional and the developmental.

Before Lynne Wheat, Norton's former principal, created the teams, she spent time watching each teacher work and sought to identify the teachers' learning styles so that they could be matched with students with similar learning styles. "I would ask teachers, 'What do you think about working with this person or that person?'" said Wheat, more recently director of administrator recruitment for the district, who assembled teams in which teachers sometimes shared each other's pupils for various subjects. In turn, the school gave parents the chance to select teachers. "Parents try to choose teachers who will work well with their children," Wheat said. "The school will switch a child during the year if the learning style of child and teacher don't match."

In Pamela O. Heatherly's third grade, a nontraditional, inquiry-based class, for example, children had latitude in choosing how to use their time. "After a while, I ask them to switch to another activity and they're more willing and more interested," said Heatherly, indicating that being self-directed—the way that she said she herself learns—the students were most amenable when they had some control over what they did.

"It's time to switch," Heatherly said to the class. "If you've been writing, you need to read. If you've been reading, you need to write." It was a class for students who crave organized independence. They set their own regulations for the classroom and posted them. They spurned restrictions on when to leave the room to get a drink of water or go to the bathroom, wanting to come and go as they pleased. They determined their homework assignments and decided at the opening of the year how to arrange the room, seeking to minimize distractions.

"I try to use their world to make things have more sense to them," Heatherly said. Her approach seemed to pay dividends for the 17 boys and 6 girls in the class, most of whom she characterized as having "high energy." Some of them, she said, might have been classified as special education students and medicated if they had been in a different setting. Heatherly seldom asked them to work as a whole class or even in large groups because, she said, "their bodies are too active" to work efficiently unless they work alone or in small groups.

Elsewhere in Norton, the High Flyers, another team, was so explicit about its learning style that on the wall next to the door of each of the team's four classrooms was a printed sign explaining that the approach inside was a combination of "traditional and developmental." According to the signs, this meant group work, hands-on activities, problem solving, writing process, and whole language in a traditional setting. One of the four teachers, Marianne Page, whose classroom combined second and third graders, said that she had seen great change "for the good" in her time at Norton. "We were straight grades, had desks and tables, and lots of workbooks," she said, describing the past from the vantage of 31 years in the classroom. "Our school does a great job of implementing different ways of learning," she explained. "If we all taught the same, we'd lose a lot of children."

For their part, most parents, too, liked Norton's approach. Angie Dortch, with a daughter in the fifth grade and a son in kindergarten, said that the traditional approach had not been successful for her daughter. She observed some of the other teachers and finally found a classroom that suited her child's learning style. Another parent, Debbie Wesslund, had her daughter in a traditional-style fifth grade, which was "working fine." Previously, her daughter was in a "developmental-style" class and that also worked. "I think parents are looking for quality teachers, whatever the style," Wesslund said. "I want a teacher who knows my daughter and how to engage her. That's what counts."

It was not as if parents at Norton, which serves some of the most af-fluent public school families in Jefferson County, are all that easy to please. The school—in a wooded, suburban setting amid sprawling resi-dential lots spacious enough for some to have horses—is just down the street from a country club. Parents, filled with high expectations, contin-ually filter in and out of the school's roomy front hall, where a coffee urn, a homey sofa, and easy chairs invite them to congregate. It is the kind of place where the parents of a third grader donated money so that bused-in students could submit orders for books for pleasure reading each month along with their more advantaged classmates.

WHAT TO DO ABOUT SPECIAL EDUCATION

Many schools today use the primary grades as a staging ground to try to ward off the need for special education placements. A stepped-up empha-sis on literacy instruction as PK–3 dictates, for instance, includes more early intervention to help struggling pupils make breakthroughs in learn-ing to read. Schools appear less inclined to accept the idea that a substan-tial number of students must spend their entire school career classified as in need of special education and put in isolated settings. "There is a movement to enable early intervention to take over the wait-to-fail model," said G. Reid Lyon, former director of the National Institute of Child Health and Human Development.[17]

A school focused on prekindergarten through third grade can adjust to the needs of children by organizing itself to more readily include spe-cial education students in programs as close to the mainstream as possi-ble. Such an approach conforms to the intent of federal law, and it increases the possibility that some youngsters who start out in special ed-ucation or as later candidates for special education may, during the form-ative years, make sufficient strides to move fully into the mainstream by the middle elementary years. The trend in this direction involves more than altruism; the more students that districts can include in the main-stream, the less money they have to allocate for separate special educa-tion, though in many cases there is the cost of the aides who accompany the students into regular classrooms.

I made the point in the second chapter that a PK–3 approach ought to reach out to all children even before they enter preschool. The Indi-viduals with Disabilities Education Act mandates such an approach for the disabled, in particular, beginning at birth. Hundreds of thousands of infants and toddlers receive services at public expense, usually in their homes. As state-supported prekindergartens expand, they undoubtedly will play a leading part in identifying and serving disabled children, but also in reinforcing the skills and abilities of other youngsters so that they will not need special education.

The emerging PK–3 programs at teachers colleges, in keeping with this role, include preparation for working with pupils with disabilities as part of the focus on the primary grades. Furthermore, No Child Left Behind, with its requirement that school systems disaggregate data for the country's 6.7 million children with disabilities to show adequate yearly progress as early as the third grade, puts pressure on schools to take this responsibility seriously.

MAKING SCHOOLS ACCOUNTABLE
FOR THE PRIMARY GRADES

Ongoing assessment plays a fundamental role in efforts by the Montgomery County Public Schools in Maryland to bolster education in the primary grades. Teachers closely monitor the progress of youngsters and respond to the results by adjusting instruction. This process begins with the primary reading assessment—inquiring into oral language, letter identification, and concepts of print—which schools administer as early as kindergarten. The claim in many districts that data drive educational decisions is questionable, but it is a fact in Montgomery County, where critics of testing would have a field day. The superintendent, Jerry D. Weast, likens the school system's approach to what he calls the medical model of diagnostics. "How do you tell if the patient is getting well?" he asks. He answers his own question: "Shoot a few X-rays."

The system does some of its most extensive data gathering in the lowest grades. "The assessments in K and first grade have revolutionized how we can teach," says Diane Hoffman, an instructional specialist for the district. This abundance of data adds up to what the school district calls its instructional management system, which through assessment provides a sort of snapshot of each elementary school student, including individual scores on state and national tests.

The data are color coded, much like the U.S. Department of Homeland Security's original warning system, to indicate the range of concerns about a student's achievement. In general, this data-heavy approach won the approval of Montgomery County educators. "For our teachers," says James Virga, former principal of Vier's Mill Elementary, who became director of the district's school improvement initiatives, "it gives clear data on how kids are progressing. Sure, it's possible to overdo it and it is stressful, but you need to gather information on how kids are doing and make adjustments."

Formerly, paper-and-pencil assessments produced scores that were then, in a separate operation, entered into computers. During the 2004–05 school year, though, schools in Montgomery County ascended to the digital age via a pilot project that distributed handheld computers to teachers from kindergarten through second grade to use as they assessed pupils individually. In a single operation, a teacher can send information directly into a central computer as she conducts assessments that the district created with a commercial partner, Wired Generation. Montgomery County Public Schools expects its collaboration to lead to a procedure for computerized reading assessments that can be sold to other school systems and reap income for the district.

Teachers administer one of the assessments three times a year to monitor students' progress and determine their reading levels. The assessment uses the running records that teachers formerly took in longhand, following a protocol, to record a student's comprehension and other details as the child reads a specific book. Wired Generation obtained permissions from publishers to create a database of thousands of books that children read in the primary grades; with a version of the specific book stored in the handheld computer, the teacher has space on the screen in which to write assessment notes with a stylus as the pupil reads an actual printed copy of the book.

In addition to these assessments for informing instruction, Montgomery County gives the TerraNova CTBS, a nationally standardized, norm-referenced test, to compare itself with school systems around the country. Along with the state's other school systems, Montgomery also administers the Maryland School Assessment. This test, complying with the federal government's No Child Left Behind law, is the basis for gauging how schools measure up to Washington's requirements for adequate yearly progress.

An advantage of gathering this wealth of data on each student is the extent to which it allows teachers to design instruction for individuals, something like a tailor taking measurements for a custom-made suit. This kind of personal approach has been available for a generation for special education students for whom federal law mandates individualized education plans. Few students in most districts, though, receive such attention without being classified as disabled. Some places, though, are starting to act on this discrepancy. A law enacted in 2004, for instance, mandates that schools in Washington state create a learning plan for each ninth grader who has yet to pass one or more of three sections of the Washington Assessment of Student Learning exam given to them as seventh graders.

Montgomery County's Ronald McNair Elementary, with input from parents, uses data that the school gathers to write what it calls an academic improvement plan (AIP) for students whose assessments in either reading or math show that they lag behind peers. "We use baseline data to determine if a student needs an AIP," says C. Michael Kline, principal at McNair. The school's improvement plan consists of specific, measurable learning goals, some of which depend on the action of cooperating parents for their realization. Thirty first graders at McNair began the 2003–04 school year with academic improvement plans. By winter, more than half were midway to their projected achievement levels and, by the end of the school year, only six had not reached grade level in their achievement. The school wrote new improvement plans for those six youngsters for the second grade.

A typical improvement plan—stemming from insights gained through assessment—sets a goal, enumerates specific interventions, names those responsible for implementing them, sets a starting date, and, afterward, lists the results. For one particular second grader, let's call him Jason, the first goal called for recognizing high-frequency first grade words at 95 percent accuracy by the end of the second quarter as measured by sight word lists and running records. Jason attained the goal at 99 percent accuracy by the end of the first quarter. Then, the teacher set a new goal for Jason: to recognize second grade sight words at 90 percent accuracy. He met that objective by the end of the second quarter. The intervention involved daily participation in a reading support class and activities with words, as well as games with magnetic letters that he used at home with his parents. Jason also had other goals involving vocabulary and reading comprehension.

MORE THAN ONE WAY TO TEST

As the practice of monitoring progress in Montgomery County shows, assessment need not be a punishment that holds high-stakes implications for students. It can be *formative*, as when a teacher assesses a child to gauge progress and adjusts instruction accordingly. The other kind of assessment in schools is *summative*, as when a score determines a final mark or whether a youngster moves on to the next grade. Attacks on testing have grown in recent years and, indeed, sometimes such criticism is warranted. Seldom, though, do critics distinguish between formative and summative assessment.

Formative assessment of young children in the early grades of school may not look like testing to those expecting to see whole classes of pupils sitting silently in rows, number 2 pencils in hand, laboring over multiple-choice questions in commercially produced booklets. The teachers, not the children, often do the writing during formative assessments as they note observations about how a student interacts with the work. They usually do this in a one-on-one situation, while other youngsters work independently or in small groups. Other times, ongoing formative assessment may consist of a series of questions formulated by the teacher to see how well students understand the work and to decide how to adjust the lesson. Formative assessment is frequent, aligned with instruction, and designed to improve both teaching and learning.

"The process of ongoing assessment should be distinguished from the administration of standardized norm-referenced tests," the Educational Testing Service urges in a report outlining a framework for monitoring the literacy development of children from preschool through second grade.[1] The report points out that evidence of whether students have achieved goals may consist of records of their conversations and samples of such work as drawings and writings—hardly the kind of high-stakes testing for which the testing service is best known.

Alignment between curriculum and assessment, incidentally, shows how foolish some critics can be when they object to *teaching to the test*. If you want second graders to learn to solve multistep word problems in math, then teach them how to do so by giving them multistep word problems to solve. Then, assess their ability by presenting them with some entirely different multistep word problems that require them to apply the principles they have learned. That's teaching to the test. Curriculum and assessment should be opposite sides of the same coin.

The William and Flora Hewlett Foundation helped lead an effort to promote formative assessment that school systems in Los Angeles, San Diego, Cleveland, and Boston have been at various stages of implementing. The Bay Area School Reform Collaborative, recipient of a Hewlett grant, called its approach to formative assessment the "cycle of inquiry," a process that goes beyond simply reviewing data. It takes the next step and searches for links between what teachers do and what students achieve. Some people refer to this approach as assessment *for* learning as opposed to assessment *of* learning.

One way this might happen is by teachers inducing students to discuss their understanding of the material, a sort of postmortem of a lesson from the perspective of a seven- or eight-year-old. This is particularly important in the primary grades, where fissures left unattended will grow into gaps too wide to fill in later grades. "[I]mproved formative assessment helps low achievers more than other students and so reduces the range of achievement while raising achievement overall," Paul Black and Dylan Wiliam found in an extensive survey of hundreds of studies of classroom assessment by teachers.[2]

The key here is *monitoring*. Formative assessment, like a thermometer used to take a child's temperature, helps guide instruction and fits perfectly with the goals of a PK–3 school. It reveals, without imposing any penalty, what the student has learned and where instruction falls short. Dick Lilly, a former member of the Seattle school board, recommended that schools "assess kids early on and base K–3 instruction on that data," warning that "a child who is not reading at grade level by the end of third grade is unlikely ever to catch up."[3]

A pitfall of individual assessment, though, is the amount of a teacher's time that it requires. Unless the teacher has an aide, the rest of the class is on its own. This challenge could be seen one day in a kindergarten class at Broad Acres Elementary in Montgomery County, where the teacher took notes as she went through a book with a child. Only 14 other children were in the room that day, but just one unruly youngster can disrupt a class. These children were remarkably self-reliant for five-year-olds.

The teacher never had to reprimand them as two children huddled over a computer, one showing something to the other on the screen; four sat quietly doing puzzles; a girl sunk into a beanbag chair, leafing through a book; another child sprawled on the floor, drawing; three, wearing earphones, listened to stories; and others played name bingo, turning over cards with names of classmates printed on them and covering the corresponding names on their bingo cards. Finally, breaking the spell, two children approached the teacher, who was still carrying out the one-on-one assessment. "Is this an emergency?" she asked, hardly breaking from what she was doing. Apparently, whatever they had in mind could wait. The youngsters retreated, taking the teacher's cue and going back to work on their own, letting her complete the formative assessment.

Portfolio assessment based on the products of actual performance offers yet another approach to accountability, combining elements of both formative and summative assessment. PK–2 schools in Glen Ridge, New Jersey, do not give standardized tests to pupils, who, instead, keep portfolios in each subject. The collection of work shows a youngster's progress over time and the material at the end of a prescribed period represents, in effect, the youngster's achievement to that point. The contents of portfolios are reviewed in November, March, and June. Teachers give parents checklists that rate students in each category according to whether they need support, are developing as expected, or are secure in their attainment.

For example, teachers in Glen Ridge rate the reading development of first graders in regard to nine categories including the degree to which they participate in group discussion, recognize vocabulary words, demonstrate comprehension, and read with fluency. Or, teachers rate the writing development of second graders in nine categories including the extent to which they organize pieces logically, apply punctuation and capitalization, edit their work, and spell assigned words correctly.

This process certainly takes more of the time of teachers than does simply administering tests and recording scores, but educators in Glen Ridge decided in 2000 that portfolio assessment was more meaningful and less stressful for young children, who face tests for the first time in the school system's third grade. Teachers pass along the portfolios from year to year to each pupil's new teacher and the children get the portfolios to keep when they leave the school at the end of second grade.

HIGH-STAKES TESTING AND SOCIAL PROMOTION

Whatever else the New York City Public Schools may or may not have accomplished with the controversial third grade promotion test that the system implemented in 2004, the examination—a summative assessment—renewed a debate about the wisdom of social promotion. The practice of moving pupils to the next grade, almost regardless of scholastic performance, became standard practice in American schools by the middle of the twentieth century. As a result, stories reverberate of students reaching the upper elementary grades and secondary schools unable to cope with the work.

Thus, it seemed a genuine attempt to reach pupils early enough to make a difference when New York City imposed stricter promotion standards, characterizing the end of social promotion as a form of tough love. There are questions, though, about whether flunking students and making them repeat a grade is in their best interests. Spurred by statewide assessments and the influence of No Child Left Behind, local school systems and a number of states considered and even implemented measures to hold back third graders. This happened in Texas, Florida, and Ohio, for instance.

Holding Back Students

In Chicago, where public schools ended social promotion before New York City did, the outcomes are not encouraging. The Consortium on Chicago School Research, whose raison d'être was to document reforms in the city's schools, examined what became of third and sixth graders during the years after they were not promoted. Students retained in the third grade scored slightly higher than their promoted peers the next year, but there was no significant difference between the two groups after two years. Classmates who had been promoted from the sixth grade outperformed those retained for the next two years, and the gap between the two groups further widened in the second year.[4]

It may not be wise to hold back even kindergarteners. A large-scale national study comparing those retained with similar pupils who were promoted to the first grade showed that the ones held back lost ground in reading and writing achievement after only a year.[5] Aside from academic consequences, retention may have a dire impact on a child's psyche. Some psychologists maintain that the practice increases anxiety to the extent that sixth graders rate retention in grade as the single most stressful event in their lives, higher even than fear of going blind or losing a parent.[6]

Nonpromotion also has monetary costs by causing school systems to absorb the expense of an additional year to educate each child. In North Carolina, where retention is most frequent in kindergarten and first grade, the annual cost for this extra year of schooling works out to $170 million. Opponents of retention assert that the state would be better off using assessments during the years from kindergarten to second grade to identify children who need extra support and then to intervene through the child's regular classroom work.[7]

It's easier not to be left behind if you don't start behind. The futures of many children are compromised for want of a better educational beginning. And the older they grow, the worse off they become as the effects of a poor start multiply; thus, the need for a PK–3 approach. Pupils who do not get a strong education from prekindergarten through third grade are three times more likely to be held back than those who build a solid foundation during this period.[8]

Reviewing data from three decades of the National Assessment of Educational Progress, the policy information center of the Educational Testing Service noted as "disturbing" the large differentials in reading scores by the fourth grade that already existed when children entered kindergarten. The portion of children who recognized letters of the alphabet at the start of kindergarten, for instance, was 80 percent for Asian Americans, 71 percent for whites, 59 percent for blacks, and 51 percent for Hispanics.[9] To a great extent, as mentioned earlier in this book, the disparities result from huge differences in the lives of very young children. Elizabeth Burmaster, state school superintendent in Wisconsin, says that improving the quality of early childhood services is one of the best strategies for closing the achievement gap.

Remedial courses in college demonstrate the interconnectedness of education. A study of students taking remedial math at a major public university showed that they had consistently performed below their classmates in high school. Moreover, their low scores on an eighth grade statewide minimum competency test were as accurate a predictor of remedial-course-taking in college as their ACT scores or high school rank.[10] Chances are that students who lagged at the eighth grade did not receive good math instruction in elementary school and suffered deficiencies before they ever left third grade. Research in Philadelphia, for instance, identified as early as sixth grade almost half the students who would become dropouts from the city's public schools.[11]

On the other hand—and contrary to the premise of this book—even a strong start in the primary grades may not be enough to prevent academic disaster. One of the researchers in Philadelphia, in a study of high schools in Chicago with high dropout rates, stated that reforms in that city's elementary grades did not "inoculate children" from the devastating effects of attending terrible high schools.[12] All of which shows that a PK–3 emphasis, while a promising improvement, is not a panacea. The remaining years of the learning continuum cannot be ignored.

Among the students who get high school diplomas throughout the country, many graduates are equipped for neither college nor the workplace. And if this happens to high school graduates, imagine the dire circumstances that await those who do not obtain diplomas. The inequities accrue exponentially. Enrollments at the most highly selective colleges and universities are increasingly skewed toward the offspring of the affluent, usually those who have enjoyed the greatest advantages in their earlier years. An orientation toward the primary grades will not make the sun rise, but it can brighten prospects for many more students.

NO CHILD LEFT BEHIND

The controversial No Child Left Behind (NCLB) legislation, whatever its shortcomings, underscores the imperative that schools do more to help students whose achievement falters. The law requires schools to test students in grades three through eight annually and to disaggregate achievement data to highlight outcomes for minority groups, special education students, and English-language learners. Every state is free to use its own standards and its own tests. Given that Washington exacts penalties if schools do not make adequate yearly progress, the states have scant incentive to make the tests too difficult or the cutoff scores too high. It's like a marksman's contest in which no one dictates how far the target has to be from the shooter or how large the target may be.

This nation for all too long accepted, as almost divinely ordained, the proposition that a substantial number of its children would not prosper in school. Only during the last 10 to 15 years, within the context of school reform and now the No Child Left Behind law, have Americans seen this resignation to failure for the cruel act that it is. Each student's lack of success represents a lamentable denial of opportunity. Human beings have varying potential, but potential far exceeds achievement for the overwhelming number for whom school proves a daunting experience. While No Child Left Behind takes no specific account of what occurs before third grade, no one should doubt that those years will go far toward determining a student's future performance.

Yet, the law's mandate to start testing at third grade infringes on the goals of PK–3. Some children whom schools label as third graders may not be ready for the test, requiring an extra year or, perhaps, at least a summer program after third grade. PK–3, after all, represents a self-contained continuum that pupils should be able to negotiate at various rates, some faster than others. Why should there be a stigma on such youngsters in an era when so many students, especially in urban districts, take longer than four years to complete high school or longer than four years to earn a baccalaureate?

Granted, one way or another, the public should hold schools accountable for the learning of students. Taxpayers, after all, spend $460 billion annually in support of elementary and secondary education. More than that, though, the lives of young people are shaped forever by what happens in classrooms. Of course, some individual stories illustrate that life does not turn out miserably for all who fare poorly in school. Most, though, will struggle to get further education, to earn a living, and to have fulfilling lives. The question is how to reconcile the need for accountability with the realities of child development.

MEASURING PROGRESS

The years from preschool through third grade offer a special opportunity for incorporating continuous progress into accountability. This period is best seen as a time when formative assessment can show degrees of improvement and reveal what individual pupils still need to accomplish. Teachers should allow latitude within the PK–3 continuum for variations among individual children, while preparing them for fourth grade, where the first administration of the No Child Left Behind test would be more appropriate. Greater use of multiage, multigrade classes like those in Kentucky would help in this regard. Most students would proceed to fourth grade at the usual age of nine, but others would do so at eight or ten.

There comes a time, though, even if a ten-year-old has not demonstrated readiness for the fourth grade, when a child simply must move on. PK–3 is meant to do as best it can to prepare students for what awaits them, not hold them captive. Schools should shower youngsters who progress slowly with academic and emotional support throughout the remaining elementary grades and try to gird them for the challenges that await them in middle school.

Continuous Progress in Kentucky

Schools in Jefferson County, Kentucky, designate learning levels as P1 for kindergarten through P4 for third grade. The school system has a special level, P5, for those who take an extra year to complete the progression. The Kentucky Education Reform Act allows for pupils to take five years to pass through the continuum and schools retain no children at any levels before the third grade, though they may be grouped with younger children for some of their work. The widespread use of multiage classrooms in Jefferson County facilitates a continuous progress model; students of different ages in the same classroom use materials appropriate to their individual levels. Many teachers believe this approach best serves children's needs. "I'm adamant about not sending them to fourth grade unprepared," said Pamela O. Heatherly, a third grade teacher at Norton Elementary, who had three P5 students in her class.

Underscoring attention to continuous progress rather than to grade levels is the fact that Jefferson County does not give students marks on report cards until fourth grade, but provides progress reports instead. Work in the lower grades is rated as Outstanding, Satisfactory, Needs Improvement, or Unsatisfactory. Everything changes in the fourth grade, when children not only start getting traditional marks, but the instructional pace picks up. At that point, they have to write down homework assignments instead of receiving printed instructions. Teachers say that the increased responsibility in the upper elementary years helps get students ready for middle school.

Even without multiage classes, though, schools can implement elements of this approach by pairing classrooms and/or letting teachers work in teams, which also happens a good deal in Kentucky. Side-by-side classrooms containing a first grade and a second grade, for example, set the stage for the two teachers to form reading and math groups that draw from both classes. Teachers combine some first graders and some second graders performing on the same level to work together in groups that correspond to their achievement level, not their age. Good schools that follow this pattern re-form groups regularly, reassigning pupils to different groups as their levels change during the term. Similar possibilities exist in classrooms that span two grade levels, consisting perhaps of both second graders and third graders. This approach conforms to a PK–3 philosophy.

Between Third and Fourth Grades

Educators around the country have fashioned various plans to deal with the need to prepare students adequately for the demands of fourth grade, the continental divide of elementary education. Randi Weingarten, president of the United Federation of Teachers in New York City, envisions a *conditional* fourth grade to serve students who don't measure up at the end of third grade and who would otherwise not be promoted. She says that social promotion doesn't work, but feels that the school system's policy of retaining students in the third grade based on test scores and other criteria doesn't offer enough for struggling pupils. So, Weingarten proposes creating conditional fourth grade classrooms with smaller enrollments, highly trained teachers providing specialized curriculums, and a full year of enriched academic and support services. Clearly, school systems around the country recognize the critical nature of the transition from third to fourth grade, one more reason why a PK–3 approach offers promise.

Teachers in St. Paul, Minnesota, identify lagging students in the fall of their third grade year and—in consultation with parents and other school employees—devise academic improvement plans for each of them. If the youngsters do not boost their performance sufficiently by the end of the year, they are eligible for the Excel program. The district designates about 250 third graders annually throughout St. Paul's 50 elementary schools for Excel, which promotes them to grade 3.5, a kind of half grade, even though they will sit in what are ostensibly fourth grade classrooms. They attend summer school before and after the fourth grade and receive academic interventions during the year. Most schools mix grade 3.5 students with regular fourth graders, but some assign them to separate classrooms containing only 3.5 students. "We continue to see good results from our elementary students, especially at the 3.5 level," says Lori Haaland, a teacher on special assignment to Excel.

Atlanta Public Schools, for the first few years of the new century, had a transitional program for students who floundered in the third grade. Those who could not pass a reading test moved into a transitional fourth grade class containing only 11 pupils and received intensive remediation, including computerized programs in reading and math. The goal of the program, which included summer school, was to help as many youngsters as possible join their peers in regular fifth grade classrooms at the end of the transitional year. Such classes operated in 22 elementary schools as recently as 2003–04. More recently, though, policies implemented at the state level effectively ended the transitional program in favor of promoting everyone to regular fourth grade classes and providing extra help to those deemed in need of it.

In Florida, schools do not promote students from third to fourth grade unless they meet at least one of three criteria—a passing score on the Florida Comprehensive Assessment Test or on a national norm-refer-enced test, or by showing mastery in a portfolio of their work. The state requires school systems to run summer reading camps at the end of third grade as a last resort for children who do not qualify for promotion. The camps offer reading instruction daily for a month, after which students have to attain a 51 percent score on a national test to enter fourth grade in the fall. Of the 18,405 who attended summer reading camp in 2004, 13,811 ended up being retained and repeated third grade.

Accountability Virginia Style

Accountability took another form in Virginia, where the Partnership for Achieving Successful Schools (PASS) identified unsuccessful schools, mostly at the elementary level, and provided technical assistance. Former governor Mark Warner promoted the program and put the prestige of his office behind it. PASS targeted 117 schools across Virginia for im-provement, based mainly on standardized test scores and student per-formance on the state's Standards of Learning examinations. The program dovetailed with No Child Left Behind in that it dealt with many of the same schools already identified under the act as in need of im-provement. The partnership designated some 32 schools, all receiving Title I funds, as priority schools for special attention.

The Standards of Learning exams didn't officially begin until third grade, so the state offered a quarterly test to second graders through PASS, seeking one more way to monitor the progress of students in schools known to need improvement. Officials encouraged principals and teachers to use the state's pacing guide and to align instruction with stan-dards. "Normally, teachers in K–2 don't feel much accountability," said James Heywood, director of the state's office of school improvement. "Principals are waking up to the fact that the reason third graders' scores are low is because teachers are not doing their job in first and second grades. This has changed the culture in those grades and more teachers are discussing lesson plans and alignment."

The importance of doing more to get teachers to link instruction and standards was seen in the fact that 87 percent of the partnership schools lacked aligned curriculums. The program emphasized improvement in reading above all else, as PK–3 would do for all schools. Virginia had an early intervention reading initiative that included diagnostic testing from kindergarten through third grade. Moreover, first graders at PASS schools had the benefit of the Book Buddies program that the University of Virginia originated. In addition, the state had a preschool initiative that its General Assembly funded for high-poverty schools. Volunteers tutored children before and after school and on weekends. Governor Warner used the influence of his office to get businesses to form partnerships with PASS schools and encouraged the businesses to provide tutors for Book Buddies. The governor visited almost every priority school and held receptions at the executive mansion for representatives from the schools and their businesses partners.

Virginia is a strong local-control state, and as such precludes state takeovers of local school districts, even making acceptance of technical assistance from the state voluntary. Governor Warner used his visits to priority schools and his statements about the program to focus the glare of the media on schools needing to improve. "To have that kind of visibility makes it difficult to avoid attention for schools that in the past were maybe less concerned than they should have been about improvement," said Heywood.

Accountability was the bottom line for PASS. While it singled out low-performing schools for attention, the goal was improvement, not punishment. The program included tough periodic reviews and demanding recommendations, but schools could avail themselves of extensive technical assistance as they sought to improve. Outside educators and teams of educators from high-achieving schools with economically disadvantaged students were available to offer advice. Teachers at priority schools could visit achieving schools with similar demographics to see how they carried out their work and coaches could be assigned to help principals.

◻ ◻

During the early 1990s the federal government espoused goals that included an aim to have all children ready to learn by the time they enter school. Now, another administration seems to have forgotten that aborted campaign. Officials in Washington today tout the promise of leaving no child behind, neglecting to acknowledge that many still board the train without tickets, lacking the benefit of early stimulation that would provide them with adequate fare for this arduous journey. Some end up abandoned at way stations, dropped from the train because they do not have the wherewithal to make the full trip. A program that focuses on prekindergarten through third grade would prepare more youngsters for a successful passage.

TEACHERS:
BECOMING EARLY CHILDHOOD EXPERTS

In Harrisburg, Pennsylvania, a new superintendent, charged with changing instructional practices in an utterly dysfunctional school system, recognized that educating the teachers would be an essential ingredient. Until that point, professional development in the school district was a willy-nilly, unfocused affair. Like those working in other fields, educators who want to improve need to learn what to do differently.

Superintendent Gerald Kohn put his early emphasis, especially in literacy, on building a formidable structure to span the distance from prekindergarten through third grade. This meant establishing preschools, implementing the High Scope curriculum, *and* preparing teachers for those new classrooms. In kindergarten, first, second, and third grades, it involved equipping teachers to use the balanced literacy approach that Kohn decided was fundamental to change. Teachers had to get rid of the basal readers on which they had depended and imbue themselves with an instructional philosophy totally new to most of them. They had to learn new ways of assessing pupils to determine what books were most suitable for each one.

He installed a coach, called an "instructional facilitator," in every elementary school, most of them former classroom teachers who had to learn as they went along how to assist colleagues. Two of the first 12 coaches, daunted by the task, left after the first year to return to their classrooms. Five more were thinking about giving up coaching the next year. Coaches found that some colleagues wouldn't take advice and some other colleagues demanded more of their time than they could afford to give them. Moreover, the coaches ran out of time to teach the model lessons designed to show classroom teachers how to handle new approaches to reading instruction. Jessica Dalinsky, the coach at Downey Elementary, who had previously taught kindergarten and first grade, felt reasonably confident aiding colleagues from the primary grades, but squirmed over suddenly donning the mantle of "expert" in dealing with teachers above the third grade.

One morning, in a typical professional development session, Dalinsky was working from strength: helping five first grade teachers deepen their knowledge of guided reading, one of the ways that balanced literacy calls for organizing and monitoring pupils. It involves gathering a group of four to six children of roughly the same ability and having them read books aloud as the teacher helps them develop strategies for navigating through increasingly challenging levels of difficulty.

After such a session, the teacher may ask one child to remain to read to her while she records inaccuracies, substitutions of one word for another, multiple attempts at words, omissions, and insertions. The flaws translate into a formula to determine the pupil's reading level. The goal is to help children become independent, silent readers who understand the books they read. Dalinsky told the teachers that she hoped to make them comfortable implementing guided reading.

THE NEED FOR
PROFESSIONAL DEVELOPMENT

Teachers across the country, like those in Harrisburg, often need professional development; they discover that their initial preparation did not equip them for all eventualities. Many districts these days combine professional development with coaching, as in Harrisburg. Superintendent Kohn decided, upon taking up the job, that if Harrisburg were to become a learning community, teachers would have to be among the learners. When it comes to education in the early grades, schools frequently have to rely on the limited training that teachers have for creating a foundation in reading and math. Professional development will be essential to any attempt to remake schools into places with a PK–3 emphasis that give more children the wherewithal for success in the upper grades.

The inadequacies of teachers appear in the picture of early education that Robert C. Pianta of the University of Virginia paints from his observations of pre-K through grade three. Teachers direct much of their instruction to the whole class, seldom interacting with children in small groups or individually, Pianta and fellow researchers found. The typical child is involved in individual or small-group interaction for only four minutes during the course of a morning. Kids spend ten times as many minutes listening as doing. High levels of routine activities and an emphasis on basic skills characterize these classrooms. Teachers devote seven times as many minutes to the basics as to thinking skills. Pianta also found scant consensus among practitioners on what should be taught to young children or on how to teach it.[1]

Such findings raise questions about coherence and equity across classrooms and across grades from preschool through third grade. Activities too seldom build successively on each other as should happen in a kind of spiral effect, especially in the primary grades. The learning environment leans toward the passive, without enough activities and engagement to support early learning. Worst of all, pupils who most need better instruction are least likely to get it. Researchers studying five different kinds of preschools, for example, found that programs serving the poorest, least-prepared children not only make available fewer books, but also have a more restricted range of books "in terms of genres, linguistic complexity, content, and topics."[2] Children spend less time than researchers had expected on literacy activities, with only 20 minutes a day in the most limited situations.

Professional development aimed at remedying such deficiencies ought to be an ongoing feature of teachers' lives, as it is for physicians, lawyers, accountants, and others. Unfortunately, such pursuits in the world of education are frequently insignificant and irrelevant, a palliative where surgery is indicated. Teachers have been able to attend workshops of their choosing—often with barely any connection to improving student achievement—to qualify for advances on the salary scale. But simply giving more time to training may not help students unless that training improves teachers' knowledge of subject matter and sharpens their insights into children's reasoning in those subjects.[3] As researchers gain more understanding of what and how teachers learn from professional development and its effect on pupil achievement, organizers of these programs increasingly link them to curriculum and standards.[4] The PK–3 school should be a learning community for teachers as well as for students.

How important is it to their later education that pupils get good teachers in the early grades? Author Philip Schlechty, an astute observer of school reform, maintains that a student who has had the right teachers in kindergarten, first, second, third, and fourth grades, can survive a bad teacher in the seventh grade. He says, though, "you're really in trouble if you had a bunch of bad teachers" in those grades "and then you get a nasty seventh grade teacher." The differences among teachers can "make much more difference in younger kids," Schlechty adds. Highly qualified teachers, knowledgeable about the development of young children, are essential to the PK–3 school.

The ability of teachers to reach their full potential also frequently depends on the extent to which principals enable them to do so. Part of leadership means facilitating the efforts of the people one supervises. Certainly, any move in elementary schools toward emphasizing education in the early grades should mean helping principals understand how they can lead teachers to take advantage of what PK–3 offers. A successful PK–3 configuration needs leaders adept at creating and protecting planning time so that teachers can confer readily with colleagues about ongoing program alignment and about issues pertaining to students' working in small groups that must be continually reconstituted to take account of individual progress.

Joseph Murphy of Vanderbilt University, who has spent much of his career exploring leadership issues, argues that faulty administrators can impede literacy instruction. In describing the role of principals in ensuring that children in their schools learn to read, Murphy says that principals should promote quality instruction, supervise and evaluate instruction, allocate and protect instructional time, coordinate the curriculum, promote content coverage, and monitor student progress.[5] In part, this implies a need for adequate professional development for principals, and it also means improving or removing principals who stand in the way of good instruction.

From the time it was reconstituted as a PK–3 school, the Children's Academy of New Albany, Indiana, recognized that improvement depended on professional development as much as on any of the contemplated changes at the school. "Professional development must be intensive and focused," the new principal and assistant principal told the central administration and the school trustees in 2005 in making the case for the new school. They pointed out that most programs to upgrade teachers and most materials that teachers use in the lower elementary years are different from those in the upper elementary years. These differences, they observed, lend themselves to separate professional development paths for primary teachers, as would be possible with the creation of the Children's Academy.

The school designed its daily schedule with blocks of time for special subjects—music, art, and physical education—so that groups of regular classroom teachers would be free during those hours to gather and advance their own learning. In addition, the district allotted funds so that teachers could meet twice a week after the instructional day. Terri Boutin, selected as assistant principal of the new school, was an Indiana Teacher of the Year, a skilled and respected educator whose responsibilities were to include oversight of professional development at the school. She had followed an unusual path into her distinguished career: She didn't go to college until her children were well along in elementary school and was close to 40 by the time she taught for the first time.

Picture this scene: One morning at a typical gathering, the school's three third grade teachers are discussing the outcomes on a language arts assessment that they recently administered to their pupils. The teachers are satisfied that the students displayed a grasp of phonics, but some students did less well on grammar and in responding to a writing prompt. The teachers search for the reasons for this spotty performance so that they can do something about it.

One teacher, Liz Ballard, thinks the students did not derive enough information from what they read. "They have to recognize that they have to reread," she says after talking about children who did not push themselves. Another teacher, Melissa Hearn, raises questions about the test itself, wondering why some students scored higher than would be indicative of their ability. Sheila Rohr, the principal, who is attending the meeting in place of Boutin (who has a conflicting appointment), tries to help the teachers extract the implications of their discussion. She suggests that perhaps the students need more understanding of how to read for information. Rohr also raises the possibility that teachers should focus on certain specific skills that students still have to develop.

PROFESSIONAL DEVELOPMENT
TO IMPROVE READING

As its name implies, Literacy First provides teachers with a process for improving reading instruction, no matter what reading programs their schools decide to use. The Professional Development Institute in Mill Creek, Washington, markets Literacy First to schools and school districts, where at least 80 percent of the teachers agree to participate in sessions over a three-year period. Instructors from Literacy First lead the sessions and coach teachers in applying what they learn. Literacy First aims to make educators more knowledgeable and skilled in teaching phonological awareness, phonics and word study, fluency, vocabulary, comprehension skills, and strategies by which pupils can figure out and make sense of what they try to read.

Educators learn how best to organize flexible reading groups and how to plan activities that promote the development of reading skills, concepts, and strategies. The program provides assessment tools for assigning pupils to reading groups and for monitoring their progress so that teachers can shift them among groups as their achievement levels change. Teachers and administrators say that all of this is not new to them. Most of them just never learned as students in education colleges and as practicing professionals to pull together the information in the systematic manner that Literacy First helps them do. "All of our staff had some training in teaching reading, but they needed consistency," says Barbara Smith, acting superintendent and former language arts supervisor in Little Egg Harbor, New Jersey.

During the first year, Literacy First provides teachers of kindergarten, first, and second grades with five days of professional development. In addition, program representatives spend five days at the school coaching and consulting with teachers. In the second year, the training continues with three more days for teachers from kindergarten through second grade and it begins with five days for third, fourth, and fifth grade teachers. During the third and final year, teachers from third to fifth grade get three more days of professional development and six more days of coaching and consulting. Literacy First makes unlimited coaching and consulting available throughout the three-year period by telephone and e-mail.

Literacy First expects the school principal and some central office administrators to participate, thereby increasing the buy-in. Initiatives in schools are apt to flounder unless principals believe in them and feel a part of the undertaking.[6] The administrators not only accompany teachers to training sessions, but also attend a leadership institute that Literacy First operates to bring together administrators from various school systems, giving them a chance to build a network and to acquire insights into practices elsewhere. The principal of a Literacy First school must agree to spend an hour a day visiting classrooms, and central administrators must pledge to spend at least an hour a week in classrooms.

Literacy First in Little Egg Harbor

Little Egg Harbor, near the shore in southern New Jersey, turned to Literacy First because some administrators thought that the tiny district's two elementary schools could teach reading better. It is a semirural place where families scrimp to make ends meet and children get limited amounts of enrichment in their homes. "We wanted to teach our teachers how to effectively teach reading," says Constance Fugere, principal of George J. Mitchell Elementary School, a one-story, red-brick building on a highway, where 800 kids attend prekindergarten, kindergarten, first grade, and second grade. "There wasn't continuity from class to class and from grade to grade."

By the time that educators at Mitchell Elementary completed their three years of sessions with instructors and coaches from Literacy First, they felt satisfied that their newly gained knowledge would enable them to improve reading instruction. Conversations about how best to teach reading grew common among faculty members, and the boost in confidence that came with more insights made them receptive to critique and advice. Their enthusiasm affected the entire culture of the school. Fugere thinks her role was redefined by the program and that she became the kind of instructional leader who exists more frequently on paper than in reality. "If I'm going to ask my teachers to undertake something so massive," Fugere says, "I want to be a part of it."

Moreover, the school created the full-time position of literacy resource specialist, as Literacy First recommends, filling it with one of its former first grade teachers, Linda Hoffman, who revels in her new role as coach and consultant to her colleagues. Fugere and Hoffman regularly visit classrooms to observe reading instruction, keeping a log of what they see, and, later, offering advice to teachers, striving to do so in a non-threatening manner that does not smack of evaluation. During these classroom visits, Fugere wears a badge emblazoned "Literacy First" to emphasize that she has pledged the hour to the program and that no one is to divert her during that precious time. "I want them to know, I'm on a mission," she explains.

Teachers from each grade level assemble with Hoffman for weekly meetings during their open periods in addition to consulting with her individually throughout the week. One afternoon in the neat, well-lit former classroom that serves as Hoffman's office, a place filled with books and materials that teachers can borrow to use in their classes, half of the ten first grade teachers have gathered to hear Hoffman describe a meeting that she had attended at state education department headquarters in Trenton.

Hoffman tells her colleagues how proud she is that Mitchell Elementary already carries out most of the recommended activities—daily blocks of at least 90 minutes devoted to reading and writing and a ban on pulling out students for other studies during that time, for instance. She concedes that the school had not yet assembled a library of at least 300 books on various reading levels for each of its classrooms. The teachers discuss techniques they use in their classrooms to extend what they began under Literacy First. Such meetings help them meet the requirement for 100 hours annually of professional development.

Educators at Mitchell Elementary are long past the exasperation and frustration of the first year of Literacy First, when they felt overwhelmed by what they were learning and didn't think they could ever make the necessary changes in the ways they taught. "I felt like I was in over my head, but at the end it was all worth it," Hoffman says of the training.

Evidence of the impact of Literacy First is everywhere at Mitchell. One day in a first grade classroom, for example, students work in twos, threes, fours, and fives performing tasks. Each of these so-called learning centers, based on the design of Literacy First and set up in every classroom, is devoted to a different aspect of instruction in reading and writing. At one spot where students' desks have been shoved together, they play vocabulary bingo, pulling words from a pile and then covering the same words on hand-lettered cards with pennies. Another group draws pictures to tell the story of Dr. Dolittle. Elsewhere pupils paste poems they have written into their journals. Still another group works on memory, turning over small paper pumpkins with words on the back as they try to find the pumpkins with the matching words that they saw earlier. Three other children sit with the teacher, reconstructing a story they have read together as they hone their understanding of sequence, gleefully reciting the final sentence together: "He caught the minnow, but he didn't catch me."

Professional development has given the teachers a structure for teaching children to read, leaving far less to chance than previously. They see Literacy First as providing a model for teaching other subjects as well. Already, teachers use one of the centers in some classrooms to teach math skills alongside other centers devoted to literacy. Fugere concedes that Literacy First advocates using literacy centers only for literacy-related activities, but says: "There's a lot of reading in math and I want them to make a connection." Professional development has introduced habits and practices that Little Egg Harbor is institutionalizing into the fabric of its schools. Fugere says: "We see such a difference in kids who in kindergarten wouldn't have known a letter [of the alphabet] if they fell over it and who now are fluent readers in the second grade. It's all because of the hard work of their teachers."

Literacy First in Daytona Beach

The experience in Little Egg Harbor is by no means unique. Educators at Turie T. Small Elementary School in Daytona Beach, Florida, feel similarly lifted by Literacy First. With almost nine out of ten of its students on federally subsidized meals, Turie T., as it is known, has the characteristics of the worst of inner-city schools. Pupil behavior was abysmal and reading scores were so low that Florida gave the school a "D" on its annual state report card. The school was a revolving door for teachers, many of whom did not remain long enough for children to get to know them. They simply gave up and shifted to jobs elsewhere in the system, replaced sometimes by teachers other schools didn't want.

Principal Betty J. Powers worked into the night to no avail; reading scores remained mired in waters seemingly as deep as the nearby ocean. The area superintendent finally told Powers that he intended to close Turie T., a warning that paradoxically provided her with an opening to pursue improvement. She asked faculty who wanted to remain to write letters explaining what they would do to make the school better. Enough of the almost 40 teachers were reassigned to enable Powers to hire 17 replacements—and, for the most part, she chose to fill the positions with novices who did not bear the stain of past failure. In 1999, Powers turned to Literacy First. "With so much pressure from the FCAT [Florida Comprehensive Assessment Test]," she said, "we had to give teachers support to show we were still there." The result, as at Little Egg Harbor, was that teachers found a way to focus their work and felt empowered by the knowledge and skills they gained for teaching reading.

"Literacy First made me a better reading teacher," says Jennifer Joseph, who taught second grade at Turie T. and later shifted to fifth grade. "I came out of college with courses in reading, but I wasn't ready for the different levels in the same classroom. Literacy First gave me a toolbox of strategies. I became more organized and able to understand the process of how kids learn to read. It changes the conversation among teachers because we have now all had the same experiences and can discuss the same strategies."

Teachers think they learned a great deal through a process in which Peggy Rivers, the Literacy First consultant, and the school's administrators observed them providing reading instruction in their classrooms. Then, while a substitute kept the class going, the teacher would leave the room and undergo an instant critique, point by point, aimed at honing her craft. "The teachers were brave and agreeable," says Nancy Gossett, the administrator who became Turie T.'s academic coach. She and others stress that the critique was "nonthreatening."

The story almost has a Hollywood ending—but not quite. FCAT scores soared and Turie T. ultimately gained an "A" on the state report card. There was a sense of mission on the campus, which comprises several separate one-story buildings without indoor corridors. The doors of classrooms open to covered walkways and grassy courtyards. A Wall of Fame in a multipurpose room has the portraits of "A" students and classmates who have distinguished themselves by improving.

But Powers and her staff look over their shoulders to keep Turie T.'s troubled past from catching up with them. They face the challenge of a persistent pupil mobility rate of 49 percent, churned by a steady stream of families on public assistance checking in and out of the dilapidated motels lining Route 1, the historic Maine-to-Florida highway just blocks away. Family reinforcement for the school remains tenuous as evidenced by low participation in a family education program. The school used Title I funds to assemble baskets containing books and a cassette player, goods worth a total of about $50, to reward those who attended all six evening meetings in a series. Only 15 families qualified for baskets. Even Mother Nature reminds Turie T. of its fragility. Three of the four hurricanes that pounded Florida's east coast in the fall of 2004 tore through the neighborhood, ripping holes in the school roof and leaving Turie T. with a half-million-dollars worth of damage.

Powers and many of the teachers think that perhaps the school should bring back Literary First to maintain their momentum. Some teachers joined the faculty while the professional development program was under way and didn't receive the benefit of the entire program, and newer teachers missed it altogether. A school, after all, is a dynamic place, always in flux. Furthermore, Powers and a number of the teachers who participated believe they could use a refresher course. School communities that rally to free themselves from the grip of adversity generally worry about retaining their gains and not slipping back, not unlike many families that make their way up out of poverty.

A Different Approach in Mississippi

For some youngsters, learning to read between kindergarten and third grade is a natural process that requires little, if any, intervention. Others face more formidable obstacles. Mississippi has a larger percentage of its population living in poverty than any other state and ranks dead last in the portion of fourth graders reading proficiently. Clearly, the stakes are extremely high during the years before fourth grade. The state is so bereft of taxable resources that even by spending the same portion of its wealth as the national average it stands no better than 49th out of 50 in per-pupil spending. In Mississippi, learning to read can be a tragic struggle.

Poverty and lack of education among adults perpetuate a situation in which only one state has a higher rate of infant mortality and none has a worse rate of low birthweight. Children arrive at school barely knowing letters and seldom having handled books in their homes. Cotton has remained king of Mississippi's cash crops and catfish farming has grown so big that the state leads the world in production, but the state continues to languish in educating its citizens. Teachers face a task of enormous proportions.

Into this breach stepped Jim Barksdale and his late wife, Sally, loyal alums of Ole Miss, to donate $100 million in 2000 to found the Barksdale Reading Institute, an enterprise meant to raise reading achievement in the state by attacking the problem from preschool through third grade. They said they wanted to give something back to their state. Jim Barksdale, a titan of Silicon Valley, made his fortune as chief executive officer of Netscape. The Barksdale Institute, based at the University of Mississippi, is as much about educating teachers to teach reading as it is about teaching children to read.

"All of the research says how critical the early grades are for getting a kid on track," says Claiborne Barksdale, chief executive officer of the reading institute and Jim Barksdale's brother. "By the time they leave third grade, if they are not reading on grade level, they may never do so. We'd like to think they all walk into kindergarten at the starting line, but they don't. This is particularly true with the population we're focused on—poverty, single moms who didn't graduate from high school. These are the children we have overwhelmingly in the schools in which we work. They lack concepts about print and phonemological awareness."

Barksdale Reading Institute annually identifies the schools throughout the state with the lowest reading scores in the primary grades and invites them to join the program. During the 2005–06 school year, 59 elementary schools—new enlistees and old—participated in the program. Most remain involved for a period of four or five years. Barksdale sends a regional reading coordinator—an experienced primary teacher with a master's degree—to every school once a week and also pays for a full-time coach to work with teachers at the school.

Each school organizes its teachers from kindergarten through third grade into a peer-coaching study team that meets for two hours of uninterrupted time every week to review data, learn about diagnostic assessment, and plan strategies for reading instruction. In addition, the school designates a primary teacher as a liaison who gets a salary supplement to handle logistical activities for the study team. Much of what occurs outside the classroom is, in effect, professional development that aims to boost the abilities of teachers in the primary grades as reading instructors. Besides the weekly meeting, the school finds time for periodic faculty study time by using teacher aides and substitutes, paid by Barksdale, to cover classes.

Teachers screen children in pre-K through third grade at the start of the year to identify those most in need of aid. The peer-coaching team, using diagnostic data, helps develop individual plans that take note of how each child decodes unknown words and derives meaning from text, as well as the pupil's reading fluency. Teachers plan one-on-one interventions. Teacher aides spend two hours a day on tutoring, and the program recruits tutors from the outside as well. Teachers themselves tutor students individually and in small groups on specific skills, a particular challenge to the program as many teachers feel most comfortable providing whole-group instruction. The program tries to prepare teachers to use cooperative learning so that other children can collaborate while the teacher devotes time to just a few youngsters.

Schools in the Barksdale network receive funds to extend reading instruction to the hours before and after school, on Saturdays, and during the summer. There is also supposed to be a parent/family literacy center in each school to provide literacy-related puzzles, games, and other materials that families can borrow and take home. Connections to homes include visits by home-school coordinators to model procedures for reading with children and talking with them. The institute intervenes at the preschool level, too, mostly through Head Start and child care centers. Only 59 of Mississippi's 152 school districts have programs for four-year-olds and usually a district has no more than two prekindergartens. A home-school coordinator, paid by Barksdale, visits the centers to train child care and preschool teachers to provide the skills that children ought to have for kindergarten.

The institute spent a total of $43 million by the end of 2005 and now expends an average of $5.5 annually, after larger outlays during its start-up years. It expects to remain a viable entity for at least another ten years, probably not long enough to solve the state's reading problems but possibly a sufficient period to create a learning community in each school so that teachers value their continuous growth as educators devoted to enhancing reading instruction. Barksdale wants schools to institutionalize the changes, to sustain the professional development, and to stress reading even as teachers and principals turn over. Whether this will happen remains to be seen. The institute dropped some schools for failure to live up to the commitment that they made to the program.

GETTING IT RIGHT AT THE BEGINNING

While professional development can deal with the bulk of the teacher corps—those already on the job—new teachers should prepare specifically for work in PK–3 schools. An infrastructure already exists to serve that purpose and officials could use it to expand the preparation of teachers for the early grades. Some states credential and license teachers to work in prekindergarten through third grade, and some colleges and universities have programs that meet those requirements. In turn, the National Council for the Accreditation of Teacher Education accredits the programs, applying standards developed by the National Association for the Education of Young Children (NAEYC).

Once, the term *early childhood education* referred mainly to programs for preschoolers and toddlers, but in more recent years it has been stretched to embrace kindergarteners, and now the first three primary grades. Thus, the term has resonance for PK–3 schools. NAEYC, in promulgating its standards, identifies its mission as "improving the quality of services for children from birth through age 8," while conceding that "states' definitions of the early childhood age span . . . vary greatly."[7] The most rigorous of the teacher preparation programs deal with early development during the critical period from birth to age three, as well as with pre-K and kindergarten, and the individual subject areas from first through third grade.

One such program, which combines bachelor's and master's studies, began in 2001 at the University of Virginia. The university's Early Childhood and Developmental Risk program leads to a credential qualifying the graduate for work anywhere along the preschool-to-third-grade continuum. This preparation is far more specific to the needs of young children than the courses of study that the majority of teachers pursue for work in elementary schools. The University of Virginia program includes studies of child development from birth to age five and preparation to teach special education students, whom federal law requires schools to include in regular classrooms to the extent possible. Students enroll in the College of Arts and Sciences and major in psychology. They begin taking courses in Virginia's Curry School of Education as juniors and after five years are eligible to receive a bachelor of arts degree and a master of teaching degree. Those with bachelor's degrees in fields other than teaching may enroll for the two-year master of teaching degree.

Paige Pullen, the program director, thinks its students get a better understanding of child development across the span from birth to age eight than they would in the usual program leading to a credential as a K–6 or K–8 elementary school teacher. Curry offers the K–6 sequence for students who don't seek special preparation for the primary grades. Undergraduates in the Early Childhood and Developmental Risk program take only one education course before the junior year, a foundations course in which they learn about the various settings that accommodate young children and then spend time in one such setting as observers. As juniors, seniors, and during their fifth year as graduate students, they add various education courses to their schedules and have practicums and student teaching in schools.

Virginia modeled its program after the University of Florida's Unified Early Childhood Education Program that started with a grant from the U.S. Department of Education and by 2006 was turning out 25 to 30 graduates a year for work along the PK–3 continuum. Florida, like UVA, admits students into the program as juniors. Their studies over five years lead to a bachelor's degree and a master's degree. Unlike their counterparts at Virginia, students at Florida are not required to major in psychology. They end up with a teaching license for K–3 and endorsements for education for teaching birth to four years old, preschool with disabilities, and English as a second language.

○ ○

When it comes to primary education, almost nothing happens unless teachers take responsibility for making it happen. A classroom door slams shut and a teacher reigns supreme over a realm bounded by four walls. Superintendents may hand down edicts and principals may issue threats, but the teacher does largely what she (probably at least 90 percent in the primary grades are women) wants to do. Her students are utterly dependent on her insight, wisdom, and beneficence. Thus, PK–3 will not fulfill its potential unless teachers get all the preparation they need to make the most of the opportunity.

BEFORE AND AFTER SCHOOL

The school day and the workday follow different, somewhat incompatible schedules. Pupils arrive at elementary schools at about the same time that their parents are expected to get to work. But the job responsibilities of most parents extend well beyond the school day, which poses a daily challenge for families with small children who have no adult waiting for them at home in the late afternoon. Youngsters during their years in prekindergarten through third grade can't be simply left on their own during the hours when the school clock and the work clock conflict. Older siblings may look after some of them, but this is an inadequate solution. So, what should happen to young school children during the hours when adults are unavailable to watch them?

More and more, wraparound programs are an answer to this important question. Part of the impetus has come from the federal government's funding of almost $1 billion annually for 21st Century Community Learning Centers. Increasing numbers of programs serve young children during the hours before and after school. Many such programs perform a dual function, providing child care while devoting at least a portion of time to academic enrichment and homework completion. Of course, wraparound programs hold value for students of all ages, but they are often essential for the youngest children whom parents leave on their own only at great peril.

Parents, educators, and policymakers recognize that after-school programs figure most importantly in the lives of the youngest children, those from kindergarten through fifth grade, who are 66 percent of the 6.5 million participants. Some 13 percent of kindergarteners and 15 percent of pupils from first through fifth grades attend after-school programs. Families of another 22 million youngsters would like to have such programs available, according to one report.[1] Other researchers, though, maintain that the amount of unmet need is based on unverifiable assumptions and that existing programs have significant numbers of open slots and absentees.[2] Whatever the actual level of demand, enough students in the early grades and their working parents need such programs to warrant linking them to PK–3 schools that expect to serve children to the fullest extent.

LATE AFTERNOON IN HARRISBURG, PENNSYLVANIA

It is almost 3:30 and the regular school day has ended, yet children continue their work in several classrooms scattered throughout Harrisburg's Hamilton Elementary School, housed in a roomy, three-story building that looks from the outside, except for an addition, like the year might still be 1901, when the school was built. But the city has changed markedly since Hamilton's construction, and one result is the need to reinforce lessons beyond normal school hours and to ensure that pupils have a supportive setting in which to do homework. Furthermore, drug sales and gang violence mean that during the afternoon children are most secure either in school or in their homes—certainly not out on the streets.

Once Harrisburg's districtwide program called EXPLORE, for Extended Learning Opportunities and Other Recreational Opportunities, included fun and games. More recently, though, academic imperatives and funding regulations have dictated that kindergarteners through fourth graders devote most of their time to tutoring and homework, with one teacher for every ten children. Their regular classroom teachers identify pupils to participate based on low reading achievement.

On this afternoon at Hamilton, Bernadette Fay, who teaches third grade during the regular day and receives a stipend for remaining beyond her normal working hours, reads *Goldilocks and the Three Bears* to ten children who have probably heard the tale so many times that they know, at any point, what will happen next. But Fay is interested in more than the story line; she stops regularly to focus on individual words. "We didn't talk about this word," she says as she prints "porridge" on the board. "What do you think it might mean?" The guesses strike close to the mark, ranging from soup to oatmeal to cereal. The children, amazingly rapt so late in the afternoon, listen as the teacher describes how Goldilocks tastes the porridge meant for the littlest bear, with whom they seem to have identified.

Fay continues, telling them that the intruder (my noun, not hers) next heads into the parlor. Another one of those words: "What's a 'parlor'?" asks Fay. Again, the guesses come—room, living room, tunnel. "All good," Fay reassures the children. "Let's find out." Strangely, she never actually defines "porridge" or "parlor" despite lifting the words out of the text. Instead, Fay returns to the trespassing young Goldilocks as she makes her way through the bears' house. "Why do you think she's going into the bedroom?" Fay inquires. Still filled with enthusiasm, the children conjecture over whether Goldilocks is merely tired and wants to sleep or wants to leave her mark in the bears' home.

The lesson completed and Goldilocks frightened out of the house after awaking in the presence of the curious and somewhat miffed bears, the children switch rooms with their counterparts next door and go to math. They will spend 30 minutes with that subject before proceeding to the computer lab, where they will drill themselves with electronic versions of worksheets in reading and math. "A lot of them look forward to it," Gene Spells, a second grade teacher and head of the after-hours program at Hamilton Elementary, says of the extra two and a half hours that the young children spend in school from Monday through Thursday. "They may not get the help with homework at home that they get here. It gives them more practice and confidence. At the end of each month their classroom teachers get printouts of how they perform here."

Spells assigned one of his own pupils to the after-school program because of lagging performance and said that the extra time made her the most improved student in the class. "I'm really proud of her and she feels good about herself," he says. The child's improvement spurred students who were at levels not much higher than she to work harder to keep up. The extended day ends in the cafeteria with a free dinner of pasta, carrots, chocolate milk, and an orange. This means that most of the after-school participants eat all three meals at school, having already consumed federally subsidized breakfasts and lunches. At 5 P.M., long after most of their classmates have departed, they clamber onto buses, still in relatively good humor.

THE IMPACT OF AFTER-SCHOOL PROGRAMS

As in Harrisburg, after-school programs throughout the country usually have an academic component. There is disagreement, though, about the extent to which these added efforts boost achievement. A review of the results of out-of-school-time programs by the RAND Corporation, a research organization, revealed that few evaluations were rigorous and that programs had, at best, a modest effect on academics.[3] Most notably, a three-year study of the 21st Century Community Learning Centers found in a series of reports stretching from 2003 to 2005 that most elementary-age pupils participating showed no academic gains.[4]

On the other hand, an examination of 53 studies of the effectiveness of such programs on achievement from reading and math found positive results, with the strongest impact in programs providing one-on-one tutoring for low-achieving students. Much to the topic of this book, students in the elementary grades received the greatest benefits.[5] Furthermore, a study that looked at various settings in which pupils from the ages of six through ten from low-income families might spend their out-of-school time found after-school programs better in promoting motivation and academic performance than merely having children spend the time with family members. It emphasized that not all after-school programs are equal and that academic-related results are highest when children find activities most engaging. The study also pointed out the importance of distinguishing, for evaluation purposes, among pupils who attend programs regularly and those who go only occasionally.[6]

In the wake of controversies over the effects of such programs, the No Child Left Behind act has shifted the focus of the 21st Century program toward tutoring lagging students. A single-minded obsession with achievement, though, can cause one to lose sight of the multiple purposes of after-school programs for PK–3 youngsters. Socialization and peer relationships figure prominently in after-school programs for children in the primary grades, who are still cementing their ties to school and to each other. They need snacks and downtime. They also enjoy and gain from recreation and from arts and crafts activities that, while having a learning component, may only indirectly connect with the lessons of the regular school day. Families of means, who pay for nannies and can afford to send their children off to lessons of one sort or another most afternoons, may not feel a need for such programs, but in less-advantaged communities after-school programs can be a godsend for children and working parents.

Surely, academic reinforcement ought to be a vital feature, but children this young cannot readily submit to two and a half uninterrupted hours of schoolwork on top of the six hours they have already endured. As a matter of fact, most families say they prefer "activities that foster interests, values, and growth" over those that concentrate on academic achievement.[7] This opinion comes from a survey of parents of students in middle schools and high schools, but would probably be similar in the lower grades. In any event, it is not as if after-school programs ignore the academic side.

LA'S BEST

For many children in Los Angeles the school day continues through the afternoon, ending at about 6 P.M. after almost three hours of additional time during which they are safe, productively engaged, and continuing to learn. This is LA's BEST, offered free of charge at 130 of the city's 449 elementary schools. The program uses its own staff of mostly 20-somethings to provide one of the country's leading after-school enrichment programs. The largest segment of the enrollment in LA's BEST comprises pupils from kindergarten through third grade, the bulk of the student population in the city's elementary schools, which mostly run through fifth grade.

A daily centerpiece is the approximately 45 minutes devoted to homework, a chance for many children to complete their assignments with some help and not have to do any further schoolwork at home during the evening, when some of their non-English-speaking parents would find it difficult to assist them in any event. Typically, a group of third graders at Grant Elementary School one afternoon busily engage themselves with various tasks in workbooks and on worksheets assigned to them during the day by their classroom teachers—reviewing vocabulary words, finding the names of animals amid scrambled letters, subtracting three-digit numbers, copying words five times each to practice spelling, and dealing with unit fractions in exercises in which they color, say, one of four sections of a square.

At Grant, like so many schools in the Los Angeles Unified School District (LAUSD) these days, the enrollment is overwhelmingly Latino (in fact, Latinos make up 82 percent of the pupils participating in LA's

BEST). Situated in a corner of Hollywood, just a block from a ramp to the 101 Freeway, Grant is distinctive, however, in that almost 20 percent of its 1,172 students are Armenian Americans, children from the largest concentration of their ethnic group in the United States. As if to testify to Grant's locale, the view from the asphalt-paved playground, framed by tall palm trees across the street from the school, features a picture-perfect view of the famous H-O-L-L-Y-W-O-O-D sign on a nearby hill. Oblivious to the fabled town's location and history, the after-school students are intent on getting their homework assignments out of the way.

"The homework is the connection to the classroom," says Debe Loxton, chief operating officer of LA's BEST, which stands for Los Angeles's Better Educated Students for Tomorrow. Carla Sanger, president and chief executive officer of the organization, calls the program's favorable impact on children's school attendance "our number one accountability factor." If Nancy Nguyen's attitude is any measure, experiences during the after-school program can, as Sanger suggests, help build a good attitude toward school in general. "It's fun," says Nancy, a third grader at Griffin Avenue School, where she participates in LA's BEST. "I get to play with my friends. I get to make new friends. I like to dance and do science. I get to learn more stuff. If I finish my homework, I don't have to do it at home and I get to do fun stuff at home, like play on my computer and watch TV. Sometimes I have homework to take home."

Good Management Makes a Difference

The program benefits from the continuity of leadership provided by Sanger, its first employee when it began in ten schools in 1988, and Loxton, one of Sanger's first hires. Operating on a budget of $23.9 million in 2005–06, LA's BEST draws funds from a multitude of sources—roughly 61 percent from the state of California, 26 percent from the city of Los Angeles, 5 percent from the federal government, 8 percent from private donors. It has a star-studded board of directors filled with members who contribute financially to the program and solicit donations from others in their lofty orbit, an approach that during the program's existence has produced $20 million in private funds and $19 million in in-kind gifts. A separate advisory board monitors program quality and assures the input of diverse constituencies.

The program has not been shy about arraying itself in the glitter of the world's entertainment capital to enlarge its visibility and gain access to gifts. For example, the headquarters of Sony Pictures served as the venue for the LA's BEST's annual family brunch in 2004, with the anchor of a morning TV news program as host and Rhea Perlman, the TV actor, among the honorees, receiving her award from Ted Danson, with whom she starred in *Cheers*. Perlman did more than lend her name to the event, having long been active in LA's BEST. Among past honorees are Hollywood's Jamie Lee Curtis, Kirk Douglas, and Andy Garcia.

LA's BEST also benefits from the clout of City Hall. Lodged in the Mayor's Office since its inception, then-mayor Tom Bradley envisioned it as a counterbalance to the gangs that were recruiting Angelenos at ever younger ages. The program acts as a kind of inoculation against a host of adverse factors that afflict children in the most troubled settings. It has operated until now in schools serving, mostly, the poorest of the poor. No school received a program unless at least 70 percent of its enrollment qualified for federally subsidized meals.

LA's BEST continues to have its corporate headquarters in the 28-story City Hall, a classic structure with an arched Romanesque interior befitting a cathedral. This arrangement gives the program a semiautonomous standing even while its operations are officially part of the school system. The program has not only endured but also expanded under five school superintendents and a succession of mayors from both political parties.

An important element in the success of LA's BEST has been its carefully designed management structure. A site coordinator oversees the program at each school, supervising program workers who deal directly with the children, generally on a 1-to-20 ratio. A traveling supervisor and an activities coordinator act as a team, taking responsibility for five or six sites and interacting with the site coordinators and program workers. The operational headquarters of LA's BEST, housed in trailers surrounded by a chain-link fence in a seedy industrial area near downtown Los Angeles, uses networked computers to pull together the day-to-day business of running dozens of program sites and provides educational, personnel, and management oversight. These various employees—about 1,600 in all—are mostly young adults, three-quarters of them enrolled in college or having recently attained degrees.

Griselda Michelle Moreno, 26, the site coordinator at Grant, for example, got her associate's degree in liberal arts at Los Angeles Community

College and was continuing on for a bachelor's degree in social work at California State University at Los Angeles. She had two children of her own and spent half the day as a teacher's assistant at Grant, where she worked the other half of the day for LA's BEST. One out of five of the program's staff members work in the schools as educational aides or teacher's assistants.

"It's like being a miniprincipal," said Yvonne Garcia, Moreno's counterpart as site coordinator at Griffin Avenue Elementary School. "I deal with some of the same issues as the principal, only I do it in afternoon situations. I go to the principal with some issues and she says, 'Now, you know what I go through.'" Like Moreno, Garcia, too, worked in her school as a teacher's assistant. Garcia, 35, had a bachelor's degree from California State University at Los Angeles, where she was pursuing a teaching credential.

LA's BEST offers children the chance to remain on the school premises and not have to travel after regular classes to some other site for the program, as happens in many other cities. This also means that school principals, while having no explicit responsibility for the program, nonetheless feel a proprietary interest as it, in effect, operates on their turf. In its early days, LA's BEST did not immediately appreciate the extent to which principals could affect the program's destiny. More recently, LA's BEST has wisely cultivated the good will of the host principals, going so far as to give them veto power over who works at their schools for LA's BEST. Many principals have become unabashed supporters of the program, acknowledging the potential benefits to their students.

"It helps stabilize the school," says Robert Bilovsky, the principal at Grant Elementary. "We have a lot of single parents who are heads of household and have to work. It provides day care and some instructional focus and safety. Without it, many of them would be latchkey children. They'd be home alone or with brothers and sisters. We would have more students getting in trouble and being couch potatoes." Bilovsky thinks so highly of LA's BEST that he intervened to establish a program at the school where he was previously a principal and was glad to find a program at Grant when he arrived.

Making an Impact on Young Children

Some parents speak just as positively about the program as Bilovsky, the principal. Marcia Salazar, a parent at Grant, likes the socialization it provides for her daughter, Tara. "It's also good to have her get help with homework that I'm not sure I could give her," Salazar says. "She gets exercise. It teaches her about nutrition and affects her attitude toward school. She's been able to make friends better. I live in an apartment in Hollywood and if she was at home in the afternoon, she would have nothing to do and would sit in front of the TV." Salazar says that her daughter also likes the field trips and that she had accompanied her on all but two of them.

Operating every afternoon, Monday through Friday, the program consists of four parts—a snack, an educational activity, a club or recreational activity, and homework. LA's BEST has few of the physical activities (like basketball) found in so many after-school programs. Instead, recreation usually means something like putting on a play. The program is a more joyful extension of the school day, with children's interests determining many of the activities.

LA's BEST builds on those interests with such offerings as the nutrition club at Glen Alta Elementary, where children one afternoon created a menu, listing healthy foods—broccoli, apples, and carrots—down one side and such unhealthy foods as cake, chocolate, and Pepsi down the other side. This was a group of mixed ages from first through fifth grade and they were also learning about the food pyramid. LA's BEST is not above inculcating healthy eating habits if its staff members can do so while keeping children interested. The staff member leading the session, Maricela Lara, took a nutrition course at Pasadena Community College, where she was one semester away from her associate's degree. She found satisfaction in introducing youngsters from the barrio to vegetables with which they were unfamiliar. "Tomorrow, we'll make smoothies," she announced as the session was ending. "I'll bring a blender."

The serious intent of the cognitive side of LA's BEST is captured one afternoon at Griffin Avenue School in Lincoln Heights, when Javier Navarro teaches a science lesson to a group of second graders. Navarro is one of LA's BEST's star graduates, having finished in the top four in the county science fair and, as a result, attended astronaut camp in Huntsville, Alabama. Now a college student, he uses the natural coloration of animals as the basis for discussing how they defend themselves. "Think about what animals need to camouflage themselves," he tells the children.

"Color," says one student.

"Yes," Navarro responds. "An animal wouldn't want to be yellow."

"No," agree several students. "They want to blend in."

Navarro has youngsters draw the animals of their choice, cut them out, and color them. He selects four students to act as predators and they leave the room while classmates hide their animal cutouts, preferably in plain sight in places where their colors will allow them to elude detection. After a discussion of what a predator does as it seeks prey, the student-predators come back into the room to search for animal cutouts. They find all but four of the animals—a lizard, a snake, and two fish, all with colors that disguise them.

"Would you change the color of your animal?" Navarro asks after the exercise. He points out that well-camouflaged animals "are not eaten as often" and speaks of natural adaptation whereby animals change over time. "Survival of the fittest," Navarro says. "The ones that are most fit survive." After talking about varieties of lizards that "actually change the color of their bodies," he holds up a picture of Nemo, the movie fish who changed colors to protect itself. The students are engrossed, clearly regarding the lesson as amusement even as they learn science.

Meanwhile, in another classroom at Griffin, where first graders are engaged in the after-school program, a program worker reads a book to them about how a mix-up over two words in Spanish led an old man to carry his door (*puerta*) to a barbeque instead of the pig (*puerco*) that he was supposed to take. The book, *The Old Man and His Door* by Gary Soto, with illustrations by Joe Cepeda, is part of AfterSchool KidzLit, a reading program that the Developmental Studies Center has tailored for after-school programs.

After hearing the story, the youngsters draw pictures based on their imaginations and on what they saw on the pages of the book. The book, like others in the series, includes several words that the accompanying teacher's guide identifies as "cool"—*village, chile, vieja,* and *avocado,* for instance. The lesson also gets the children thinking about relationships as they reflect on the many people whom the old man had helped solve problems as he trod his route, mistakenly carrying the door on his head and shoulders.

KidzLit is an academic enrichment program that aims to foster social, emotional, and ethical development. It offers materials that employees without college degrees—who account for many of those who look after children in after-school programs—can use effectively. An implementation guide accompanies each of the 120 age-specific books in the series, providing advice to the site worker, who, after reading aloud to the children, tries to engage them in conversations about the story. Then, the site worker can use suggested activities involving writing, drama, or art—also popular in after-school programs—to extend the lesson.

Despite the ostensible academic nature of some parts of the LA's BEST program, it makes no attempt, other than through homework, to replicate or directly extend specific classroom work of the regular school day. LA's BEST prefers to originate its own projects, often with academic intent but of the program's making, trying to ensure that activities tap into the kids' interests. An exception to this policy is Literacy Leap, which reinforces the Open Court reading program used by the district during the regular school day. The principals at the five schools where Literacy Leap is incorporated into the after-school program insisted on this accommodation.

One reason LA's BEST does not ordinarily try to continue the academics of the school day is because few of its on-site employees are credentialed teachers. The program pays site coordinators $17.50 an hour and traveling supervisors get $19.42 an hour, amounts probably insufficient to entice many public school teachers to agree to remain on campus every afternoon. Furthermore, program workers, who provide most of the direct contact with the children, earn only $12,400. The pay may not be high, but the responsibilities can be weighty. The experiences of many of the young people working for LA's BEST as coordinators and supervisors are potentially excellent preparation for careers not only in the classroom but also in management and administration.

A STEW OF OFFERINGS

The farrago of offerings that make up the nation's system of after-school programs is so disparate as to defy categorization. Even under the auspices of a single school system, the programs tend to be separate enterprises, sometimes isolated and uncoordinated. Los Angeles Unified was one of the first districts to try to bring order out of chaos when in 2000 it placed all of its on-campus, out-of-school-time programs, including LA's BEST, under a single administrator to oversee expanded-day enterprises. Some programs around the country, like LA's BEST, are on school premises, but many others involve busing to locales away from the school. These off-campus programs have a host of sponsors from such nonprofits as the YMCA and the Boys' and Girls' Clubs of America to such for-profit tutoring centers as Sylvan and Huntington. Boys' and Girls', which originated in 1906, says that it alone serves 4 million children in 3,400 clubs in all 50 states.

A report in 2005 from the National League of Cities urged mayors, council members, and other municipal leaders to involve themselves in systemwide issues that affect after-school programs—access, quality, staffing, funding, and transportation. The report said that they ought to make sustainability a priority, and that programs should not overlook such funding sources as those dedicated to youth development, crime prevention, obesity, child care, health and human services, family support, and nutrition. After-school programs should link academic and enrichment activities to the school curriculum to reinforce and expand on learning that occurs during the school day, the report recommended.[8]

The brief history of 21st Century Community Learning Centers demonstrates the depth of demand for after-school programs. Funds for this program soared from $1 million to $1 billion in just five years during the late 1990s and early 2000s. It reaches 1.2 million children, mostly in the elementary grades, at 6,800 schools. Congress has been so supportive that it maintained the funding level rather than cut support by more than half, as the Bush administration had proposed. The program changed sharply under No Child Left Behind, however, explicitly focusing on academic enrichment, especially in high-poverty neighborhoods, playing down its role of providing recreation and community services. Many programs also became state-recognized tutoring providers in conjunction with No Child Left Behind.

A distinction of 21st Century Community Learning Centers, besides its size, is its role as a prominent example of a financial partnership between the federal government and a private philanthropic organization, the C. S. Mott Foundation. Such a collaborative model bears consideration for replication for various aspects of the PK–3 school. The Mott Foundation has been a partner to the U.S. Department of Education since the program's inception, taking responsibility especially for technical assistance, training, and identification of best practices.

Beyond the funding streams that flow from government sources, 21st Century programs depend heavily on the largesse of corporate, foundation, and philanthropic coffers—making finances relatively unpredictable and uncertain. Business has a stake in after-school programs, just as it does in child care, given the fact that employees, particularly mothers, want to know that while they work their children are in good hands. It was therefore not surprising that Corporate Voices for Working Families, a partnership of 47 major corporations, issued a call in 2004 for high-quality after-school programs to which all youngsters have access.[9]

During the Great Depression, the community school concept emerged and held the promise of making public schools places that would remain open from sunrise to long after sunset with a full array of programs for the entire family. Such an arrangement, had it proliferated and endured, could have helped meet today's need for before- and after-school programs. Instead, the country developed a patchwork that not only offers insufficient access but varies greatly in quality. Just as in child care, pay for before- and after-school workers is low and, as a result, the employees have only modest qualifications.

Such cutting-edge programs as LA's BEST have found ways to cultivate their own talent, but by and large, in most locales across the country, these are part-time positions without benefits and with all of the attendant shortcomings that such a situation implies. Only a minority of staff members hold certification as teachers, which underscores the academic constraints. Ideally, there would be links, however subtle, from the educational goals of the school to programs before and after school hours. In a program connected to a PK–3 school, this would mean that these various parts of the day would meld together in a coordinated plan to advance learning and development.

AFTER-SCHOOL LESSONS LEARNED

Lessons learned from an analysis of 60 programs in 20 communities that were part of the Wallace Foundation's Extended-Service Schools Initiative bear examination. Though this initiative concentrated on students in the fourth to eighth grades, it faced many of the same challenges as programs for younger children. The key to high quality was not so much the topics or skills being addressed as the abilities of staff members,[10] a reminder that the best after-school programs must be more than babysitting and should exercise care in selecting staff.

Attendance appears to be an issue in many after-school programs that hope to affect academic outcomes, especially when, unlike LA's BEST, no attendance requirement exists for those who want to participate. One can hardly expect much of an impact from a program that lets children be absent as they please. Moreover, spotty attendance rates complicate planning, staffing, and budgeting. The study of Wallace's Extended-Service Schools Initiative found that registration and attendance requirements can increase participation for complying youngsters but dampen overall participation.

The hours immediately following the official end of the school day are perhaps the most problematic for children of all ages. Teenagers and students in the upper elementary grades have the greatest potential for getting into trouble during this time, when many receive little or no adult supervision. Youngsters in the early primary grades, while less apt to flirt with some of the worst dangers that stalk older children, nevertheless may wander into harm's way for lack of proper monitoring. As it is, some 8 million youngsters between the ages 5 and 12 get no supervision whatsoever after school. The problems come not only from being on the street or hanging out at a mall. One large-scale survey found that pupils in elementary schools who spend a lot of time home alone after school are, in general, less often engaged with their families concerning their education than peers who do not spend these hours alone. In turn, they also more frequently engage in delinquent classroom behaviors.[11]

Let's say it straight out: No child between the ages of four and eight years old should be alone or very far from the eyes of an adult after the school day ends. After-school programs should be widely available for this age-group to ensure adult supervision, especially for the most vulnerable children in America's most troubled neighborhoods. The idea of No Child Left Alone should be part of No Child Left Behind. Many parents have few options when it comes to finding places for their children once the final school bell has rung. Ultimately, parents are forced to make less than satisfactory arrangements for older youngsters. But part of building a network of support for children still in the primary grades should include proper care in the hours before school and during the late afternoon, until the time when most parents can reasonably resume their protective role.

FACING REALITIES IN EARLY EDUCATION

Children who attend public school in Glen Ridge, New Jersey, begin their education in an intimate and nurturing setting made possible by the district's PK–2 configuration. Between them, the district's two primary schools—Forest Avenue and Linden Avenue—serve the entire enrollment until the children continue on to Ridgewood Avenue School for third through sixth grades. It is an arrangement that assures that Glen Ridge's youngest schoolchildren will spend four years, from prekindergarten through second grade, in safe places where literacy instruction reigns and they and their parents feel close ties to the teachers.

Forest Avenue School, for instance, is a 1920s, two-story, red-brick building with long, old-fashioned windows in a century-old suburb 15 miles west of Manhattan, where gracious homes whisper prosperity. Glen Ridge is so quintessential a bedroom community that its tiny commercial base of tax ratables has little more than one shopping strip with only a drug store, a dry cleaner, and a luncheonette. Nonetheless, the school system serves as a magnet for families willing to pay top dollar in property taxes to support their schools. The average annual real estate tax bill in the district of 1,830 students is $14,022.

So homey is Forest Avenue School that the chimney running up its front denotes the fireplace in one of its kindergarten classrooms. Parents, some carrying coffee mugs from home and others pushing tots in strollers, assemble with their children at the edge of the playground each morning. In almost any kind of weather, Deborah Fitzpatrick, the principal, and her teachers are outside the school to meet the families and to usher pupils to their classrooms at 8:30. "Early learning skills are thematic throughout the building," says Daniel Fishbein, the superintendent. "The focus, as it should be, is on literacy."

The PK–2 configuration helps teachers, formally and informally, maintain that focus. Every six days, teachers with classes on the same grade level meet for common planning for a half-hour, either before or after school. Each teacher meets monthly with Fitzpatrick for a 40-minute planning session and the faculty gathers en masse once a month for professional development. The narrow age range of the students means that teachers think about and act on pretty much the same learning issues. "We're all primary-minded," says Kathleen McArdle-Stewart, who teaches first grade.

Teachers at Forest Avenue—where all but two are tenured and hardly anyone ever leaves—don't hesitate to approach colleagues who taught their pupils the previous year with pertinent questions about a child, as McArdle-Stewart does every now and then with the kindergarten teachers. The second grade teachers, following the same philosophy, went as a team to visit the third grade teachers at Ridgewood Avenue School to answer questions about the children they had sent to that school in the fall.

What has to happen to get more school systems to appreciate the merits of focusing on the youngest students? This is not the most propitious time to think about schools that concentrate on children from prekindergarten through third grade. The finances of state and local governments have recovered somewhat from the dreadful setback after 9/11, but money is not as plentiful as in the late 1990s. Competition for public funds has never been more intense. Moreover, the No Child Left Behind act has diverted the attention and energy of educators to the upper elementary grades and secondary schools.

Yet, PK–3 offers a compelling vision. Students will be prepared to show adequate yearly progress to meet No Child Left Behind requirements only if they have a firm foundation for learning. Now that the achievement gap finally commands the attention it deserves, no initiative offers more promise of narrowing it than highlighting what happens to children before they reach the fourth grade. For even more advantaged pupils, like those in Glen Ridge, fulfilling potential also depends on getting the right start. The evidence has never been stronger that investments in the early years pay education's largest dividends. Against this backdrop, though, one must weigh the political, educational, and fiscal realities of what it will take to win support for the PK–3 concept.

POLITICAL REALITIES

The effort to establish universal prekindergarten (UPK) across the United States remains incomplete; nevertheless, it offers a model for what advocates of PK–3 might pursue. Preschool did not attract widespread attention simply on its merits. A well-orchestrated plan enlisted politicians, editorial writers, parents, business people, and even law enforcement officials. This could be seen in such states as Florida, Massachusetts, and New Mexico, each of which was the target of a concerted UPK campaign. Such foundations as the Pew Charitable Trusts have invested in this mission. Pew stated proudly in 2005 that it was helping to lead a broad-based movement with the primary goal of providing access to preschool for all three- and four-year-olds.

Pre-K proponents wisely sought the support of governors, the key figures presiding over the educational apparatus in each state. Such advocacy groups as pre[k]now cultivated the backing of the National Governor's Association and other influential organizations that weigh in on education and social policy. UPK ultimately depends on adoption state by state, and support in legislatures has been bipartisan, though Democrats have tended to be more reliable allies than Republicans.

Tennessee's Phil Bredesen, New Mexico's Bill Richardson, Louisiana's Kathleen Blanco, Iowa's Tom Vilsack, and Illinois's Rod Blagojevich were among the more responsive governors praising early education and proposing increased support for it. In their successful gubernatorial campaigns in 2005, Virginia's Timothy M. Kaine pledged to work for universal pre-K and New Jersey's Jon Corzine proposed $24 million for full-day kindergarten and other early childhood programs. In addition, ballot measures that originate either as initiatives or referendums have become major vehicles in recent years to advance the cause of early child care and education.[1]

Some economists see so strong a case that they argue for pre-K as a form of economic development, superior to other ways that localities promote their region. Art Rolnick and Rob Grunewald of the Federal Reserve Bank of Minneapolis made this point in relation to subsidies to locate a discount retail store and an entertainment center in downtown Minneapolis, a corporate headquarters in the suburbs, and a computer software firm in downtown St. Paul. "Can any of these projects, which combined represent an estimated quarter of a billion dollars in public subsidies, stand up to a 12 percent public return on investment?" they asked, citing the benefit to society that they estimated for the Perry Pre-School Project.[2]

Among the strategies used to promote prekindergarten, surely one of the most ingenious was the creation of an organization known as Fight Crime: Invest in Kids. Its membership comprised sheriffs, police chiefs, and prosecutors—not teachers, principals, and superintendents. Fight Crime predicated its support on statistics showing that children of low economic circumstances who attend pre-K are less likely than peers to become delinquents and to engage in antisocial behavior. This group sponsored such people as Pittsburgh Police Chief Robert W. McNeilly Jr. and Allegheny County Sheriff Peter DeFazio to speak at a news conference in Pittsburgh about research demonstrating that graduates of good preschool programs are less likely to commit crimes later in life than their contemporaries without preschool experience.

Fight Crime ran a nationwide publicity and lobbying effort for preschool that relied on the law enforcement community to present the arguments in news conferences and in meetings with editorial boards and members of Congress. The approach captured the attention of journalists who, like the rest of the public, were fascinated by the image of conservative, hard-bitten law enforcement personnel making the case for prekindergarten. Issues of self-interest and economics underpinned the campaign. Fight Crime, in effect, gave people a reason to care about other people's kids, even the poor ones.

Similar efforts to inform people of the importance of reinforcing the gains that children make in pre-K and kindergarten could help make the case for PK–3. Advocates could cite evidence attesting to the idea that sustaining these improvements depends on aligning the early grades so that they build on one another like a structure made of Lego blocks.

EDUCATIONAL REALITIES

Imagine what the governors who have led the push for preschool could accomplish if they lent their support to PK–3 as a coordinated and comprehensive continuum that embraces children from preschool through third grade! The first governor who grabs this idea will be a pacesetter whose initiative will capture attention. PK–3 requires not so much additional funding—though striving toward smaller teacher-student ratios in the early years would help—as a determination to spend money differently. School systems can reconfigure enrollments in existing buildings. The classrooms mostly exist and most of the teachers are already on the payroll. The students, except for the expansion of prekindergarten, already attend the schools. Schools just have to organize classes and teachers in new ways and pay close attention to program alignment. PK–3 does not require the court battles, lotteries, constitutional amendments, and referendums that have played midwife to pre-K. A change of mindset is needed.

Ernest L. Boyer encouraged a fresh way of thinking about the primary grades in the mid-1990s with his vision of the Basic School, which shared several attributes with PK–3. Boyer's "new place . . . for the first years of formal learning" included teachers organized into horizontal and vertical teams that set aside time for professional collaboration, literacy as the first and most essential goal, benchmarks to monitor student progress, and after-school and Saturday enrichment. Boyer, the late president of the Carnegie Foundation for the Advancement of Teaching, promoted the concept vigorously in speeches and a book,[3] thousands of copies of which his foundation distributed free to educators and opinion makers. (I contributed to the research and writing of that book, which brought little change.)

The idea of reconfiguring schools to emphasize a particular age group and a different philosophy, while radical, has precedent. Advocates for preadolescents persuaded districts across the country during the 1970s to alter the structure so that middle schools replaced junior high schools. At that time, the Edna McConnell Clark Foundation and other backers convinced educators and policymakers that it made more sense to gather this age group in school buildings from the sixth to the eighth grade instead of from the seventh to ninth grade. The issue wasn't simply the grade span, but the kind of personalized, interdisciplinary program that the middle school featured.

The campaign for middle schools was so successful that by the early twenty-first century junior highs enrolled no more than 5 percent of young teens.[4] Proponents of PK–3 could hardly find a more encouraging model to show the possibilities for achieving change with the right kind of approach. The irony, though, is that now the middle school has fallen into disfavor and new arrangements for educating preadolescents, especially K–8 schools, are growing popular. Supporters of this configuration argue that preadolescents fare better in a more nurturing setting, more like an elementary school. It also means that children can remain longer in the same building without having to endure the strains that come with moving into a new setting.

This emerging interest in a K–8 configuration has implications for children in the primary grades. Just how much attention would they receive in a school with students as old as 13 or 14? When *The School Administrator*, a magazine for superintendents, dedicated an issue to what it called "the elemiddle school" (in other words, K–8), the lead article labored over questions of what would best serve students from sixth to eighth grades, wasting nary a word on how the youngest children would fare in such a school.[5] One worries that a K–8 school would concern itself mainly with the testing required by No Child Left Behind and the preparation of its oldest pupils for the demands of high school.

NEW MODELS FOR PK–3

Like the people in New Albany, Indiana, discussed earlier in this book, some educators in other parts of the country also are in the process of considering and implementing the PK–3 configuration and aspects of its approach. Three examples can be found in Colorado, North Carolina, and Michigan.

From Airport to PK–3 in Denver

The future of PK–3 education in Denver will likely take physical form on what had been a runway of the old Stapleton International Airport. A committee spent the 2005–06 school year laying plans to convert Westerly Creek School into a PK–3 school, starting with three-year-olds, in a paired arrangement with a school under construction less than a half-mile away that would accommodate Westerly Creek's students from fourth through eighth grade. The prospective setup underscores the ease with which school systems can adapt the PK–3 concept if they summon the will.

Stapleton International closed in 1996, when Denver opened a sprawling new airport, making available for development the 4,700 acres of publicly owned land that the airport had occupied for 65 years. The Stapleton Foundation, overseeing the vast project, engaged private developers to build a new community representing an extension of Denver, a grid of streets and avenues that connects with the thorough-fares surrounding the former airport. Newly built houses—colonials, Victorians, craftsman-style—echo the styles of the city's older neigh-borhoods. And, with young families pouring into Stapleton so fast that some blocks had more baby strollers than cars, schools were very much part of the project.

Westerly Creek, which opened in 2003, was slated to be a PK–5 school, and the nearby unnamed school was to house preschool through eighth grade classes. Planners decided, though, that both schools would benefit from a unified campus without overlap at any grade level. The Stapleton Foundation and the school system convened meetings throughout 2005 to solicit opinions and discuss the future of the two schools. More than 90 percent of those surveyed approved the PK–3 and 4–8 configurations.

Those favoring this approach liked the idea that professional devel-opment could readily be tailored to each school with its own separate mission. They also thought that the PK–3 school could be a center for modeling best practices in early childhood education, featuring Colorado Bright Beginnings, Head Start, pre-K, and full-day kindergarten. Mean-while, the 4-to–8 school would have the critical mass of students for an ambitious system of elective subjects at the upper elementary grades. The planning committee expected that the schools—officially one PK–8 school in two separate buildings—would have a single principal and ad-ministrative staff, one parents' association, a joint budget, and alignment between their educational programs. Plans called for modifying facilities at Westerly Creek to add more kindergarten classrooms and play areas for young children.

Westerly Creek and its partner school would be only part of the edu-cational infrastructure being developed on the former airport land for what will be a community of 30,000 residents within the Denver city lim-its. Developers expect 35,000 people to come to work each day in the hundreds of thousands of square feet of office space under construction. Among the houses, apartment and office buildings, retail space, and 1,100 acres reserved for parks and open land, there will eventually be more than a dozen elementary and secondary schools. As a goal, the Sta-pleton Foundation hopes to provide facilities for life-long education, ranging from a satellite college campus to a family resource center that imparts parenting skills.

A "First School" in North Carolina

Early childhood experts in North Carolina set out to create a model for PK–3 education in the United States. Calling their project First School, a team from the Franklin Porter Graham Development Institute at the University of North Carolina received planning grants from several foundations to formulate what they envisioned as the start of a network of schools across the country to provide a coordinated learning experience from the ages of three through eight. Supporters of First School expect it to operate as part of the Chapel Hill–Carrboro Schools system, with a projected 2009 opening in a new building made possible by a donor. They hope its architecture will reflect the interests and needs of small children.

Planners tested their ideas for First School in focus groups in 2005. They heard some reservations about whether three-year-olds might be too young for formal schooling and whether eight-year-olds might be too old and better off among older children. Some people worried that the word "First" in the school's name might imply that parents were not children's first teachers. Some respondents encouraged planners to think creatively about family involvement; others said they should solicit ideas from other units of the university, churches, business, child care providers, and a host of social service agencies—all of which would tie in with the planners' goal to maximize services in the school.

Eventually, First School expects to have a "national experts panel" of representatives of major education organizations to offer ongoing advice. Some see First School as a place to conduct research and demonstrate best practices in early education, particularly as a school that shows how to accommodate in the same classrooms pupils with a wide range of needs and backgrounds.

The school system's regular budget would likely cover most costs for operating First School. Federal funds and state money for children-at-risk would be available for some preschoolers as the Chapel Hill district is the local grantee for Head Start; planners want to supplement those revenues to enroll children not eligible for that support to reflect the composition of the entire community. Many PK–3 schools, of course, face this issue of underwriting the costs of preschoolers who do not qualify for subsidized programs targeted at children from needy families.

Multiage Grouping in Michigan

Officials in the Carman-Ainsworth School District, abutting Flint, Michigan, spent the 2005–06 school year considering how they might convert one of their six elementary schools into a multiage, multigrade school, an arrangement very much in keeping with the PK–3 philosophy. If the plan goes ahead, Carman Park Elementary would probably become a magnet school, with children throughout the district eligible for the continuous progress approach. Innovation has characterized Carman-Ainsworth, which already has one K–3 school and where Superintendent Dan Behm has advocated non-graded education. "I question the blind faith that all ten-year-olds need to be learning the same things and working on the same skills at the same time," Behm said.

FISCAL REALITIES

In 1997, when New York State authorized universal prekindergarten, the state intended to phase in the program with gradually increasing allocations projected to reach $500 million in 2001. Instead, legislators marooned the funding on a $200-million plateau and the program reached only 60,000 children, more than two-thirds of them in New York City. Thus, parents in New York, as in most other states, will continue for the foreseeable future to pay most of the cost for the settings in which children younger than five spend time outside the home.

The challenge of finding more money for education today is not unlike that which the country faced during the depths of the Great Depression as officials sought to fund initiatives to put people back on their feet. When Harry Hopkins, the savvy advisor to President Franklin Delano Roosevelt, spoke to a group of farmers in his native Iowa one summer day in 1935, he described FDR's burgeoning vision of government-sponsored jobs and social services to rescue a beleaguered nation. Hopkins's skeptical audience asked him how the United States could possibly afford so a lavish plan. "This is America, the richest country in the world," declared Hopkins. "We can afford to pay for anything we want."[6] Indeed, the country apparently has the wealth to underwrite whatever it wants to do as shown by the more than $1-billion-a-week cost of the Iraq war. It's a matter of priorities.

Priorities were on the minds of lawmakers in Washington state in 2004, when they sought advice on how best to spend the public's money among various prevention and early intervention programs. The Washington State Institute for Public Policy, a research group, found that intervention programs for juvenile offenders had the highest payoff, but also discovered that early childhood education programs for low-income three- and four-year-olds—while not producing as large a benefit—"provide very attractive returns on investment."[7] A separate analysis showed early learning to be more efficient and productive than, for instance, expenditures farther down the line to improve the skills of workers who have not attended college or even allocations to hold down tuitions for those who attend college.[8]

If Congress chose to, it could adopt a plan akin to that proposed by the Progressive Policy Institute for a partially federally funded preschool program to incorporate matching funds from the states.[9] But the young must vie with the demands of an aging population that wants to sustain Medicare and Social Security, as well as the soaring cost of Medicaid for the indigent, which now consumes more of the states' budgets than elementary and secondary education. Furthermore, a nation that has the date September 11 branded into its collective psyche faces perhaps a generation-long battle against terrorism that will consume increasing sums for security and defense. Thus, education advocates must employ bold and creative ways to find traction.

This sometimes means exploiting some of people's baser instincts. Georgia's universal preschool was built on the hopes of citizens who bought lottery tickets. Tennessee and North Carolina followed this example, initiating lotteries of their own in support of UPK. California pumped hundreds of millions of dollars into programs of early care and education by taxing tobacco products. The school board in Jefferson County, Kentucky, beseeched state legislators to aid education with gambling revenues from casinos at racetracks. Ohio tried unsuccessfully to put slot machines at racetracks to support early childhood education. Sin and education: America's new best friends.

SHARING THE COST

One way to implement portions of the PK–3 agenda that require extra funds—pre-K and full-day kindergarten, for instance—would be to ask beneficiaries who can afford to do so to help finance them. Opponents of this approach argue that all taxpayers should help underwrite every public service. They point out that since public schools do not charge students' families for first grade through sixth grade, they should not expect them to pay extra for pre-K or kindergarten. There are many precedents, though, for what amount to user taxes. States charge car owners for drivers' licenses and auto registrations, as well as for highway and bridge tolls. Students at state-supported universities pay tuitions that go beyond the basic tax support for those institutions.

Some school districts charge for adult education and summer school, activities placed outside those underwritten by general funds. Parents in some school systems contribute voluntarily to subsidize salaries of foreign-language teachers or music teachers that the basic budget does not cover. New York state formerly required school boards to adopt austerity budgets when citizens voted down budgets. This set in motion a process under which families had to pay added amounts for their children to participate in interscholastic sports, extracurricular activities, and transportation.

Charging for Pre-K and Full-Day Kindergarten in Denver

Denver Public Schools expanded enrollments in half-day preschool and full-day kindergarten by levying tuition on families most capable of paying it. In 1992 the state instituted the Colorado Preschool Program for the neediest children who did not attend Head Start, and the district itself provided limited funding for an additional number of pupils. Still, almost half of the city's four-year-olds did not have preschool classes to attend.

The impetus for Denver's tuition-based approach for both pre-K and full-day kindergarten came in the spring of 2003, when the state reduced the school system's allotment for preschool. At the same time, district officials felt they could no longer justify spending more than a million dollars in general funds on preschool when that money was really meant for K–12. The district turned to a sliding-scale tuition plan to replace the lost funding and to expand enrollment in pre-K and in its small full-day kindergarten program. Payment was optional as no one had to send children to either program. Furthermore, half-day kindergarten was available for those who chose not to pay for a full day.

A family of four—if its annual income was more than $56,550—paid full tuition for either preschool or kindergarten. Family income and family size determined tuition levels all along the scale. Annual full tuition was $1,755 for pre-K and $2,430 for full-day kindergarten. Full tuition for kindergarten covered the cost of providing the classes, but full tuition in pre-K did not cover the costs and was subsidized by the district. The school system used a lottery to select pupils for both programs and assigned each school some "scholarships" to cover full tuition, based mostly on poverty statistics in the school's feeder zone.

"They recognize it's a good deal," Anita Theriot, principal of Southmoor Elementary School, said of families' reactions to the tuition-based programs. Southmoor stands in the southeast corner of the school district, one of Denver's more affluent neighborhoods. Theriot said that the children in each preschool class of 20 had a certified teacher who was a regular member of the school's faculty, as well as a paraprofessional teacher. Altogether, the 5,500 Denver children who attended pre-K in 2005 under the auspices of the school system or at one of the federally sponsored Head Start centers represented just under half of the city's four-year-olds. Private preschools enrolled an undetermined number of others.

An advantage of tuition-based pre-K in Denver's public schools, which brought in children from higher socioeconomic groups, was the opportunity to mix children from many backgrounds. "Kids with less language and less experience have peer models," said Roberta Genty, a pre-K teacher at McKinley-Thatcher Elementary School. "The mix allows me greater flexibility in my teaching and broadens the range I teach to. I am also able to mix children in small groups by socioeconomic background. They teach each other."

Full-Day Kindergarten in Westwood, Massachusetts

Public schools in Westwood, Massachusetts, abandoned their free, full-day kindergarten program in the spring of 2005 when the district sought to cut $2.4 million after voters rejected the annual budget. Superintendent Paul Ash said that only the morning portion of kindergarten would remain free and that families wanting to leave their children in school for the afternoon would have to pay for it. Even at that, Westwood would underwrite more than half of the afternoon program, which Ash estimated would cost $300,000. Fees would generate only $125,000 of that amount. There would be no tuition for students from families poor enough to qualify for federally subsidized meals, as well as for those repeating kindergarten and certain special education pupils.

Westwood expected more than 80 percent of its kindergarteners to enroll for full-day kindergarten, from 8:45 A.M. to 1:30 P.M. Dismissal for the rest would be at 11:30 A.M. The school system planned to save additional money by not making buses available to children in the half-day program; it would be up to their parents to arrange for their transportation home.

Such policy changes, almost anywhere, stir controversy. Some families said they moved to Westwood, just west of suburban Boston's circumferential highway, expressly for the full-day kindergarten. Families that didn't want to pay for the afternoon kindergarten session worried that their children would miss an important part of instruction. Ash said, however, that Westwood would not change the morning portion of the program, when most literacy and numeracy skills were taught, conceding only that those not in attendance in the afternoon "would get less program."

Deep in the Heart of Texas

Some school systems offer a model for combining education and child care. Plano, Grapevine-Colleyville, McKinney, and other districts in the Dallas suburbs added self-supporting, after-school programs in the same buildings where pupils attended regular classes. In many cases, the programs—for which primary pupils formed the largest group—included academics as well as recreation and supervision. The motivation of the schools went beyond altruism. They charged fees and made the after-school hours a source of income. Plano, for instance, netted almost a million dollars annually from the after-school venture.

It operated from 2:45 to 6:30 P.M. in all 43 of Plano's elementary schools, enrolling 3,800 of the 25,456 students in those schools. Parents paid $205 a month for one child and $169 for a second youngster. Monthly fees for families eligible for federally subsidized meals were $133 or $100, depending on whether they qualified for reduced-cost or free meals. Regular teachers, including some retirees, received $25 an hour to lead the hour of academics integral to the after-school program.

Critics can argue about whether private dollars should help finance activities at public schools, but their objections will not make the money appear. Grapevine-Colleyville, a system only a quarter the size of Plano, included morning child care beginning at 6:30 A.M. and offered it through the summer so parents could rely on the service year-round. The before- and after-school program, like some others, was self-supporting, generating $620,000 a year for the school district's general fund, enough money to help hire back some of the 100 regular school day personnel dropped from the payroll for lack of funds a few years earlier.

CREATIVE FUNDING FROM THE OUTSIDE

Singling out primary education for special emphasis requires recognition of the importance of the early years to later achievement. This is a no-brainer. Nonetheless, many schools take it for granted that whatever has to occur from pre-K through third grade will happen. Paul Revere, an elementary school that runs through eighth grade in Chicago's Grand Crossing neighborhood on the South Side, was one such school. But when they reflected on the unsatisfactory performance in the school's upper grades, administrators concluded that hopes for improvement resided in bolstering the lower grades.

Paul Revere's interest in PK–3 led the school to explore the possibilities with the Erikson Institute, a graduate school in downtown Chicago that prepares educators specifically for work in preschool through the third grade. Paul Revere was not about to cut loose its youngest pupils and create a separate PK–3 school, but during the 2005–06 school year it edged closer to giving unprecedented attention to those grades.

This was a school accustomed to taking bold steps. One of its alumni, Gary Comer, had already provided millions of dollars through his Comer Science and Education Foundation to revitalize Paul Revere and the surrounding neighborhood. Comer, founder of catalogue retailer Land's End, showed up at the school one day in 1999 evincing an interest in the architectural origins of the century-old structure that has been enlarged by two additions. He ended up paying to rewire the school, install computers, and hire a technician. One project led to another for Comer, and he extended his commitment to the surrounding neighborhood, feeling that it, too, would have to change if the school were to improve.

Comer was the moving force behind a $25-million community center erected two blocks from the school. The community center, which a subsidiary of Comer's foundation expects to operate, was planned as a place for family members to pursue adult education and, eventually, as a locale to teach parenting skills to mothers and fathers of toddlers and preschoolers. This would complement the contemplated PK–3 mission of Paul Revere. Comer also helped create Revere Run, a nonprofit enterprise to build 90 1,600-square-foot, single-family houses over a three-year span on empty lots on the blocks surrounding the school. Comer intends the new houses as anchors in a neighborhood where mobility thwarts the ability of the school to make a long-term commitment to educating its children.

Wealthy philanthropists are not apt to emerge from the ranks of every school's alumni, but the experience at Paul Revere illustrates a possibility that few schools have tapped. Comer's involvement raises another issue as well—the limits of what schools can do on their own. Geoffrey Canada, an activist long involved in education in Harlem, concluded that he would need to widen his scope if schools were to alter outcomes. His Harlem Children's Zone directed its efforts at youngsters living between 116th and 132nd Streets, extending the school day, the school week, and the school year for them, but also injecting a host of social services along with guidance to parents. "Most programs deal with only a slice of a child's life," he said. "We want to rebuild a sense of community and build a best-practice program at each developmental stage in a child's life." Proponents of PK–3, in other words, would do well to consider the bigger picture and should connect schools to their communities as well as to social service agencies.

Schools in Glen Ridge, New Jersey, where only 6 percent of the revenues come from state aid and only 5 percent from commercial property taxes, benefit from local residents above and beyond the substantial amounts they pay in property tax on their homes. Between them, the Home & School Association and the Glen Ridge Foundation have, for instance, provided Forest Avenue School with cubbies for the kids' belongings, mats in the gym, air conditioning in the multipurpose room, a library of books graded by reading levels, and innovation grants for the teachers.

In less affluent communities, there is enormous room for the growth of school-college partnerships to enhance PK–3 education at relatively low cost. This kind of collaboration has been discussed for more than a quarter-century with far too few results. Such an omission is underscored by the location of Teachers College at 120th Street and Broadway, on the Columbia University campus, at the edge of Harlem. Teachers College, regularly ranked by *U.S. News & World Report* among the country's premiere graduate schools of education, reposes in its glory within walking distance of some of the worst public schools in America.

Finally, in the first decade of the twenty-first century, bolstered by a million-dollar grant from a trustee, Teachers College set out to create the "TC Edzone Partnership" with neighboring elementary schools in northern Manhattan. The effort began with four schools, the closest a mere two blocks from the back door of the college. Graduate-level students got tuition scholarships in return for going into the schools as "reading buddies" and "math buddies." The TC students provided one-on-one tutoring daily in reading to the six lowest-performing students in each first and third grade classroom. They gave help in math three days a week to 16 children in each third and fourth grade classroom, working with them in groups of four. The students tutored in math were also invited, along with their parents, to a Saturday morning program at the college.

As Dawn Arno, director of the program, described it, the goal was "to break the cycle of failure in a community with a high incidence of educational neglect." In addition, graduate social work students at Columbia became interns, counseling the students—and sometimes parents, as well—on nonacademic issues. Essentially, the cost of the program was Arno's salary and a half-time salary to the person who oversaw the social work interns, plus the tuition scholarships. Imagine the boost for primary education if every teacher preparation program in the country involved itself in neighboring schools in this way.

A NEW ERA

It appears that schools and colleges have moved into a new era, given the pressures on tax-based sources of support. This is a time when limits on taxes and more competition for slices of a finite pie will require imaginative searches for money—in effect, high-stakes scavenger hunts. Leading public universities increasingly privatize portions of their mission as they obtain more funding from nongovernmental sources. Like it or not, public schools may have to travel this route as well, calling on parents who can afford to pay more of the cost to do so. But public schools will remain one of society's greatest bargains, especially in the context of the growing recognition of the crucial nature of primary education.

The New York State Board of Regents, one of the most influential bodies overseeing education policy in any state, for instance, acknowledged the importance of the early years in their January 2006 policy statement calling for strengthening education from birth through fourth grade. The 11 components put forth by the Regents included services from birth through age two; statewide prekindergarten; compulsory full-day kindergarten; alignment of standards, curriculum, instruction, and assessment from pre-K through fourth grade; integrated services for students with disabilities and English-language learners; partnerships to make parents coaches in their children's education; and professional preparation that includes more focus on teaching literacy skills. It was left to the legislature, though, to provide funds to bring the measures to fruition.

When legislatures don't act, courts may intervene, as occurred during the waning days of 2005 in South Carolina. A judge in that state ruled the school finance system unconstitutional because some districts did not have enough money to pay for the prekindergarten classes that he deemed essential to academic success. Ordering the state to fund preschool for low-income children, Judge Thomas W. Cooper concluded that at-risk pupils need "intervention from prekindergarten through grade 3" . . . to ensure them "the opportunity to receive a minimally adequate education."[10]

Those who believe in giving children the best possible start have only to resolve to lift out this portion of schooling and provide it with the separate integrity and distinct prominence that it deserves. The best way to do this will be through an identifiable PK–3 approach, whether the primary grades have their own separate buildings or wings or autonomy within an elementary school that includes the upper grades. Deborah Fitzpatrick, the principal at Glen Ridge's Forest Avenue, a freestanding PK–2 school put it best: "These children should be recognized as different from those in other grades and we should treat them differently."

Notes

CHAPTER 1

1. Dick Kaukas, "ISTEP Scores for Southern Indiana School," *Courier-Journal*, Feb.17, 2005, B3.
2. National Center for Public Policy and Higher Education, "Income of U.S. Workforce Projected to Decline *If* Education Doesn't Improve" (San Jose, CA: Nov. 2005).
3. Thomas Jefferson, *Notes on the State of Virginia*, Introduction to the Torchbook Edition (New York: Harper & Row, 1964), xiv.
4. Joseph Murphy, *Leadership for Literacy: Leadership-Based Practice, Pre-K to 3* (Thousand Oaks, CA: Corwin Press, 2004), 4.
5. National Association of State Boards of Education, "Right from the Start: The Report of the NASBE Task Force on Early Childhood Education" (Alexandria, VA: 1988).
6. Edward Zigler, "The Effectiveness of Head Start: Another Look," *Educational Psychologist* 13, (1978): 71–77.
7. "Closing the Achievement Gap: Head Start and Beyond," *Evaluation Exchange*, Summer 2004, 11.
8. National Academy of Sciences, "From Neurons to Neighborhoods: The Science of Early Childhood Development" (Washington, D.C.: 2000), 2.
9. Derek Gillard, "Education in England: A Brief History," revised and updated May 2004, www.kbr30.dial.pipex.com/edu19.shtml
10. "OFSTED Primary Education," www.archive.official-documents.co.uk/document/ofsted/ped/ped–02.htm
11. Nancy Hoffman, "Add and Subtract: Dual Enrollment as a State Strategy to Increase Postsecondary Success for Underrepresented Students," *Jobs for the Future*, March 2005.
12. Lawrence Cremin, *American Education: The Metropolitan Experience 1876–1980* (New York: HarperCollins 1988), 644.
13. U.S. Bureau of the Census, *Historical Statistics of the United States*, Series H641; and idem, *Statistical Abstract: 1987*, Table 199.
14. David Tyack and Larry Cuban, *Tinkering toward Utopia: A Century of Public School Reform* (Cambridge: Harvard University Press, 1995), 91.
15. National Association of Elementary School Principals, "Leading Early Childhood Learning Communities: What Principals Should Know and Be Able To Do" (Alexandria, VA: 2005), 2.
16. David L. Angus, Jeffrey E. Mirel, and Maris A. Vinovskis, "Historical Development of Age Stratification in Schooling," *Teachers College Record* 90, no. 2 (Winter 1988): 213.
17. Joel Klein, WNYC, 7:30 A.M. news report, Sept. 14. 2004.

18. Kristie Kauerz, Annual Forum of Foundation for Child Development in New York City, Oct. 18, 2002.
19. Joint Committee to Develop a Master Plan for Education, "School Readiness Working Group: Final Report" (Sacramento, CA: Joint Committee, Feb. 2002).

CHAPTER 2

1. NICHD Early Childhood Research Network, "Multiple Pathways to Early Academic Achievement," *Harvard Educational Review* 74, no. 1 (Spring 2004): 1–29.
2. James J. Heckman and Amy L Wax, "Home Alone," *Wall Street Journal*, Jan. 23, 2004, A14.
3. Betty Hart and Todd D. Risley, "The Early Catastrophe: The 30 Million Word Gap by Age 3," *American Educator,* Spring 2003.
4. Kenneth C. Land, "The 2005 Index of Child Well-Being (CWI)," Foundation for Child Development Policy Brief Series No. 2 (March 2005), 3.
5. "Building Concepts through Verbal Interaction: The Key to Success in School?" *Carnegie Quarterly* V, no. 27, N. 1 (Winter 1979).
6. Phyllis Levenstein, Susan Levenstein, and Dianne Oliver, "First Grade Readiness of Former Child Participants in a South Carolina Replication of the Parent-Child Home Program," *Applied Developmental Psychology* 23 (2002): 331–53.
7. Washington State Institute for Public Policy, "Benefits and Costs of Prevention and Early Intervention Programs for Youth" (Olympia, WA: Sept. 17, 2004).
8. Bureau of Labor Statistics, U.S. Department of Labor, "Employment Status of Mothers with Own Children under 3 Years Old by Single Year of Age of Youngest Child and by Married Status, 1999–2000 Annual Averages" (Washington, D.C.: 2001).
9. Jennifer Ehrle and Gina Adams, "Who's Caring for Our Youngest Children? Child Care Patterns of Infants and Toddlers" (Washington, D.C.: Urban Institute, 2001).
10. W. Steven Barnett and Donald J. Yarosz, "Who Goes to Preschool and Why Does It Matter?" (New Brunswick, N.J.: National Institute for Early Education Research, Preschool Policy Matters), 8 (Aug. 2004): 3.
11. John Dewey, *The School and Society: The Child and the Curriculum* (Chicago: University of Chicago Press, 1990), 6–7.
12. National Research Council, *Eager to Learn: Educating Our Preschoolers* (Washington, D.C.: National Academy Press, 2001), 25.
13. "Ready to Learn: The French System of Early Education and Care Offers Lessons for the United States" (a report of the French-American Foundation, 1999), xi.
14. Brian P. Gill, Jacob W. Dembosky and Jonathan P. Caulkins, "A 'Noble Bet' in Early Care and Education: Lessons from One Community's Experience" (Santa Monica, CA: RAND, 2002), 21–22.
15. Teresa Heinz, "To Our Readers," *h magazine* (Spring 2002): 3.
16. David M. Halbfinger, "Kerry Steers Message with Eye to the Nation's Center," *New York Times*, Aug. 8, 2004, 22.
17. Presentation at the Pocantico Conference Center, Nov. 14–16, 2001.
18. U.S. Department of Education, "Third National Even Start Evaluation" (Washington, D.C.: 2003–5).
19. Sue Miller Wiltz, "Bringing Parents on Board," *Harvard Education Letter* 20, no. 1 (Jan./Feb. 2004): 2.
20. Jeanne Brooks-Gunn, "Questions & Answers," *The Evaluation Exchange*, 10, no. 4 (Winter 2004/05).
21. Jeanne Brooks-Gunn and Lisa B. Markman, "The Contribution of Parenting to Ethnic and Racial Gaps in School Readiness," *The Future of Children* 15, no.1 (Spring 2005): 139–68.
22. National Institute of Child Health and Human Development, Early Child Care Research Network, *Child Development* 76, no. 4 (July 2005): 795.

CHAPTER 3

1. Robert Pianta, "Transitioning to School: Policy, Practice, and Reality," *Evaluation Exchange* (Summer 2004): 5.
2. James Heckman and Dimitriy Masterov, "The Productivity Argument for Investing in Young Children" (paper presented at the conference of the Committee for Economic Development, Washington, D.C., Dec. 3, 2004).
3. L. J. Schweinhart et al., "The High Scope Perry Preschool Study through Age 40" (Boston: Strategies for Children, Nov. 2004).
4. "The Effects of Oklahoma's Universal Pre-Kindergarten Program on School Readiness" (Washington, D.C.: Georgetown University Center for Research on Children in the U.S., Nov. 2004).
5. Jeanne Brooks-Gunn, Testimony to Subcommittee on Human Resources of U.S. House of Representatives Committee on Ways and Means, May 10, 2000.
6. National Center for Education Statistics, "Children's Reading and Mathematics Achievement in Kindergarten and First Grade" (Washington, D.C., 2002).
7. National Center for Education Statistics, "From Kindergarten through Third Grade: Children's Beginning School Experiences" (Washington, D.C., 2004).
8. Arthur J. Reynolds, *Success in Early Intervention: The Chicago Child-Parent Centers* (Lincoln and London: University of Nebraska Press, 2000), 166.
9. Reynolds, *Success in Early Intervention: The Chicago Child-Parent Centers.*
10. Anne W. Mitchell, "Education for All Young Children: The Role of States and the Federal Government in Promoting Prekindergarten and Kindergarten" (Working Paper Series, Foundation for Child Development, April 2001), 13.
11. National Research Council, *Eager to Learn: Educating Our Preschoolers* (Washington, D.C.: National Academy Press, 2001).
12. Robert Dallek, *An Unfinished Life: John F. Kennedy 1917–1963* (Boston: Little, Brown, 2003), 640.
13. Margaret Bridges et al., "Preschool for California's Children: Promising Benefits, Unequal Access" (Berkeley: Policy Analysis for California Education, policy brief, Sept. 2004).
14. David K. Dickinson, "Shifting Images of Developmentally Appropriate Practice as Seen through Different Lenses," *Educational Researcher* (American Educational Research Association) 31, no. 1 (2002): 26.
15. Steven Herzenberg, Mark Price, and David Bradley, "Losing Ground in Early Childhood Education" (Washington, D.C.: Economic Policy Institute, 2005).
16. Janet Currie and Duncan Thomas, "Does Head Start Make a Difference?" (Santa Monica, CA: RAND, 1995).
17. "Head Start Impact Study First Year Findings" (Rockville, MD: Westat for U.S. Department of Education, 2005).

CHAPTER 4

1. Council of Chief State School Officers, "Key State Education Policies on PK–12 Education, 2004" (Washington, D.C.: Council of Chief State School Officers 2004).
2. Marguerita Rudolph and Dorothy H. Cohen, *Kindergarten and Early Schooling* (Englewood Cliffs, NJ: Prentice-Hall, 1984), 95.
3. Bernard Spodek, "Development, Values, and Knowledge in the Kindergarten Curriculum," in *Today's Kindergarten: Exploring the Knowledge Base, Expanding the Curriculum*, Bernard Spodek, ed. (New York: Teachers College Press, 1986), 41.
4. Evelyn Weber, *The Kindergarten* (New York: Teachers College Press, 1969), 20–21.
5. Ibid., 119.
6. Mason-Dixon Polling & Research, "National Kindergarten Teacher Survey 2004" (commissioned by Fight Crime: Invest in Kids, Washington, D.C., 2004).

7. The Citizens Budget FY 2005, Montgomery County (MD) Public Schools, 10.
8. Debra J. Ackerman, W. Steven Barnett, and Kenneth B. Robin, "Making the Most of Kindergarten" (National Institute for Early Education Research, March 2005), 6.
9. Debra Viadero, "Full-Day Kindergarten Produces More Learning Gains, Study Says," *Education Week*, Oct. 19, 2005, 1.
10. WestEd, "Full-Day Kindergarten: Expanding Learning Opportunities" (San Francisco: WestEd, April 2005).
11. Education Commission of the States, "Full-Day Kindergarten" (Denver: Education Commission of the States, June 2005).
12. Debra J. Ackerman and W. Steven Barnett, "Prepared for Kindergarten: What Does 'Readiness' Mean?" (National Institute for Early Education Research, March 2005), 2.

CHAPTER 5

1. Kimber Bogard and Ruby Takanishi, "PK–3: An Aligned and Coordinated Approach to Education for Children 3 to 8 Years Old," *Social Policy Report* 19, no. 3 (2005).
2. Susan J. Kinsey, "Multiage Grouping and Academic Achievement," ERIC Digest, ERIC Identifier: ED 448935, 2001. www.ericdigests.org/2001–3/grouping.htm.
3. Bruce A. Miller, "Children at the Center: Implementing the Multiage Classroom" (Portland, OR: Northwest Regional Educational Laboratory, 1994).
4. David L. Angus, Jeffrey E. Mirel, and Maris A. Vinovskis, "Historical Development of Age Stratification in Schooling," *Teachers College Record* 90, no. 2 (Winter 1988): 218.
5. Ibid., 227.
6. Connie Belin and Jacqueline N. Blank, International Center for Gifted Education and Talent Development, "A Nation Deceived: How Schools Hold Back America's Brightest Students" (College of Education, University of Iowa, 2004).
7. National Education Commission on Time and Learning, "Prisoners of Time" (Washington, D.C., 1994).
8. Barbara Heyns, *Summer Learning and the Effects of Schooling* (New York: Academic Press, 1978).

CHAPTER 6

1. Joseph K. Torgesen, "Preventing Early Reading Failure," *American Educator*, Fall 2004.
2. Catherine Snow, "From Literacy to Learning," *Harvard Education Letter*, July–August 2005.
3. U.S. Department of Education, "Reading Tips for Parents" (Washington, D.C., 2003).
4. Yange Xue and Samuel J. Meisels, "Early Literacy Instruction and Learning in Kindergarten: Evidence from the Early Childhood Longitudinal Study—Kindergarten Class of 1998–1999, *American Educational Research Journal* 41, no. 1 (Spring 2004): 191–229.

CHAPTER 7

1. Debra Viadero, "Math Emerges as Big Hurdle for Teenagers," *Education Week*, Mar. 23, 2005, 1.
2. Devora Davis and Macke Raymond, "Singapore Math Curriculum: Final Project Brief" (Stanford, CA: Center for Research on Education Outcomes, Hoover Institution, Stanford University), Nov. 8, 2004.

3. David Klein et al., "The State of State Math Standards 2005," Thomas B. Fordham Foundation, 2005, www.edexcellence.net/foundation/publication.cfm?id=338& published=1.

4. Louis Menand, *The Metaphysical Club: A Story of Ideas in America* (New York: Farrar, Straus & Giroux 2001), 153.

5. Megan Schleppenbach et al., "Extended Discourse in Chinese and U.S. Math Classes" (paper prepared for 2005 American Educational Research Association Annual Meeting, April 2005, Montreal, Canada), 35.

6. Deborah Loewenberg Ball, Heather C. Hill, and Hyman Bass, "Knowing Mathematics for Teaching," *American Educator,* Fall 2005, 14–46; also, "Knowing and Using Mathematical Knowledge in Teaching: Learning What Matters" (paper presented as keynote to the Southern African Association of Mathematics, Science, and Technology Education, Cape Town, South Africa, Jan. 14, 2004).

7. American Institutes for Research, "What the United States Can Learn from Singapore's World-Class Mathematics System" (Washington, D.C., Jan. 28, 2005).

8. Tom Loveless, "The 2004 Brown Center Report on American Education: How Well Are American Students Learning" (Washington, D.C.: Brookings Institution, 2004).

9. Tom Loveless, "Computation Skills, Calculators, and Achievement Gaps: An Analysis of NAEP Items" (paper prepared for 2004 American Educational Research Association Annual Meeting, San Diego, Apr. 12–16, 2004).

10. Herbert Ginsburg, *Children's Arithmetic* (Austin, TX: Pro-Ed, 1977), 21.

CHAPTER 8

1. National Science Resources Center, "2005 NSRC Inquiry-Based Science Education Program" (Washington, D.C.: National Science Resources Center, 2005), 9.

2. Keith C. Barton and Linda S. Levstik, *Teaching History for the Common Good* (Mahwah, N.J.: Laurence Erlbaum, 2004).

3. Stephen J. Thornton, *Teaching Social Studies That Matters* (New York: Teachers College Press, 2005), 12–13.

4. "The Bayer Facts of Science Education X Survey: Are the Nation's Colleges and Universities Adequately Preparing Elementary Schoolteachers of Tomorrow to Teach Science?" Market Research Institute, May 2004.

5. National Science Resources Center, *Science for All Children* (Washington, D.C.: National Academy Press, 1997), 9.

6. "Critical Links: Learning in the Arts and Student Academic and Social Development" (Washington, D.C.: Arts Education Partnership and National Endowment for the Arts, 2002).

7. Kevin F. McCarthy et al., "Gifts of the Muse: Reframing the Debate about the Benefits of the Arts" (Santa Monica, CA: RAND Corporation, 2004).

8. Center for Applied Linguistics, "Foreign Language Instruction in the United States: A National Survey of Elementary and Secondary Schools" (Washington, D.C., 1997).

CHAPTER 9

1. Randy Capps et al., "Promise or Peril: Immigrants, LEP Students, and the No Child Left Behind Act" (Washington, D.C.: Urban Institute, 2004), 7.

2. Ibid., 12.

3. Randy Capps et al., "The New Demography of America's Schools" (Washington, D.C.: Urban Institute, 2005), 13.

4. Stuart Anderson, "The Multiplier Effect" (Arlington, VA: National Foundation for American Policy, 2004).

5. Sharon B. Adarlo, "Top Students Have Come a Long Way," *Newark Star-Ledger*, June 23, 2005, 1.
6. Clemencia Cosentino de Cohen, Nicole Deterding, and Beatriz Chu Clewell, "Who's Left Behind? Immigrant Children in High and Low LEP Schools" (Washington, D.C.: Urban Institute, 2005), 4.
7. Harold L. Hodgkinson, "Leaving Too Many Children Behind" (Washington, D.C.: Institute for Educational Leadership, 2003).
8. Randy Capps et al., "Promise or Peril," 2004, 14.
9. Randy Capps et al., "The New Demography of America's Schools," 2005, 17.
10. Randy Capps et al., "The Health and Well-Being of Young Children of Immigrants" (Washington, D.C.: Urban Institute, 2004), ix.
11. Timothy A. Hacsi, *Children as Pawns: The Politics of Educational Reform* (Cambridge, MA: Harvard University Press, 2002), 100.
12. American Educational Research Association, "English Language Learners: Boosting Academic Achievement," *Research Points* 2, no. 1 (Winter 2004).
13. Hsiu-Zu Ho, Carol Dixon, and Vishna Herrity, "A Four-Year Study of Family Literacy: Promoting Parent Support Strategies for Student Success" (presented at the annual meeting of the American Education Research Association, 2004, San Diego).

CHAPTER 10

1. James Fallows, "Japanese Education: What Can It Teach American Schools?" *Concerns in Education* (Arlington, VA: Educational Research Service, 1990), 8.
2. Flavio Cunha, James J. Heckman, et al., "Interpreting the Evidence on Lifecycle Skill Formation" (Bonn, Germany: Institute for the Study of Labor, Discussion Paper no. 1675, July 2005), 22.
3. Ibid., 5.
4. Lauren B. Resnick, "From Aptitude to Effort: A New Foundation for Our Schools," *Daedalus* 124, no. 4 (Fall 1995).
5. Deborah Stipek and Kathy Seal, *Motivated Minds* (New York: Henry Holt, 2001), 61.
6. Deborah Stipek, *Motivation to Learn: Integrating Theory and Practice* (Boston: Allyn and Bacon, 2002), 18.
7. Tommy Tomlinson, "Issues in Education—Hard Work and High Expectations: Motivating Students to Learn" (Washington, D.C.: U.S. Department of Education, April 1992).
8. Anne M. Seitsinger et al., "Parent Involvement and Academic Performance at the Elementary Level" (paper presented at the annual meeting of the American Educational Research Association, April 2005, Montreal, Canada).
9. Gene I. Maeroff, *Altered Destinies: Making Life Better for Schoolchildren in Need* (New York: St. Martin's Press, 1998), 2.
10. "Teaching Interrupted: Do Discipline Policies in Today's Public Schools Foster the Common Good?" (New York: Public Agenda, May 2004), 2.
11. Ross A. Thompson, "Development in the First Years of Life," *The Future of Children* (Princeton University—Brookings Institution) 11, no.1 (Spring/Summer 2001): 25.
12. Molly Ball, "8-Year-Old Arrested after Biting Administrator," *Las Vegas Sun*, May 13, 2005.
13. "Prekindergarteners Left Behind: Expulsion Rates in State Prekindergarten Programs" (New York: Foundation for Child Development, May 2005).
14. Kathleen Kennedy Manzo, "Researchers Urge Broad View on How to Build Character," *Education Week*, Dec. 14, 2005, 1.
15. Stephen Brand et al., "Guiding School Improvement at the Elementary Level: Systematic Assessment of School Climate" (paper presented at the annual meeting of the American Educational Research Association, 2005, Montreal, Canada).

16. National Institute of Child Health and Human Development, Early Child Care Research Network, "The Relation of Global First-Grade Classroom Environment to Structural Classroom Features and Teacher and Student Behaviors," *Elementary School Journal* 102, no. 5 (May 2002): 367–387.

17. Kathleen Kennedy Manzo, "Basic Measures," *Education Week: Quality Counts 2004*, Jan. 8, 2004, 39.

CHAPTER 11

1. Jacqueline Jones, "Early Literacy Assessment Systems: Essential Elements" (Princeton, N.J.: Educational Testing Service, 2003).

2. Paul Black and Dylan Wiliam, "Inside the Black Box: Raising Standards through Classroom Assessment," *Phi Delta Kappan*, Oct. 1998.

3. Dick Lilly, "It's Time to Put a Real Focus on Reading in Our Schools," *Seattle Times*, April 7, 2004, op-ed page.

4. Jenny Nogaoka and Melissa Roderick, "Ending Social Promotion: The Effects of Retention" (Chicago: Consortium on Chicago School Research, 2004).

5. Guanglei Hong, "Effects of Kindergarten Retention Policy on Children's Cognitive Growth in Reading and Mathematics," *Educational Evaluation and Policy Analysis* 27, no. 3 (Fall 2005).

6. Gabrielle E. Anderson et al., "Grade Retention: Achievement and Mental Health Outcomes," National Association of School Psychologists, www.nasponline.org/pdg/graderetention.

7. FPG Child Development Institute, "North Carolina Early Grade Retention in the Age of Accountability" (Chapel Hill, NC, undated).

8. Arthur Reynolds et al., "Paths of Effects of Early Childhood Interventions on Educational Attainment and Delinquency: A Confirmatory Analysis of the Chicago Child-Parent Centers," *Child Development* 75, no. 5 (2004).

9. *ETS Policy Notes*, ETS Policy Information Center, Education Testing Service, Spring 2003, 2.

10. Geoffrey Maruyama and Chi Keung Chan, "High School Math Performance of Students Taking Postsecondary Remedial Courses in Mathematics" (paper presented at the annual meeting of the American Educational Research Association, April 2005, Montreal, Canada).

11. Robert Balfanz and Liza Herzog, "A Dropout Prevention Study by the Philadelphia Education Fund and Johns Hopkins University" (paper presented at the Philadelphia Education Fund's Middle Grades Symposium in Philadelphia, March 2005).

12. Robert Balfanz and Nettie Legters, "Locating the Dropout Crisis" (Baltimore: Center for Social Organization of Schools, Johns Hopkins University, June 2004), 19–20.

CHAPTER 12

1. Robert C. Pianta, "Standardized Classroom Observations from Pre-K to Third Grade: A Mechanism for Improving Quality Classroom Experiences during the P–3 Years" (unpublished paper, Oct. 2003).

2. Anne McGill-Franzen et al., "Learning to Be Literate: A Comparison of Five Urban Early Childhood Programs," *Journal of Educational Psychology* 94, no. 3 (2002): 443–467.

3. "Teaching Teachers: Professional Development to Improve Student Achievement," *Research Points* (American Educational Research Association) 3, no. 1 (Summer 2005): 4.

4. Hilda Borko, "Professional Development and Teacher Learning: Mapping the Terrain," *Educational Researcher* 33, no. 8: 3–15.

5. Joseph Murphy, *Leadership for Literacy: Leadership-Based Practice, Pre-K to 3* (Thousand Oaks, CA: Corwin Press, 2004), 25–32.
6. Gene I. Maeroff, *Team Building for School Change: Equipping Teachers for New Roles.* (New York: Teachers College Press, 1993), 80–97.
7. National Association for the Education of Young Children, "Accreditation of Baccalaureate and Graduate Degree Programs," www.naeyc.org/faculty/degrees.asp.

CHAPTER 13

1. "America after 3 PM," a report commissioned by the Afterschool Alliance with funding from J.C. Penney Afterschool Fund, May 2004.
2. "Making Out-of-School-Time Matter" (Santa Monica, CA: RAND Corporation, research brief, 2005).
3. Ibid.
4. Mathematica Policy Research, Inc., "When Schools Stay Open Late: The National Evaluation of the 21st Century Community Learning Centers Program Final Report," 2005.
5. Mid-continent Research for Education and Learning, "The Effectiveness of Out-of-School-Time Strategies in Assisting Low-Achieving Students in Reading and Mathematics: A Research Synthesis" (Aurora, CO, 2003).
6. Joseph L. Mahoney, Heather Lord, and Erica Carryl, "An Ecological Analysis of After-School Program Participation and the Development of Academic Performance and Motivational Attributes for Disadvantaged Children," *Child Development* 76, no. 4 (July 2005): 811–825.
7. Ann Duffett and Jean Johnson, "All Work and No Play?" (New York: Public Agenda, 2004).
8. National League of Cities, "The Afterschool Hours: A New Focus for America's Cities" (Washington, D.C.: National League of Cities, 2005).
9. Corporate Voices for Working Families, "After School for All" (2004).
10. Jean Baldwin Grossman et al., "Multiple Choices after School: Findings from the Extended-Service Schools Initiative" (Public/Private Ventures and Manpower Demonstration Research Corporation, 2002).
11. Anne M. Seitsinger et al., "Parent Involvement and Academic Performance at the Elementary Level" (paper presented at the annual meeting of the American Educational Research Association, April 2005, Montreal, Canada).

CHAPTER 14

1. National Women's Law Center, "Power to the People: The Effectiveness of Ballot Measures in Advancing Early Care and Education" (Washington, D.C.: National Women's Law Center, 2005).
2. Art Rolnick and Rob Grunewald, "Early Childhood Development: Economic Development with a High Return," *The Region* (Federal Reserve Bank of Minneapolis), Dec. 2003, 10.
3. Ernest L. Boyer, *The Basic School: A Community for Learning* (Princeton, NJ: Carnegie Foundation for the Advancement of Teaching, 1995).
4. Kimberly Reeves, "Figuring and Reconfiguring Grade Spans," *The School Administrator* 62, no. 3 (March 2005): 18.
5. David L. Hough, "The Rise of the 'Elemiddle' School," *The School Administrator* 62, no. 3 (March 2005): 10–14.
6. June Hopkins, *Harry Hopkins: Sudden Hero, Brash Reformer* (New York: St. Martin's Press, 1999), 1.

7. Washington State Institute for Public Policy, "Benefits and Costs of Prevention and Early Intervention Programs for Youth" (Olympia, WA: Washington State Institute for Public Policy, Sept. 17, 2004).

8. James J. Heckman, "Policies to Foster Human Capital," *Research In Economics* 54 (2000): 50.

9. Sara Mead, "Open the Preschool Door, Close the Preparation Gap" (Washington, D.C.: Progressive Policy Institute, 2004).

10. *Abbeville County School District et al. v. State of South Carolina et al.* (Case #93-CP–31–0169 3rd Jud. Cir., Manning, SC, Dec. 29, 2005), 167.

Index

Gene I. Maeroff and granddaughter Chloe

Gene I. Maeroff was Founding Director of the Hechinger Institute on Education and the Media at Teachers College, Columbia University, where he is now Senior Fellow. He is a former national educational correspondent for the *New York Times* and is the author of over a dozen books, including *The Guide to Suburban Public Schools, Team Building for School Change, School Smart Parent, Altered Destinies,* and *A Classroom of One*. He is the grandfather of Romy, Max, Harrison, Chloe, Dalia, and Alan.